BLOOD AND BONE
THE CALL OF KINSHIP IN SOMALI SOCIETY

BLOOD AND BONE

THE CALL OF KINSHIP IN SOMALI SOCIETY

Ioan M. Lewis

THE RED SEA PRESS
Publishers and Distributors of Third World Books
11 Princess Road, Suite D
Lawrenceville, NJ 08648

The Red Sea Press, Inc.

11 Princess Rd, Suite D
Lawrenceville, NJ 08648

Copyright © Ioan M. Lewis 1994

First Printing 1994

Book design: Jonathan Gullery
Cover Design: Carles J. Juzang

Library of Congress Cataloging-in-Publication Data

Lewis, I. M.
   Blood and bone : the call of kinship in Somali society / I. M. Lewis.
      p.   cm.
   Includes bibliographical references and index.
   ISBN 0-932415-92-X. -- ISBN 0-932415-93-8 (pbk.)
      1. Patrilineal kinship--Somalia. 2. Family--Somalia.
   3. Political anthropology--Somalia. 4. Somalia--Social conditions.
   5. Somalia--Politics and government. I. Title.
   GN650.5.S65L43   1994
   306' .096773--dc20
                                              93-47165
                                              CIP

CONTENTS

PREFACE

The evocative power of kinship as the axiomatic "natural" basis for all forms of social co-operation and as the ultimate guarantee of personal and collective security is deeply and pervasively rooted in Somali culture. For the weaker and less successful members of the Somali lineage, kinship is an indispensable source of protection and safety - readily manipulated by their stronger more politically ambitious clansmen for whom kinship is an elastic resource, conveniently accessible and infinitely negotiable. "Our kinsmen, right or wrong" is the basic motto of Somali social life. As the foundation of social co-operation, kinship enters into all transactions between and amongst individuals. There is no significant area of Somali social activity where the influence of kinship is absent. It is not without significance, therefore, that a recently coined Somali term for "anthropologist" means literally "one who knows (or understands) kinship" (*tol yaan*).

This book brings together a series of related studies of different aspects of Somali kinship ideology and behaviour. Written at various times over a period of some thirty years, the original versions of these essays have been revised and up-dated to take account of subsequent developments and research. The last two chapters dealing with current politics at the "national" level, and which follow organically from the preceding chapters, have been included to complete the study of "traditional" rural and contemporary urban kinship. They illustrate the devastating force of kin loyalties manipulated by totally unscrupulous "modern" political leaders, in destabilising and ultimately destroying the Somali state.

One objective, especially at this catastrophic stage in their history, is to present as full as possible an account of Somali kinship in action, which I hope will be of some value to those who have the awesome task of rehabilitating the nation. This, of course, means not only Somalis themselves but also expatriate relief workers. Naturally, at the same time, I seek to contribute to the fuller anthropological understanding of the workings of such lineage-based societies and hence address a variety of "theoretical" issues. My title reflects the way in which kinship (or lineage solidarity: *tol*) is conceptualized by the Somali people and the fact that, unlike many other patrilineal systems, here people derive *both* their blood and their bones from their father and his ancestors. In this respect once again, in light of comparative anthropology, Somali culture appears in a maverick role as I have noted with reference to other features in many previous publications.

It is now generally accepted that anthropological accounts should include an examination of the anthropologist's field situation and his relations with those whom he presumes to study. In this spirit, chapter one, based on an article published in 1977, offers an autobiographical account of the circumstances of my fieldwork and my involvement with Somalis as I see these in retrospect. Somalis, of course, have made, and will continue to make their own assessments of my activities. Chapter two, published originally in 1962, has been extensively revised to highlight salient features of Somali kinship and family organisation - which is, naturally, the source of the production and reproduction of the abiding kin values which are utilized holistically in such a wide range of social contexts. Here we see how Somali theories of conception, attributing both blood and bone to the paternal side, depart from those taken for granted by anthropologists as characteristic of patrilineal systems generally. Another initially puzzling feature of Somali kinship, the use of reciprocal kin terms between parents and children, is analyzed in chapter three (published in 1991). The structure of genealogies which conserve and convey kinship entitlements is explored in chapter four (originally published in 1962) which shows how their historical content varies at different genealogical levels. Chapter five explores how kinship has been employed to provide chains of trust linking pastoral producers and livestock traders, and migrant workers. The importance of this aspect of kinship is dramatically illustrated by the fact that in the decade of 1980-1990 most of the Somali Republic's foreign exchange moved through these "unofficial" kinship channels. Chapter six (first published in 1969) analyzes the changes in kinship and political organisation linked with the transition from pastoral nomadism to cultivation in southern Somalia, and the persistence, in mutated form, of kin and clan ideology.

In the early 1970s, under the banner of President Siyad's rustic version of "scientific socialism," Somalia officially renounced clan and kinship ties following the slogan "socialism unites, kinship divides." Chapter seven (published in 1979) assesses the success of this military exercise and analyzes the real powerbase of the Somali dictator which turned out to be based on a prudent and fully traditional use of kinship. This phase marks the climax of the absurd political pretension that Somali nationalism had triumphantly overcome and completely supplanted kin and clan solidarity. Chapter eight, based like the previous chapters essentially on anthropological oral research but in this case relying on interviews with specific "key" figures (carried out by Dr. G.

P. Makris, Dr. Seid Abdi and myself), illustrates the strengths and weaknesses of segmentary kinship as a basis for political organisation in the modern context. The tension between transcendant nationalism and lineage-based loyalties is lucidly highlighted in this case study of the organisation of the most effective recent Somali political movement, a tension explicitly recognised by its leaders who have been remarkably consistent in their political activities. Finally, chapter nine examines the collapse of the Somali state and the pervasive re-emergence of extreme lineage particularism which underlies the 1992 Somali disaster.

As will be apparent, it was indeed during the height of this Somali tragedy (while I was recuperating from heart failure) that this book was put together. Along with other Somali specialists, I have been as active - nationally and internationally - as my health permitted in trying to encourage and support those individuals and organisations working for peace and harmony (or, as Somalis say, "peace and milk" - in opposition to "war and famine") and reconstruction in the Somali region. I would thus like to pay particular tribute to the Somali *Ergada*, the "traditional" elders in Somaliland, and to all those non-governmental organisations working so courageously in the field. I am also grateful to Margaret Bothwell and Ann Seale for typing parts of this book at various stages, and to Andrew Canessa for his help in editing the text and assembling the bibliography.

I. M. Lewis
London, May 1993

ACKNOWLEDGEMENTS

This book has developed from the following:

Chapter 1: "Confessions of a "Government" Anthropologist," *Anthropological Forum*, IV, 2, 1977; pp. 226-238.

Chapter 2: *Marriage and the Family in Northern Somaliland*, East African Studies No. 15, Kampala, 1962.

Chapter 3: "Parental Terms of Reference : a patrilineal kinship puzzle," in W. Shapiro (ed.), *On the Generation and Maintenance of Person - Essays in Honour of John Barnes, Australian Journal of Anthropology*, 1990, 1:2-3, pp. 83-96.

Chapter 4: "Historical aspects of genealogies in Northern Somali Social Structure," *Journal of African History*, 111, 1962, pp. 35-48.

Chapter 5: "Lineage continuity and modern commerce in Northern Somaliland" in P. Bohannon and G. Dalton (eds.), *Markets in Africa*, 1962.

Chapter 6: "From nomadism to cultivation : the expansion of political solidarity in southern Somalia," in M. Douglas and P. Kaberry (eds.), *Man in Africa*, Tavistock, London, 1969, pp. 59-78.

Chapter 7: "Kim Il-Sung in Somalia : the end of Tribalism" in W. A. Shack and P.S. Cohen (eds.), *Politics in Leadership*, Oxford, 1979, pp. 13-44.

Chapter 9: "Il nazionalismo frammentato della Somalia," *Politica internazionale*, No. 4, 1992, pp. 35-52.

The author thanks the editors of these publications for permission to reprint their material in its revised form here. The author is also grateful for research assistance provided through small grants from the Nuffield Foundation and the London School of Economics Staff Research Fund.

Orthography

Individual personal names are rendered in their common Anglicized versions. The names of groups and other Somali terms use doubling to represent long vowels. The Cushitic Somali voiced post-alveolar plosive is not differentiated, nor is the pharyngal fricative. Native speakers and Somali specialists will know how to read words containing these without their being specially marked. I have deliberately avoided the current written Somali orthography in the interests of accesability to non-Somali speakers.

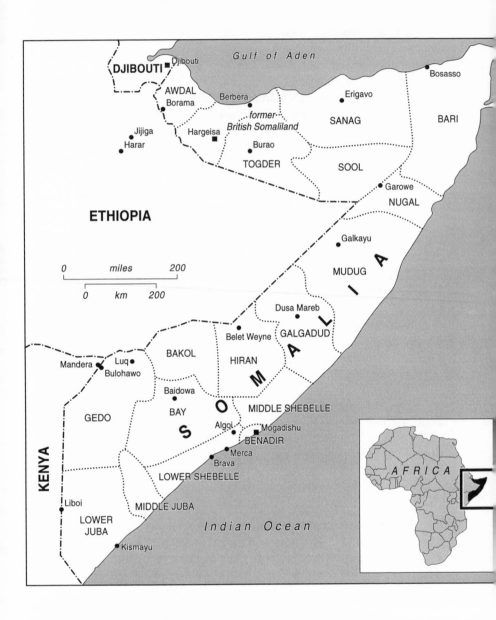

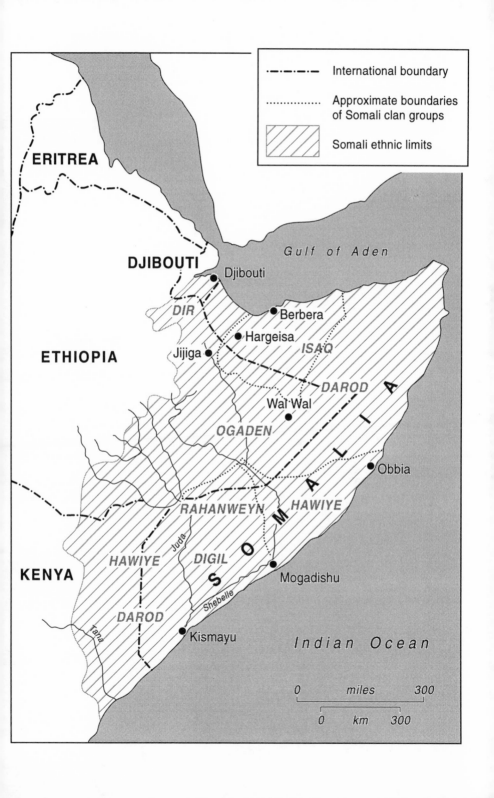

Chapter I

AN ANTHROPOLOGIST AT LARGE

IN THE

"CINDERELLA OF EMPIRE"

"I had another reason which made me less forward to enlarge his
Majesty's dominions by my discoveries. To say the truth, I had conceived a few scruples with relation to the distributive justice of princes
upon these occasions. For instance, a crew of pirates are driven by a
storm they know not whither, at length a boy discovers land from the
topmast, they go on shore to rob and plunder; they see an harmless
people, are entertained with kindness, they give the country a new
name, they take formal possession of it for the king, they set up a rot-
ten plank or a stone for a memorial, they murder two or three dozen
of the natives, bring away a couple more by force for a sample, return
home, and get their pardon. Here commences a new dominion
acquired with a title by divine right. Ships are sent with the first
opportunity, the natives driven out or destroyed, their princes tortured
to discover their gold; a free licence given to all acts of inhumanity
and lust, the earth reeking with the blood of its inhabitants; and this
execrable crew of butchers employed in so pious an expedition, is a
modern colony sent to convert and civilize an idolatrous and bar-
barous people."

— Swift, *Gulliver's Travels*, 1726. Chapter 12.

Somali Apprenticeship

This familiar passage provides a salutary reminder that awareness
of the dangers of the misuse of ethnographic information is scarcely as
novel a hazard a some of the "radical" critics of Anthropology appear to
think. It seems to me self-evident, in any case, that whatever the political persuasions of its individual practitioners, Social Anthropology is by

its very nature one of the most unashamedly exploitive of the vicarious professions. Here, for once, that notoriously elusive Amerindian guru, Don Juan, hits the nail firmly on the head when he bluntly calls his anthropological interpreter and surrogate, Carlos Castaneda, (1974:81) a "pimp."

This unedifying identification will hardly commend itself to the enthusiastic new recruit. And I certainly would have indignantly repudiated it forty years ago as I worked on a thesis in Somali Studies as a graduate at the Institute of Social Anthropology, Oxford, under the benign direction of that immensely erudite scholar, Franz Steiner. Steiner had undertaken to write an ethnographic survey on the Somali and related peoples of North East Africa for the International African Institute. On his untimely death I assumed this responsibility, reworking my B.Litt thesis accordingly (see Lewis 1955/1969). In the course of this library research, I became increasingly intrigued by the people and culture I was learning about second hand. It was very fortunate and probably decisive for me that my first encounter with a living representative was with the distinguished Somali poet and folklorist, Muse Galal, then working at the School of Oriental and African Studies as a research assistant to B.W. Andrzejewski who, in turn, became my teacher and close friend. Through these exciting initial contacts and Andrzejewski's infectious enthusiasm, I was drawn into a wider circle of Somali acquaintance and soon discovered a Somali cause to fire my youthful idealism. This was the campaign organized by political leaders in the British Somaliland Protectorate to recover the important Haud grazing region, recognized as Ethiopian by Britain in 1897, but finally surrendered to effective Ethiopian control only in 1954. When the movement's leaders came to London to present their case as forcefully as they could, I was naturally excited to be able to meet them and to play a minor role in helping with the publicity arrangements.

My romantic ambition to go and study the nomads who were being so harshly treated was fired by these contacts. The problem was to find any organization that was prepared to pay for such research. In common with my peers at Oxford and Anthropology students elsewhere who were similarly desperate to find financial support for their prospective fieldwork overseas, I pursued every possible source. The Colonial Social Science Research Council (financed by Colonial Development and Welfare Funds) awarded one or two research fellowships for anthropologists each year, and these much-prized grants were fiercely sought after. Only a few charitable trusts were prepared to make grants for similar purposes, so that competition was inevitably keen and it was necessary to be patient as well as persistent. The many improbable approaches that

I tried included one to the owners of a famous French trading company with Aden and Somali interests. Through the help of a friend who had recently completed his military service in Somaliland, I even tried to join the Somali Camel Corps (or "Somali Scouts" as it was then known) with, alas, an equal lack of success. Eventually in 1955, while marking time working as a research assistant to Lord Malcolm Hailey who was engaged in revising his magisterial *African Survey* at Chatham House, I had at last the good fortune to secure a research fellowship from the Colonial Social Science Research Council. The Council's Anthropology Committee was chaired at this time by the editor of the *Sunday Times* and Evans-Pritchard, my professor at Oxford, was an influential member. Sally Chilver, who was then Secretary, made all the practical arrangements with a brisk incisiveness that inspired confidence even in callow postgraduates like myself.

My delight at this news was tempered by the information which I received from Mrs Chilver that certain conditions attached to my proposed research. These, it turned out, had nothing to do with my proposed research - a general study of the social and political organization of the Somali nomads - but concerned the issue, at first sight even more delicate, of my position in Somaliland, and relationship with the Protectorate administration. The authorities in Somaliland, I was told, were not prepared to have a strange unattached social researcher roaming the country without let or hindrance. Virtually every expatriate there was an official employee of the government, and ambiguous creatures like me would represent bizarre anomalies which, if left to their own devices and outside official control, might "offend the Somalis" (a phrase with which I was to become very familiar in the ensuing months). Besides, in a territory where a British political officer had recently been shot in a tribal feud, it was emphasized that it would be essential for my own personal security (as well as that of my wife, who was coming with me) to be incorporated within the Protectorate administration. I had of course been taught at Oxford to give colonial officials as wide a berth as possible. But my serious misgivings on this proviso turned out, to be totally misplaced. This was partly, though not entirely, a consequence of the strong pro-Somali ethos of the Protectorate administration.

The Somali Protectorate: a "parental" expatriate regime

Here it is important to have some appreciation of the political history of British interests in the Somali coast. The main factors can be quickly outlined (cf. Lewis 1988:40-62). At the close of the nineteenth century, Britain had reluctantly established a British Somaliland

Protectorate opposite her strategically important base at Aden with two principal aims. There was first a need to ensure a steady supply of Somali mutton for the hungry Aden garrison, and second a broader political interest to curtail the French presence in the Horn in the light of British and French rivalry in Egypt, the Sudan and Ethiopia. If Aden had been rudely seized in 1839 in the spirit so brilliantly satirized by Jonathan Swift, Britain's entry into Somali affairs proceeded very differently. In the wake of earlier trade treaties with the British East African Company, representatives of most of the northern Somali clans readily signed Anglo-Somali treaties of "protection" for "the maintenance of our [i.e. Somali] independence, the preservation of order, and other good and sufficient reasons." Some treaties referred explicitly to the new uncertainties created by the Egyptian withdrawal from Harar, the ancient Muslim center of eastern Ethiopia, a consequence of the dismantling of the Turko-Egyptian administration in the Sudan and its replacement by Anglo-Egyptian rule. From the British point of view this meant excluding hostile or potentially hostile parties such as France. On the Somali side it was the expansion of Ethiopian conquest, under Menelik, that presented the greatest threat. It also seems probable that each individual group of Somali dignitaries viewed their particular treaty with the British as a protective device in the context of local clan quarrels and feuds. As the Somali proverb puts it:, "He who is weak has found the European as his protector." In any event, here, as throughout the course of subsequent Somali history as I have frequently emphasized (cf. Lewis 1961: passim; 1988:40ff, 116ff), when they took it to be in their interest, Somali clans and lineages sought to involve third parties in their internal struggles.

With these minimal and essentially secondary and derived interests in what was later aptly dubbed "a cinderella of empire" Britain was appalled to find herself plunged in 1900 into an extremely costly and unproductive series of campaigns stretching over twenty years against the chimerical forces of the tyrannical, but brilliantly resourceful Somali guerilla leader and national hero, Sayyid Mohamed Abdille Hassan (see Andrzejewski and Lewis 1964; and Lewis 1988: 63-91; S.S. Samatar 1982). The war ended, ironically, with the British more entangled in local Somali affairs than had ever been intended. The expatriate administration consequently received stern admonitions from London that nothing was ever to be done again that could possibly provoke the Somalis. The spectre of another "Mad Mullah" rising in Somaliland haunted the Colonial Office. The latter Ministry had now reluctantly assumed responsibility for the territory from the Foreign Office (via Aden). Caution and appeasement were now the administrative watchwords in Somaliland. Modern developments were thus introduced with tact and patience, and soft-pedalled if the prickly Muslim Somalis responded unfavourably. No attempt was made to impose direct taxes on the turbulent nomads, for fear of a very strong reaction, and Christian missionary activity was henceforth strictly prohibited. It was firmly and repeatedly drummed into all who served in Somaliland that nothing must ever be done that might seriously antagonize the local population. It was bad enough trying to regulate their endless and often bloody clan feuds without risking any wider embroilment. The Somaliland Protectorate, consequently, was ruled with a light, sympathetic touch befitting its situation as a territory with no European settler population.

When my wife and I arrived in 1955, the entire Protectorate establishment consisted of less that 200 senior officials, of whom twenty-five were locally recruited Somalis. The country was divided into six administrative districts and, of the District Commissioners, one was a Somali officer. There were also senior Somali officials in the Education Department, the Information Department and the police force where the highest ranking Somali at the time was an assistant superintendent.

We arrived in Somaliland in September 1955 with all the usual initial fieldwork anxieties increased in my case by my apprehensions regarding the implications of my attachment to the Protectorate administration. I had found that I had been turned into a one-man department (the Protectorate administration tending, like those it served, to segment into a rich profusion of sub-divisions), known officially and somewhat grandiloquently as "The Anthropologist." I was answerable, I discovered, to the Chief Secretary through the Commissioner for Somali Affairs, and financially responsible to the Accountant-General. This entailed keeping a detailed record of financial transactions which had to be passed for approval to the Accountant's office and, just before I left my minuscule enterprise, was subjected to an official audit by a three-man committee. This was an educational and very traumatic experience for someone as inept at book-keeping as myself. I had many entertaining exchanges with the accounting people. When I recorded "gifts to informants," this was rendered by an Indian clerk as "gifts to informers." Toy giraffes, elephants and other animal gifts for children also caused trouble; the word "toy" was inadvertently omitted, and I received a stern request to explain what on earth I was doing. There were other equally trivial misunderstandings: as many on my side as on the part of what, at the time, I tended to dismiss contemptuously as "officialdom."

More seriously, while I soon gathered that various senior officials would have liked me to investigate particular issues (relating, for instance, to local government, self-help schemes etc.), I was actually given carte blanche to do what I liked. The Governor of the territory, Sir Theodore Pike (to whom I had been commended by John Beattie, then a lecturer in Anthropology at Oxford), was extremely understanding and insisted that I was to get on with my own research without any interference. Other key members of the administration and its departments (especially Natural Resources) were equally encouraging and helpful in many crucially important practical ways. Hence, in practice, my assimilation to the role of official which also made my presence seem more natural to the Somali population had many additional advantages. My truck which was on its way from England would be driven by an experienced Somali driver; I was to have four camp assistants (retired rural policemen, selected from different lineages) and access to all the usual facilities supplying camping gear and maintenance available to more orthodox departments. I could even send free telegrams, and in lighthearted moments considered adopting the telegraphic address "Anthropol" - until I discovered that this was the name for a very unpopular locust bait.

Initially, since I was clearly connected with education, it was suggested by the then Commissioner for Somali Affairs and Acting-Chief Secretary (Phillip Carrell, another source of most valuable advice) that my wife and I should live at the center of the Protectorate's principal boy's secondary school, where I would be able to learn from Somali teachers the rudiments of their culture and social institutions. This was located at Sheikh (the old hot-season Protectorate headquarters) on the edge of the Ogo mountain escarpment, with breath-taking views down the precipitous Sheikh pass to the coast. It was an ideal place to get acclimatized to local conditions, but far removed from the centers of major clan activity. After six weeks in that secluded setting where we had our initiation into the usual stomach illnesses that afflict foreigners, and having taken delivery of my new Bedford pick-up,[1] with its special desert tires, we were ready to move to a politically more lively base. I had selected this myself and negotiated with the local District Commissioner the use of an empty house as our headquarters. From this centre (Burao) I was well placed to cover the principal grazing movements of the eastern Somali clans, and within convenient distance (one or two days by road) of their main watering centers. I now felt able to dispense with the services of the distinguished old ex-government interpreter who had been generously provided by the administration. His presence had in any case become insufferable since whenever I asked different people the same questions, as I needed to, he would say that I must be very stupid to have already forgotten the previous answers! Before leaving England, I had received a crash course in basic Somali from by friend, B.W. Andrzejewski, who was an exceedingly patient teacher, and necessity finally emboldened me to launch forth into often grammatically weak but increasingly idiomatic Somali. Some eight months later, we moved from Burao to the Protectorate capital, Hargeisa, which provided an ideal base for working among the western clans, and enabled me to investigate the changes associated with the adoption of cultivation in the fertile Ethiopian border area.

I owe a great deal to the Protectorate authorities in allowing me complete freedom of action and providing such crucial ancillary facilities as information on rain distribution and nomadic movements. Most of the officials I encountered, and upon whom our safety ultimately depended, were hospitable and kindly: those who understood and were interested in my bizarre activities especially so. These included the genial Director of Natural Resources (an accomplished archaeologist), the Senior British Liaison Officer in the Haud, and successive Commissioners for Somali Affairs. One of these officials was a member of the British Communist Party, and resolutely refused to have anything to do with the local expatriate staff club as long as it excluded Somalis from its membership. (The nearest thing I can recall to government intervention in my affairs occurred when I was off on a long trip to Zaila and French Somaliland, and received an uncharacteristically terse telegram from the Commissioner saying I had left my wife for long enough, and it was time to return to base!)

The Protectorate administration as a whole attracted a high proportion of people of exceptional character, including many unusual individuals, whose eccentricities often found valuable and agreeable expression. The local population was regarded, not without justice, as notoriously difficult and challenging. Anyone who could successfully put down a Somali in debate, or out-manoeuver such naturally accomplished politicians as the clan elders, deserved respect. In such taxing conditions, expatriates regularly succumbed to nervous breakdowns - despite the deliberately short tour periods, and frequent leaves which were designed to mitigate the hardship of service in Somaliland. Perhaps capitalizing on adversity, the Protectorate administration tended to present itself as a kind of miniature replica of the prestigious Indian Civil Service (an association encouraged by its original affiliation to the India Office). In many respects, to an outsider like myself, it seemed almost as elitist and robustly individualistic as the people it served. Expatriates who proved unsuccessful in their dealings with Somalis had small hope of promotion in the service, and were encouraged to pursue their careers elsewhere.

This identification with Somali interests, which was so striking, had significant repercussions on British involvement in the Ethio-Somali "boundary" dispute. The social distance between the Protectorate Governor and the British Ambassador in Addis Ababa reflected that between the two neighbouring counties. These rival attachments fed back to Whitehall, where the Colonial Office tended to be pro-Somali while the Foreign Office clearly considered that it was more important to maintain cordial relations with Ethiopia than to accommodate the interests of obscure tribesmen in Somaliland. Thus, contrary to the simplistic view which sees colonialism as the ruthless single-minded pursuit of metropolitan interests, here it was rival local attachments that were attempting to determine colonial policy. Two separate tails were, in effect, trying to wag one ill-coordinated and rather lethargic domestic dog. This tension was dramatically highlighted when, in November 1954, Britain at last implemented the terms of the 1897 Anglo-Ethiopian treaty (contracted in defiance of the antecedent Anglo-Somali clan treaties; see above, and Lewis 1988: 40-62) and relinquished the administration of the vital Haud grazing areas of Ethiopia.

As the India Office had prophesied at the time of the unfortunate 1897 treaty, this transfer (which directly affected thousands of nomads moving back and forth into this area across the Protectorate frontier) had immediate and widespread local repercussions. Vociferous demonstrations occurred throughout the Protectorate. Somali delegations, as we have seen, were despatched to London and New York, and a new coalition party, the National United Front, was formed to coordinate the campaign, pressing for the return of the Haud and for early independence for the Protectorate. The British Colonial Secretary of the day announced in the Commons in 1955 that he regretted the original 1897 Anglo-Ethiopian treaty but found it "impossible to undo it." Nevertheless, such was the pressure mounted by the Somalis with the support of the Protectorate administration as well as by a group of MPs in London, that the Parliamentary Under-Secretary for Foreign Affairs was sent out to Ethiopia to attempt to buy back the Haud from the Emperor. Needless to say he did not succeed: and, with an increased input of Colonial Development and Welfare funds, it was left to the Protectorate authorities to make amends by preparing their wards for self-government as thoroughly and as effectively as they could.

Anthropological Fieldwork in the late 1950s

This, roughly, is where I came in. Moving about among the nomads toward the end of 1955 and early in 1956, I generally encountered an initially hostile reception. Why, I was repeatedly asked, had I (or my gov-

ernment, which was much the same thing) sold the Somalis out so treach-
erously to their traditional foes, the Ethiopians? Day after day, wherever
I went, I had to listen to the same angry tirades about Britain's betrayal
in an atmosphere which was scarcely conducive to effective ethnographic
research. My hesitant ethnographic enquiries were brusquely thrust aside
as my accusers resolutely refused to accept the passive role of informants.
As I sat with a group of elders, each new arrival would renew the debate
from scratch and I would have to listen attentively again to the same
series of denunciations, making what rejoinder I could. The fact that I
agreed entirely and strongly sympathized with these bitter criticisms made
them all the harder to bear. Protesting my innocence, and disclaiming
responsibility for the actions of the government with which I was identified cut little ice. Fieldwork, I had been taught at Oxford, would be difficult; but I never imagined that it would be anything like this. I wondered
whether it would have been different if I had not been attached so directly
to the Protectorate administration. I concluded, however, that this was
not a significant factor since, whatever my real position, I would still
have been identified by the Somalis with the British Government and at
worst regarded as a "spy."

Fortunately for me, this traumatic introductory phase gradually
passed and eventually people began to recognize that (in common with
most of the expatriate officials) I shared their resentment about their
shabby treatment at the hands of successive British governments and
had even helped to publicize their cause. So, as time wore on, I came
increasingly to be seen as a fairly harmless eccentric, exchanging food
and other gifts for information about Somali customs and history. I was
clearly one of the more peculiar branches of the Protectorate service.
My most striking and regularly infuriating characteristic was an apparently unlimited capacity to ask questions, to which the answers were
usually patently obvious, my feeble intelligence and deplorably weak
memory (as was pointed out on several occasions) being all too obvious in my irritating habit of repeating the same questions on different
occasions. "We've told you that already," or "We explained that to you
last week". were retorts that I found as annoying as my questions seemed
to my reluctant informants.

Of course, many still regarded my work with suspicion. Yes, they
knew that I said that I was simply trying to record for posterity as much
as I could learn of their culture past and present. But why was I doing
this: what was my real object? In common with most anthropologists,
whether in colonial or post-colonial circumstances, I was certainly suspected by some of being a government spy, engaged in assessing the size
of the animal and human populations for tax purposes. Religion (Islam)

was also a regularly sensitive issue. Some accepted that I was as attracted to Islam as I claimed; others were more dubious. One shaikh with whom I had many entertaining exchanges once parried one of my questions on a religious topic by saying that he would have to seek divine guidance before we could proceed further. When I met him a few days later, he solemnly informed me that he had been instructed not to reveal Islam's secrets to one who was probably an "infidel." On another occasion an important Islamic dignitary who evidently felt he could trust me, took me inside his house and, having carefully locked the door, unexpectedly produced from the locked chest in which he kept his valuables an Arabic translation of the bible. This, as he explained with a roguish, conspiratorial air, had been given to him by a well-known English Arabist who had visited Somaliland in the course of collecting information on Islam in Africa.

Another religious exchange began very badly, but had consequences which were as gratifying as they were unforseen. While working in the east of the Protectorate, I had a series of encounters with a local man of religion, whose manner was so aggressively suspicious that I began to have serious fears for my personal safety. We eventually parted, with the shaikh still obviously deeply troubled and puzzled by my activities. I felt that I had been subjected to the most searching, covert scrutiny and was relieved to move on unmolested. On a subsequent visit to Somalia almost a decade later, I was amazed to meet this shaikh in Mogadishu and to discover that he had become an oral historian and was busy travelling round the country collecting the poems of Sayyid Mohamed Abdille Hassan, recording variant versions and interpretations in an exemplary style, He had, he told me, carefully examined my work and methods and had reached the conclusion that I was engaged in a worthwhile endeavour which he could also do, with the added benefit, at least in fields such as oral literature, of much greater expertise than I could command. I had unwittingly made a professional convert. Foreign anthropologists sometimes report how they encounter amateur, native counterparts who help them with their work. The situation here was refreshingly different, and is all the more remarkable in that without the benefit of any Western academic training, Shaikh Jama has since produced a definitive, annotated edition of the poems of Mohamed Abdille Hassan unique in Somali Studies and, by any other standards, a work of outstanding scholarship (Shaikh Jama Umar/ Ise 1974). Other work is in progress. If suspicion was never completely allayed in all quarters, as the months passed most of those I met arrived at a shrewd assessment of my situation. While the ultimate purpose remained somewhat obscure, it was clear that I wanted information from my informants and, since I presented myself as a student, it was only right and proper that I should pay my teachers. After all, as many pointed out, I would not have gone to so much trouble to travel so far from my own country unless I hoped to derive commensurate profit. Since, additionally, my hosts were very important people, possessing a unique civilization, I should accordingly pay the appropriate rate. This embarrassingly accurate estimation of my position as an exploitative visitor was also shared by some expatriate officials who were understandably impatient of work which did not manifestly contribute directly to the well-being of the local people. Many of these men were actually engaged on projects of immediate benefit to the Somalis. What was I doing that was of use to anyone except myself?

Somalization and Independence

I now find hard to assess what part discomfort caused by such awkward questions played in my increasing interest in modern Somali politics. I had come to study traditional political organization and found myself more and more fascinated by the transformation of traditional institutions and their accommodation to the changes that were then so prominent. Following the unsuccessful attempt to retrieve the Haud from Ethiopian control, this was a time of growing nationalist fervour and activity. These trends received a generally favourable response, as the Protectorate administration proceeded with the initially gradual and thorough preparation of the country for self-government. the Protectorate's first legislative council was formed in May 1957, just before I left. Thus, throughout my research, I had close relations with many of the new political leaders and bureaucratic elite as well as with traditional political and religious leaders.

Another spur to the pace of development in the Protectorate was the rapid march of events in the neighbouring United Nations Trust Territory of Somalia scheduled to become independent in 1960, and where the Italian trusteeship authorities were busily engaged in making the necessary preparations. I spent some four weeks there in August-September 1956, visiting all the main centers. Despite some minor diplomatic difficulties concerning the impounding of my truck at the Italian frontier and its subsequent clandestine removal from official custody by my driver, the Italian and Somali officials were very hospitable, and understandably eager to display the many developments then in progress. We were fortunate to be touring the country a few months after the formation of the first elected Somali government (30 April 1956). A substantial transfer of power had also just taken place in the administration and police. All the Provincial and District Governors (many of whom I met) were now Somalis, although their Italian "assistants" still played an important role. Similarly, command of the carabinieri-trained Somali police force had just been handed over to its most impressive Somali commander, Mohamed Abshir Muse who was to become one of my closest friends.

These developments made a deep impression and I returned elated to Somaliland full of missionary zeal. Having participated in local meetings of the Somali Youth League, the ruling party in Somalia, I now attended similar gatherings in the Protectorate, and was even brazen enough to attempt a few speeches. I recall patronizingly informing my audience that, whereas in Somalia, day had already dawned, it was still dark night in British Somaliland, and that the local Somali political leaders should get a move on if they did not want to be left lagging far behind. (My colourful choice of metaphor, I am afraid, owed much to my still primitive command of Somali). Some Somalis must have resented my well-intentioned hectoring tone. More interesting to me at the time was the indifference shown by the Somaliland administration. The Protectorate authorities never once asked me what I thought I was up to, nor advised me to keep out of politics. Perhaps no one had told them what I was doing. That, at any rate, was the impression I formed when I was once talking to the police officer whom I understood to be the local security chief. He raised an eye-brow, I thought, but made no other comment as I casually mentioned that I had taken it upon myself to harangue a Somali Youth League meeting. Nor did I subsequently receive any reproof, caution, or other pressures. I was also allowed ready access to various confidential administrative files relating to tribal politics and personalities, and experienced little difficulty in discovering what I wanted to know from official sources.

All this is partly intelligible in terms of my harmlessness and lack of importance (for anthropologists regularly form very exaggerated estimates of their significance). But it also reflects my assimilation in a benevolently paternalistic administration whose policies were unambiguously directed toward preparing the local population for self-rule. I was also able to take advantage of my official status to address to the Kenyan government long critical requests for information on the underprivileged status of the Somalis as I saw it, in the Northern Frontier District there. Fortunately for me, the Chief Secretary in Nairobi was an old "Somali hand" who had served in northern Kenya. But, as I read through our correspondence now, I still marvel at the politeness, candour, and attention to detail with which such a senior official (later Governor of two British colonial territories), grappling with critical issues in conflict-torn Kenya, responded to the often terse queries of a callow graduate student whom he had never met. Part of the answer, as the reader will have gathered, is of course to be found in the very binding attachments which those expatriates who have enjoyed working among Somalis characteristically develop. Here, as in comparable cases elsewhere, their "transference" is at least as intense, and sometimes more sincere, than that professionally required of anthropologists. Evidence of the reciprocal nature of these Anglo-Somali loyalties can be found in the employment, by independent Somali governments, of former expatriate colonial officials in such key positions as principal adviser on foreign affairs to the Prime Minister, and adviser to the chief of police.

The benefits that flowed from my official status in such an organization seem even more striking in retrospect than they did at the time, when I tended to take them for granted. My only formal obligation to the Protectorate administration was to prepare a report on my research. This was a small return for everything I had received, and turned out to be a very useful exercise. I wrote it in Somaliland some weeks before I reluctantly left the territory to return to Oxford to write my D.Phil. thesis. This forced me to try to piece together my findings and ideas while I was still in the country and in a position to check contradictory data and to rectify omissions which only then began to come to light. The report I completed in April 1957, a month before leaving, runs to 140 roneoed foolscap pages and is pompously titled: *The Somali Lineage System and the Total Genealogy: a general introduction to basic principles of Somali Political Institutions* (Lewis 1957). Its tone towards the local administrators is shamefully patronizing, and I blush to read it now. It reflects all the native arrogance I had learnt to cultivate at Oxford. Forty pages were devoted entirely to the development of Somali nationalism, and the presentation of my argument throughout emphasized process and political change: in short, those major themes those of us who worked in this period are so often alleged to have ignored. I also forcefully argued that it was impossible (not simply undesirable) to try to understand Somali lineage politics under Protectorate rule without taking into account (as the Somalis most emphatically did) the presence of the alien administration.

My report was circulated to various members of the Protectorate government, producing a wide range of interesting and often valuable criticisms. One of the most enthusiastic commentators wrote that he had read it through "three times and found it of absorbing interest;" it was, he said, "a scholarly, interesting and accurate work whose publication would be of advantage not only to Somalis themselves but also to those who serve them." Other readers had reservations about some passages, particularly those referring to the government's maintenance of law and order as "somewhat fitful" and some Somali critics objected to certain renderings of their genealogies. In the present context, it may be of interest to record that many of the expatriate officials commented that they wished this material had been available a decade earlier. My installation as a "government" anthropologist was thus I fear untimely if not anachronistic. Certainly it did not, in any significant way, serve the interests of the government who had so generously financed it. It is possible, I suppose, that my findings may have played a minimal role in the de-colonization process. But then, of course, progress toward self-government was precisely what the Colonial Development and Welfare Fund had been established to facilitate.

Protectorate Anthropology in retrospect

As I have stressed throughout this account, the changing situation in which I found myself strongly affected the direction of my research and analysis. (It is interesting to find much the same emphasis in the works of the late A.A. Castagno, the distinguished political scientist who became a specialist on the Horn of Africa. [See e.g. Castagno 1964].) To have neglected to respond to these currents would have required the oblivious dedication of a blind ostrich. My biggest problem was not in fending off obtrusive administrative pressures, but rather in acknowledging the inadequacy of the model of Somali society I had built up in Oxford in imitation of Evans-Pritchard's brilliant analysis of the Nuer lineage system. It was this intellectual colonial heritage that had to be radically revised in the light of my own first-hand findings, a process that was in some respects all the more difficult in that I had already published a comprehensive account of the Somali, based on my library research, prior to undertaking fieldwork. The Somalis in many vital respects were, alas, not quite what I had expected them to be. (Compare Lewis 1955 [pre-fieldwork] and Lewis 1961 [post-fieldwork].) Emrys Peters' publications (Peters 1967) on the Bedouin of Cyrenaica seem to bear witness to a similar intellectual struggle directed toward achieving a more flexible segmentary lineage mode.

Since leaving Somaliland in 1957, I have revisited the country on a dozen occasions, most recently in 1992; in 1974 and again in 1978 I spent two months trying to evaluate developments achieved by the "socialist" military regime that seized power in October 1969 (see Lewis 1972a, 1972b, 1976, 1979). In one capacity or another, I have thus had dealings with every Somali government since independence in 1960. I have also written about every government before and after independence. This continuing interest in contemporary Somali affairs has generally been encouraged by Somali politicians, for whom a foreign anthropologist prepared to present current political issues sympathetically is not a totally negligible asset. In this vein, the most effective Somali Prime Minister, Abdirazaq Haji Hussein once introduced me to his cabinet as "that chap who writes about us. We don't always like what he says, but the important thing is that he writes about us!" Even the military dictator, Mohamed Siyad Barre, reluctantly tolerated me for many years despite publications (such as chapter seven) which he found far from sufficiently adulatory. (Indeed, I have been told by one of his presidential aids that the President had written on a copy that found its way into his hands such enlightening marginal comments as: "Who is this shit?"). However, there were limits. In 1986, at the height of the tyrannical oppression of northern Somaliland, in newspaper articles I urged that Western countries should suspend aid to Somalia until Siyad showed some respect for human rights and it was at this point that I was refused a visa. When it was offered a year or so later, I told the London ambassador that I had now broken off relations with his government and would not be participating in the forthcoming Somali Studies conference in Mogadishu which I saw as a public relations exercise!

My earlier diplomatic adventures in Somalia took place in less sombre circumstances. In the late 1960s as an impecunious young researcher, on the advice of my friends in the Somali police while working in Mogadishu I pitched a tent on the outskirts of the city beside a "police well." My police friends neglected to tell me that this was on land leased to the Italian embassy. In due course, a permanent secretary in the foreign ministry happened to mention that the Somali government had received an official complaint from the Italians about a foreign "vagabond" camping on their property and that he had been charged to investigate the matter. I was able to help him bring it to a prompt conclusion! In 1974, when General Siyad was chairman of the Organization of African Unity and I was in Somalia studying "scientific socialism," I received a message from a Portuguese friend and former colleague who was then working as a personal assistant to the Portuguese Prime Minister. He asked me to try and set up a meeting between his Prime Minister and President Siyad: the object was to negotiate with the freedom fighters in Mozambique and Angola through the OAU presidency. This was achieved through the Somali foreign minister who asked my Portuguese friend to come to Mogadishu as a preliminary to the formal meeting. My friend's visit was shrouded in secrecy, but he managed to escape his National Security Service watchers to sample the Mogadishu night-life so successfully that for years afterwards I was asked how my Portuguese friend (who has since become a distinguished diplomat) was getting on.

The danger here, however, is that the anthropologist who accepts this engagé role (which may be very flattering to his self-esteem) may become a kind of part-time official chronicler, and ultimately simply a propagandist for a particular power elite. Thinking back, I am most conscious of this during the 1977-78 Somali-Ethiopian Ogaadeen war when I was broadcasting virtually every week on the BBC World Service, on one program or another, commenting on the course of the conflict. I have certainly been more subject to pressures, often elusively subtle ones, in post-than in pre-independence Somalia. Reflecting on this, I now think that I have sometimes tended to be less critical and objective (too guilty of the professional anthropological "charity" Ernest Gellner [1962] rightly criticizes) about the policies and actions of successive independent Somali governments. With the benefit of hindsight, I can now see that I should have been more appreciative of the often exemplary dedication of many expatriate officials in the Protectorate administration. Here, as elsewhere, the historical perspective seems salutary if not essential.

This is not simply because it was so much easier then than it is now to carry out unrestricted research in Social Anthropology. For, in principle, I support the policy, now commonly adopted by Third World governments, not to allow themselves simply to be treated as passive "subjects for study" and requiring foreign social scientists to make some positive contribution to local problems. The trouble, however, is that it is precisely here that the most challenging ethical problems arise. As I found when teaching at the University of Rhodesia and Nyasaland (now the University of Zimbabwe) during the ill-fated Central African Federation (1957-60), it is easy to swagger around protesting one's dedication to the overthrow of a right-wing colonial regime. Some issues are morally very clear-cut. But it is much more difficult to decide where, in an independent Black state, the anthropologist's loyalty lies when there is an irreconcilable conflict between local-level and national, indigenous interests. Nor are these problems eased when one confronts a despotic regime (particularly if it claims to be left-wing) whose "enlightened" development plans and projects would automatically receive support from most well-intentioned anthropologists. More and more this is the real "crisis" with which those anthropologists who value research more than rhetoric have to contend.

Notes

1. Professor Burton Benedict, who was the other anthropologist to receive a C.S.S.R.C. fellowship in 1955, tells me that whenever he applied from the field for urgent supplementary funds he was told that none were available owing to the exorbitant cost of my transportation in Somaliland. Actually the total cost (approx. £4,000) of my project (C.D. and W.Scheme R.632), covered approximately twenty months' fieldwork, followed by a writing-up period of about four months at Oxford where I presented my D.Phil thesis in October 1957, two years after our arrival in Somaliland.

Chapter II

The Roots of Kinship:
Marriage and the Family

Somaliland (formerly the Northern regions of Somalia, and prior to that the Somaliland Protectorate), much of which is semi-desert, presents an arid environment in which the bulk of an estimated population of nearly one million live as pastoral nomads.[1] Some cultivation, chiefly of sorghum, is practised in the west of the territory, and outside it in Hararghe Province of Ethiopia. There is, however, no sharp distinction between nomadic pastoralists and cultivators; different individuals and segments of the same clan and lineage engage in both, and many of those who cultivate in local settlements also leave livestock in the care of nomadic kin. Although the cultivators are of the same clans as their pastoral kin, having turned to agriculture only within the last few decades and sharing the same institutions, their region is nevertheless one of social change where new values are being given to traditional pastoral institutions. and for this reason I exclude them from this account and concentrate here on marriage amongst the nomads.[2]

The northern Somali have a segmentary lineage organization of which, only the salient features need be mentioned here (cf. Lewis, 1957; 1961; 1982). Descent is traced patrilineally, and through his genealogy (abtirsiinyo, "reckoning of ancestors") each individual has an exact place in society. Patrilineal descent (tol) indeed is all pervasive: most corporate activities are contingent upon it; in the veneration of local lineage saints Islam is interpreted to some extent according to it; and politics stem from it. Everyone is born into a patrilineage, and thereby into a system of highly segmented patrilineal descent groups. In northern Somaliland the largest effective units are nine patrilineages which from their size and distinctiveness may conveniently be called "clans." These range in population from 20,000 to 130,000. Other smaller northern Somali clans can be ignored here. At a higher level of genealogical grouping, these clans are grouped in three larger units which I refer to as "clan-families." These are the Dir in the west; the Isaaq in the centre; and the Daarood in the east. (The Hawiye, who are mainly pastoralists live in central, southern Somalia, with the two remaining clan-families the Digil and Rahanwiin practising agro-pastoralism in the inter-riverine area of the south). Although clan-family membership has political implications, in the traditional structure of society the clan-families never act as united corporate groups for they are too large and unwieldy and their members too widely scattered.[3]

As clan families are segmented agnatically by reference to apical ancestors in their genealogies and by uterine ties or 'complementary filiation' (cf. Fortes, 1953), so clans are similarly divided into a series of component patrilineages. While to the ancestor of his clan-family a person commonly counts twenty named generations or more, to the eponym of his clan he usually counts between fifteen and twenty ancestors according to its size. Within the clan the largest most clearly defined subsidiary group can conveniently be termed a "primary lineage." This unit usually represents the limits of exogamy; amongst its segments marriage is forbidden, although not considered incestuous, and most marriages are between people of different primary lineages. In genealogical span this lineage has a depth of from six to ten named generations. (See chart opposite)

Finally, within the segmentation of his primary lineage a person most frequently acts as a member of a "dia-paying group," and this is the basic jural and political unit of northern Somali society. It is a lineage or coalition of a few small lineages tracing descent to a common ancestor from between four and eight generations. Its male strength ranges from a few hundred to a few thousand. In Somaliland there were more than three hundred and sixty such groups in the 1950s. The name "dia-paying group" which became standard administrative usage under the British derives from the Arabic diiya (Somali, mag), meaning blood-wealth. The dia-paying group is essentially a corporate agnatic group whose members are united in joint responsibility towards outsiders. The most important aspect of their unity is the collective payment of blood-compensation. If one member of a dia-paying group is injured or killed by another group, or if his property is attacked, the wronged group is pledged to collective vengeance, or if reparation is made, to sharing the compensation paid amongst all its male members. Conversely, if a person of a dia-paying group commits homicide or injury outside his group, all the other members are collectively responsible for his actions and jointly concerned in effecting reparation.

Genealogy of man of 'Ali Geri lineage showing
main points of lineage segmentation

Kablallah Daarood	*clan-family*
Koombe Kablallah	
Harti Koombe	
Si'iid Harti (Dulbahante)	*clan*
Muuse Si'iid	
'Abdalle Muuse	
Habarwaa 'Abdalle	
Shirshoore Habarwaa	
Faarah Shirshoore (Faarah Garaad)	
Ahmad Faarah	
'Ali Geri Ahmad	*Primary lineage*
Suubaan 'Ali Geri	*dia-paying group*
Khayr Suubaan	
'Igaal Khayre	
Heyri 'Igaal	
Faarah Heyri	
Mahammad Faarah	*individual elder*

Dia-paying groups act similarly in less serious issues and the interests of their members are defined by written treaties (sg. *heer*) which are lodged in District Offices. Their actual terms vary from group to group with size, degree of internal segmentation (a general concomitant of size), wealth, and other factors. But in principle all northern Somali accept that a man's life is worth 100 camels and a woman's half that number. It is important to stress that the "dia-paying group" owes its unity to a formal contract by which its members, who are agnatic kin, bind themselves together. Political unity in northern Somaliland is not merely a matter of agnatic loyalty but equally a question of formal political contract (*heer*).

Dia-paying contracts thus define the basic jural and political status of the individual and are so regarded by the administration in the settlement of disputes. In recognition of their importance, stipended local authorities (*Akils*) were appointed by the British government as the heads of the larger dia-paying groups, and smaller dia-paying groups had un-salaried but government recognised headmen. Such leaders, however, have little effective authority whatever their position in relation to the government, and are usually little more than mediators between their groups and the administration. During the socialist period of General Siyad's military regime, the term *Akil*, (properly, *'aakil*) was replaced by "peace-seeker" (*nabad doon*).

This is in keeping with the general character of northern Somali political structure which lacks chiefly offices to a marked degree. The only traditional political office occurs at the level of the clan and, in the case of very large clans, at the level of those lineages within them which may be distinguished for their size as "sub-clans." And even clan-heads (commonly styled "Sultan") have little instituted authority. At every level of political division policy is made by the elders (sg. *oday, duk*) concerned meeting in *ad hoc* councils (sg. *shir*) in which every adult male has traditionally the right to speak. This democratic organization has been preserved and is little affected by the appointment of government headmen for the dia-paying groups. During the colonial period, hardly any attempt was made to artificially erect a system of Indirect Rule. Nor, unlike the situation in the Northern Province of Kenya, was a poll-tax ever imposed.

The orders of political division distinguished in the foregoing represent the main lines of lineage cleavage. In practice, every point of lineage segmentation — every ancestor in the genealogies — is at least potentially an axis of political division and unity. From time to time concerted political action takes place not only at the level of dia-paying group, primary lineage, and clan, but at other orders of segmentation within the clan-family. Since political unity is always based on formal political contracts, when agnatic kin combine together at any level in the genealogies, they define the scope of their collective solidarity by a specific agreement. This means that in general any lineage which acts as a separate political unit in relation to others is at the time of its unity a "dia-paying group."

Thus dia-paying unity is not restricted only to the level of the minimal political units which I have called dia-paying groups. Equally the minimal dia-paying group which defines the individual's primary jural and political allegiance has only relative stability. Moreover, contract which is of fundamental importance in the constitution of political units and which normally complements agnation may sometimes override it. Since in northern Somali society, even under modern administration, self-help remains the basic arbiter in group relations and collective strength is at a premium, small groups find it expedient, if not essential, to unite against their stronger collateral lineages. Such lineage alliances sometimes run counter to the genealogical positions of groups. Coalitions of this kind within the framework of agnatic kinship often follow uterine cleavages, but whether this is so or not they always require contracts. Thus inconsistencies between the genealogical positions of lineages and their actual political status in terms of fighting strength can be resolved by contractual alliances, with or without the benefit of uterine connection, rather than by genealogical fictions. In comparison with other segmentary lineage societies fictional kinship seems strikingly rare in Somaliland.

Only at the level of the clan is there usually some association between lineage and territory. As pastoral nomads, members of a given lineage are generally widely deployed with their sheep and goats and herds of camels in the pastures. Grazing is regarded as a gift of God to man in general rather than allocated to specific groups. Pasture is thus not subject to ownership in the ordinary sense, and the right to graze in an area depends upon its effective occupation. Thus, ultimately, men and their stock move where they will subject only to their ability to maintain their position against others, if necessary by force. It is usually only in time of war, or when there is exceptional pressure on available grazing, that prescriptive rights of use are claimed and, if they are challenged, these can be maintained effectively only by force. Nevertheless, while pasture is not owned and clans do not occupy determinate territories at all seasons of the year, or in all years, usage backed by effective fighting potential and administrative recognition creates some degree of customary association with particular areas. So, at the level of the clan particularly, there is some regularity in grazing movements from year to year. This incipient localization is reinforced through the ownership of wells by groups and individuals in particular areas, and through local interests in the trading villages and small towns which are the oases of Somaliland. While there is great seasonal mobility in the population of such centers, and a constant movement between them and the pastures, there are almost always some villages in which some members of a clan are permanently domiciled. Within the clan, at subsidiary levels of lineage division, attachment to territory is less well-defined and grazing movements present a less regular pattern.

The basic herding units

There are two basic herding units in the northern Somali pastoral economy: the "nomadic hamlet," which is essentially a sheep and goat herding unit; and the "camel camp," which contains only camels. This division reflects the superior powers of endurance of camels and their less exigent watering needs in comparison with sheep and goats. In the dry seasons sheep and goats require regular watering every few days and must move in close proximity to water-points. Camels, on the other hand, can go without water for fourteen days or longer on dry grazing and have a correspondingly wider range of movement. The nomadic hamlet (*guri* or *reer*)[4] consists of a group of nuclear families, whose heads are closely related agnatic kin, with their flocks, burden camels to transport their collapsible tents (sg. *aqal*) and effects, and occasionally a few milch camels or cattle. A hamlet may be no more than the domestic group of a man and wife, or wives, and their young children with the livestock necessary for their support. Often, however, it consists of several nuclear or polygynous families of brothers, or more commonly of close agnates of the same dia-paying group with their dependants. Affines and other non-agnatically related men are frequently also included: in a sample of fifty-seven hamlets drawn from three grazing encampments and containing one hundred and eighty married women and widows, each with their own tents, 32%. of the hamlets contained affinally and other non-agnatically related men. The kinship structure of the hamlets is shown in the table.

Hamlets whose male members are all agnates

Man with or without widowed mother (or wife's mother) and
    with wife or wives and children 16
Extended family of brothers, with or without father,
    and with their wives and unmarried children...........................8
Kinsmen, other than brothers, of the same dia-paying group
    and with their wives and unmarried children..........................15
Total agnatically structured hamlets 39

Hamlets including affines or other non-agnatic kin

Affines living with nucleus of single or extended family...................7

Affines living with nucleus of agnates of the same
    dia-paying group...6
Other relationships 5

Total hamlets whose male members are not
    all agnatic kin..18
Total hamlets 57

The hamlet itself is an unstable unit, constituted as essentially a domestic group of a man with his wife or wives, with his father and brothers and their families, or only the latter, or more frequently of close agnates of the same dia-paying group with their families. Its composition fluctuates considerably through the seasons and from year to year. This is not merely the effect of changes in composition due to different stages in the formation, growth, and dispersal of families. All men do not leave the hamlet of their father when they marry, nor do all brothers separate to found new hamlets on their father's death. Many of the changes in hamlet membership are quite independent of such developmental processes. At one time a man's several wives may live together in the same hamlet, at other times they move as widely separated units amongst whom the husband shares his time and affection. Again, men attach their families now to one group of close kin, now to another. In the grazing movements of a single season the same individual families often assume quite different patterns of grouping within the general field of agnatic kinship. Thus the composition of hamlets fluctuates partly in accordance with domestic affairs, individual convenience, and lineage politics. No hamlet has a rigid structure which is only changed by the developmental phases through which its members pass.

On the average the nomadic hamlet contains three nuclear families. On occasion, however, it may swell to five or six families, but rarely more. Whatever its composition, it is generally led by the eldest man of the lineage whose members are in the majority in the hamlet. Physically it consists of a cluster of nomadic tents made of skins and mats which are attached to a hemispherical frame of wooden boughs. Each married woman or widow has her own tent, and the tents are arranged within a roughly circular fence of thorn bushes for protection against wild animals and other marauders. In the centre of the hamlet thorn bush pens are erected in which the sheep and goats are kept during the night. Usually each married woman has a separate pen for her flock and the husbandry of sheep and goats is essentially the province of women and unmarried girls. As soon as they reach the age of about seven or eight years, boys are sent out to join the camel herders in the camel camps to learn the hard art of camel husbandry.

The herding of the grazing camels, most of which are females, is exclusively the work of men. It is rare to find a married man with the camels since after marriage men usually move with the nomadic hamlets; although in the dry seasons when the grazing camels are brought in from the pastures to the wells every two or three weeks, their owners in the hamlets assist with their watering. The youths and boys -sons, younger brothers, nephews and occasionally hired servants of the camel owners - who are out in the camel camps live mainly off the milk of the camels. They are often without means of cooking and sleep out in the open. In the dry seasons, particularly, when milk and water are scarce their lot is especially hard. In addition to the physical rigours of their existence - constant movement with the herds to new pastures, and in the dry seasons, the regularly repeated long treks to the wells - they have to be constantly on the watch for stock thieves and raiders.

Livestock and agnation

Physically, a camel camp (*geelher*) consists of a large rough thorn fence, which, where several herds are corralled together, is divided internally into separate pens. Each camp contains the herds of a few close agnates and some conception of the kinds of kin who regularly herd their stock together can be gained from the following table. In contrast to the nomadic hamlets the camel camps very rarely contain the stock of non-agnates. Although individuals have primary rights over camels, they are also regarded as part of the joint stock-wealth of a lineage, and, in contrast to sheep and goats which carry the brands of their individual owners, bear a lineage brand (*summad*) usually that of the dia-paying group. Thus camels, in a sense, represent agnation, and in distinction to the nomadic hamlets which are essentially domestic groups, camel camps contain the capital resources of agnatic kin. For a man to transfer his camels from the herds of his kin is tantamount to a renunciation of his lineage solidarity.

In relation to their differing grazing and watering needs these two stock-units generally move separately and to some extent quite independently of each other. They tend to be closest together in the wet seasons when stock feeding on green pasture need little or no watering and the sheep and goats have correspondingly greater mobility. In the dry seasons when the grazing movements of the hamlets are most restricted, the camel camps are often far distant. And like the hamlet, the camel camp does not have a permanent composition. Men move their herds from one camp to another frequently, but always place them with those of kinsmen usually of the same dia-paying group. Nor does the fact that two kinsmen move together in the same nomadic hamlet mean that their camels will be together in the same camp. There is not a corresponding camel camp for each hamlet.

Where pasturage is sufficient, groups of hamlets or camel camps congregate to form temporary encampments (*degmo* from *deg*, to settle or pitch camp). These are not firm local units, they have no formal leader, and as the grazing is exhausted, or in response to reports of better pasture elsewhere, they split up at random, each hamlet or camel camp moving sometimes separately to a new area of grazing where a new and equally ephemeral encampment is formed with a new composition. Nevertheless, despite this shifting picture, where people settle in such transitory clusters they tend to distribute themselves according to

Composition of Camel Camps

Camels of one man herded separately 9
Camels of an extended family of brothers with or without the father...............2
Camels of other kinsmen of the same dia-paying group...................................16
Camels of kinsmen of different dia-paying groups..1

Grazing Encampment

(Hidhid Region: area approx 5 square miles, February 1956)

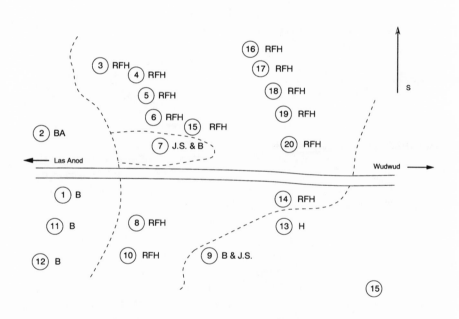

Key

RFH	Reer Farrah Hagar
B	Barkad
BA	Bah Ararsame
J. S.	Jaama Siyaad
H	Hawiye

their lineage affiliation.[5] This applies both to the temporary encampments of hamlets and of camel camps and is most marked in time of war when kinsmen cluster together for support and safety. But at other times, except in the case of very small lineages of only three or four generations, all the men of a lineage are rarely found together in the same grazing encampment.

War and feud occur frequently in Somaliland and constitute a further hazard to the pastoralists in their movements. In an arid environment in which overgrazing is general and where the human and stock populations press heavily upon the sparse grazing resources available there is constant competition for access to pasture and water and frequent lineage strife. This is most acute in the dry seasons but is generally characteristic of the pastoral life as a whole. Feud is thus endemic and, moreover, is not easily controlled in an arid country whose population is widely dispersed and where rifles[6] and motor vehicles are commonly employed in battle.

With the corresponding belief in the ultimate power of force as the decisive factor in lineage relations, agnatic solidarity is at a premium. In the last analysis the individual's security depends upon the strength of his dia-paying group and upon the number and power of his agnates. This is true even when external intervention prevents open hostility between groups and forces a settlement. For to a significant extent the amount of compensation offered and the alacrity with which it is paid is a function of the size and power of the lineages concerned. At the same time, the pastoralist is equally dependent on his kinsmen for assistance in the herding and watering of his stock, particularly his camels, and relies upon them for help in time of misfortune and famine. Thus in addition to common property interests in camels, the force of agnation, regulated and given political definition by contract, is extremely strong.

Moreover, the struggle between lineages is extended into other spheres to an unusual degree. Lineages compete in trade and there is constant rivalry over the granting of trading licences; in appointments to all kinds and ranks of employment in the public service; and since the late 50s also in national politics (cf. Lewis, 1988 pp 139-205). These patterns of lineage allegiance persist strongly in the modern towns and trading villages of Somaliland which economically and politically are essentially part and parcel of the pastoral social system. And although these settlements, the market centers for the trade of the interior, are now also the centres of social change and of nationalism, for the most part the social relations of their inhabitants, many of whom alternate between town and pasture, are based on the same clan and contractual ties as operate in the interior. Thus in a wide range of activities and spheres of social interaction beyond the strictly political, agnatic allegiance is of fundamental importance and its moral force is exceedingly strong (seen chapter 5).

In keeping with the weakness of territorially based social ties, agnation supplemented by contract has an ideological primacy which kinship does not appear to possess in other similar segmentary societies with less shifting land relationships and more binding local loyalties. In discussing the compelling moral force of kinship Somali compare agnation (*tol*) to iron or to the testicles. It is something which in principle, and generally in practice also, cannot be effaced or forgotten. With these associations the strength of agnation is contrasted with the weaker allegiances which arise through marriage, either affinally or matrilaterally, in the phrase *hayn iyo hiniin*, literally the undergarments worn by women, and the testicles.

This expression, however, while indicating the priority of agnation, is not meant to minimise the importance of non-agnatic and affinal ties. The wide network of affinal and matrilateral ties which each individual possesses is used to the full as a subsidiary basis in social relationships. This is drawn upon to gain access to pasture and water held by non-agnates, to gain help in time of distress, and in the wider sphere of social relations in employment and in many other ways. It is partly in relation to these considerations that Somali marriage is to be understood. The nature of marriage, the rights and duties established by matrimony between individuals and lineages, has to be viewed in relation not only to the exclusiveness of agnation but also in relation to the importance which affinal and matrilateral ties often assume in linking lineages.

The Nuclear and Polygynous Family

The northern Somali practise polygyny within the limits of Islamic Law which permits a man to possess up to four wives at any one time. In my experience it is unusual for a middle-aged man of from 40 to 60 years in age not to have married at least twice, either in concurrent or successive unions. In a sample of seventy-seven married men[7] between the approximate ages of thirty and sixty years, thirty-four (44.2 per cent) had only one wife; twenty-eight (36.4 per cent) had two; ten (13 per cent) had three; and five (6.5 per cent) had the legal maximum of four wives. In general polygyny tends to increase with age and status; older men have generally more wives than young men and usually also more livestock. Greater wealth in livestock, particularly in sheep and goats, not only enables a man to pay new bride-wealth but often also leads him to seek a new bride to cope with the husbandry of a flock which has become too large to be managed easily by one woman and her unmarried daughters. As the accompanying table illustrates, the average flock managed by a married woman contains about 150 head of sheep and goats and it is unusual for a wife, unless her daughters are very numerous, or unless she is helped by a widowed mother, to effectively manage a flock of more than two or three hundred head of stock. The minimum flock upon which a wife with a family of four or five young children can normally subsist contains about fifty or sixty animals.[8] For rarely half any flock are in milk at the same time, and at the end of the dry season the number of animals in milk is often very small. The minimum camel (or cattle) requirement is 10-15 milch animals. Depending on the family's own labour supply, a flock of two hundred or more sheep and goats may require additional help from women relatives. (For sales patterns, see chapter 5).

Thus most marriages are polygynous and most men between the ages of forty and sixty have succeeded in establishing a polygynous family. The polygynous family is known as *raasas* or *haasas*, the plural forms of *raas* and *haas*, the nuclear family. The expression *haas* particularly connotes weakness and refers to the demanding water requirements of the flocks and to the vulnerability of a mother and her young children whose leader, the father, is not always with them. For a man has to share his time out amongst his co-wives who are often not in the same hamlet, and especially in the dry seasons is forced to spend much time away from his children at the wells where his camels water.

A man's first wife and her children form the "great house" (*minweyn*) in contrast to the families of subsequent marriages each of which in relation to the first is described as a "little house" (*minyar*). Successive families, however, are not arranged in a strict order of precedence and it is the distinction between the first wife and other secondary wives which is most important. The first wife normally directs the domestic life of the polygynous family when the several nuclear families live and move together as a unit. Over her co-wives (*dangalo*, literally "those whose interests cross") the senior wife exerts a tenuous authority which is tempered by the preference which most polygynous husbands display for their newest and youngest bride. The senior wife is not the focus of the economic nexus of the polygynous family for each wife has her own tent and flock for the subsistence of her children. Nevertheless, where co-wives co-operate either in moving camp or in the domestic life of the family where they live together, the senior wife takes the lead and her house is usually the first on the right as one enters the outer-fence of the hamlet.

Distribution of Livestock (1955–56)

A. Nomadic Dulbahante

	No. of Wives	Camels	Sheep and Goats	Cattle
1.	2	6	60	
2.	3	108	430	30
3.	2	36	200	
4.	1	24	120	
5.	4	200	1400	20
6.	2	84	300	
7.	2	35	160	
8.	2	126	180	14
9.	1	40	150	
10.	2	60	250	
11	1	44	200	
12	4	40	300	
13	3	55	160	
14	2	60	150	
15	3	100	1000	
16	2	100	200	
17	1	40	120	
18	2	500	1100	
19.	2	500	1100	
20.	2	50	100	
21.	1	24	100	
22.	1	60	60	
23.	1	20	50	
24.	2	300	1100	
25.	2	14	50	
26.	2	80	600	
27.	3	60	120	

B. Nomadic 'Iise

	No. of Wives	Camels	Sheep and Goats	Cattle
28.	3	20	400	
29.	1	4		
30.	4	170	400	200
31.	2	11	120	200
32.	1	12	120	
33.	1	4	50	
34.	4	20	400	10
35.	3	15	470	
36.	2	25	360	

All a man's children bear as surname his first-name. Thus if a man called Mohamed has a son Ahmad and a daughter Qamar, they are known as Ahmad Mohamed and Qamar Mohamed and jointly referred to as 'children of Mohamed' (*ilmo Mohamed*). Within the polygynous family children are distinguished according to the uterine nuclear families to which they belong. Thus if Mohamed has three wives, Deeqa, Dulmar and Sureer, all of whom have children, then the three uterine families (*baho*, sg. *bah*)[9] are distinguished as Bah Deeqa, Bah Dulmar and Bah Sureer.

All the children are siblings (*walaallo*) to each other, the term siblings (sg. *walaal*) being applied only to children of the same parent and not extended to patrilineal cousins (sg. *ina'adeer*). Full siblings are distinguished from uterine half-siblings, and the children of the respective uterine families fully described as "siblings of the same father but different mother" (*walaallo waana is ku aabbe, waana kala hooyo*).

In the hamlet each uterine family has its own flocks on which it is primarily dependent for milk, the staple diet of the pastoralist, and in the dry seasons when sheep and goats are killed, for meat. Commonly, when a widowed mother lives in the same hamlet as a married son or daughter, the two flocks are penned and herded together. And sometimes the flocks of co-wives who are kin, or of women married to two brothers, are penned together. Although the husband is the legal owner of the flocks of all his wives, each wife controls her own flock and has considerable autonomy in her management of it, sometimes killing sheep and goats, or buying and selling a few animals without consulting her husband. Each uterine family is thus mainly dependent for day to day subsistence on its own family flock: clothes and other occasional expenses are usually paid for directly by the head of the family. Not every uterine family, however, has sufficient burden camels for its needs, and it is here particularly that there is co-operation between co-wives, or other families of the same hamlet.

In distinction to the flocks which essentially serve subsistence needs, all the camels of the polygynous family are herded and penned together in the camel camp. In principle only men own grazing camels and normally, at birth, a boy is given a she-camel known as the 'navel-knot' (*huddunhid*) which represents the nucleus of his future herd (sheep and goats are often also given). As he grows up, his navel-knot stock increase and he may acquire other stock as gifts from kinsmen. These, however, are not separated from those of his full and half-brothers but remain within the polygynous family herd in the final control of the family head. At marriage, a young man's increasing rights in camels are usually formalised and a portion of the herd allocated to him as bride-wealth. If, after paying for his bride, he has any camels left, these usually remain with those of his brothers and father in the same herd, unless they are very numerous when the newly married man may decide to form a separate herd. Thus the polygynous family camels are pooled, representing as they do the collective capital[10] of the family as a whole, and are not usually separated into new herds until the father dies or decides before his death to divide his stock. On the death of the head of the polygynous family, the camels as well as the sheep and goats are distributed by uterine estate. In the division of the inheritance (*dahal*) the first-born son (*'urad*) of the "great house" is customarily entitled to a larger share than his brothers. If however some of his younger brothers are still unmarried, and if he wishes to show generosity, he may waive part of his rights in favour of them, arguing that he has already benefited by drawing his bride-wealth from the herd. The first born son's privileges here reflect the fact that on his father's death he becomes titular head of the family. Where his brothers are already married, and separate from him, this may have little practical significance although it remains his duty to lead in family ritual.

Betrothal and Marriage

Despite the distinction in status between the "great and little houses," the procedure of contracting marriage, whether for a first or second wife, is much the same. There is some indication that infant betrothal may have been common in the past, but whether this is true or not, it is certainly not the general practice today. Girls marry for the first time between the ages of fifteen and twenty, and men usually marry a little later, between the ages of eighteen and twenty-five. Some control over the age of the first marriage is exerted by the principle that uterine brothers should marry in the order of their birth, and it is sometimes said that men who succeed in marrying prematurely will be destined to a luckless union. I have heard of extremely bitter conflicts between brothers where a younger brother married out of turn. This practice relates to the joint rights of siblings in the uterine estate from which bride-wealths are normally paid. Where, however, an unmarried elder brother has, through working in the government service or through other employment, an independent source of income, his precedence may be ignored.

A young man's parents, especially his father, and other senior agnates still exercise considerable control in his choice of a bride, particularly where a marriage is arranged to forward the interests of the families and lineages concerned, where in other words it is desired to forge an advantageous social link between groups. Elopements are fairly common despite this control, especially in first marriages. Many marriages, however, reflect some degree at least of personal preference on the part of the partners.[11] Clearly older men making a second or third or subsequent marriage enjoy much greater freedom of choice, although this may not apply equally to the girls they choose, but even young men contracting their first union often succeed in marrying the bride of their choice with the consent of both sets of parents.

The favourite season for seeking a bride is the spring (*gu*) when, after the rains, water and pasture are abundant, and social life expands as people find themselves less heavily burdened with herding tasks. At this time of year the two herding units - the nomadic hamlets and camel camps - are closer together than at any other period, and the young camel herders drive their beasts close to the hamlets. For the camel boys, separated for weeks and sometimes months on end from all contact with women, spring has a romantic flavour. And for some young men the transition from the long period of isolation in the camel camps is so overwhelming, that their first sight of young women drives them into a state of frenzy, which is regarded as a form of spirit possession, and which is only alleviated by the mounting of a cathartic dance in which women participate.[12] This, however, is not a very common phenomenon today, and more generally the young camel herders simply approach the hamlets of the girls tending the flocks and serenade them, inviting them to come and dance. The girls, if they are interested, reply in song, usually obliquely since the traditional convention is that little direct reference should be made to love (*ja'ayl*); for the pastoralists are puritanical and regard the open demonstration of affection towards women as unmanly.[13]

In response to such invitations the girls usually mount their own dance, and sometimes the two groups join, although this is frowned upon by many religious leaders. This gives the youths and girls an opportunity of exchanging covert glances. A bold suitor may, on these occasions, make a direct proposal of marriage in the form of a song boasting the strength of his lineage and the extent of his livestock. If his words fall on ready ears the girl to whom they are directed may, without answering the youth's proposal directly, sing a teasing reply asking for more information about his lineage, his parents, etc. Such dances, however, are conducted with decorum. Pre-marital relations are extremely formal and love-play and sexual intercourse before marriage generally regarded with abhorrence. A high value is placed on virginity in women at marriage, and the practice of female infibulation is considered as being specifically designed to protect maidenhood.[14]

From such meetings as this, young men select girls whom they would like to marry. Many different attributes make a woman attractive. Physical beauty is an important consideration. Men appreciate women of good height and stature, with good hips and breasts, and plump but not fat. A reddish tinged skin is thought highly of in preference to a dark dull black; and dark shining gums are regarded as a mark of beauty (*cf.* Laurence, 1954, p. 10).

Apart from their physical attraction, women are valued according to the standing and wealth of their families, their reputation or "name"(*maga'*) as the pastoralists put it, their decorum and character, and their physical strength. A girl who is thought to be clever and capable is strongly preferred to one who is considered foolish or flighty.

There is usually little direct courting. Sometimes, however, a youth may strike up an acquaintance with a girl whom he meets with her sheep in the pastures, or try to arrange a meeting with a girl whom he has first seen at a dance. Sometimes, again, a suitor will go with several of his cousins to the hamlet of the girl he is interested in, and if her parents regard him with favour the party may be allowed inside the tent to engage in light banter (*hodhodasho* or *haasaawe*) with the girl. On these occasions girls are usually very coy and display much embarrassment. Where the man's honourable intentions are clear, however, the prospective bride may submit with a show of unwillingness to displaying her breasts, and sometimes even her private parts to prove her virginity. Very rarely is this a prelude to premarital sexual intercourse. It is rather in the nature of a test of a girl's eligibility for marriage. Generally the suitor does not achieve such intimacy before marriage and many husbands have indeed very slight acquaintance with their brides before the formal marriage arrangements are made. The formal approach for a girl's hand in marriage is normally made by the suitor's father or by another senior agnate. Thus the initiative almost always comes from the side of the prospective husband. In very rare cases, however, if a girl has not succeeded in attracting a suitor and has passed the normal age of first marriage, custom entitles her to present herself at a hamlet where she knows that she can find a marriageable man. The group so approached is then obliged either to provide a husband for the girl or to pay damages to her lineage. For in refusing her the group concerned is held in Somali law to have insulted her lineage. This, however, happens very rarely and I know only of a few cases in which a woman has had to resort to such desperate tactics to secure a husband.

Once the girl's parents have been formally approached and if both parties agree to the match, discussion of the appropriate betrothal and marriage gifts begins. The first of these is called *gabbaati* and may be dispensed with, especially when the marriage ceremony takes place at once.

Often not more than a few pounds in value, and paid in money, live-stock, or other currency, this gift to the girl's parents establishes the engagement of the couple.[15] It is liable to be forfeited if the suitor breaks off the engagement or is unreasonably slow in concluding the final marriage arrangements. Equally it can be reclaimed by the suitor if the girl marries someone else while the marriage arrangements are pending,[16] or if the girl compromises herself by associating openly with other marriageable men.

Normally, however, the betrothal gift is the prelude to the marriage prestations proper. These consist of a reciprocal transfer of wealth between the woman's and man's families and their lineages. The gifts made to the woman's family which I shall refer to as bride-wealth are known as *yarad*, and those returned to the bridegroom and his family and lineage which I shall refer to as dowry are called *dibaad* (various other expressions occur with slightly different shades of meaning, *diiqo* being commonly used in north-western Somaliland). *Yarad* refers mainly to the bride-wealth agreed to between the parties and paid at the time of marriage or shortly after; but all subsequent gifts from the groom and his lineage to that of his bride are regarded as falling into the same category.

Bride-Wealth and dowry

As the following table shows, the amount of bride-wealth varies widely with the standing of the parties, and according to the desirability of the match, both in relation to the personal qualities of the bride and to the aims of the groups concerned in establishing a link between their lineages. As I shall explain in more detail later, a girl is sometimes given in marriage as part of the settlement of a dispute between lineages. The lowest marriage payment which I recorded amongst the pastoralists in 1956 was one of three camels (a camel varied in value between East African, 70 and 200 shs. according to age and sex). In lack-lustre unions, between impoverished townsmen which are often very transitory, smaller amounts are sometimes paid. Here the bride-wealth becomes little more than the outlay necessary for providing the wedding feast and is referred to derogatively as *sooriye* (from *soor*, food). Bride-wealth, however, is not generally lower in towns than in the interior. Between persons of standing -merchants, government officials, teachers and the like - high bride-wealths are paid, especially for educated girls.[17] There was, for example, great competition between rich merchants and government officials for the girls attending the first Intermediate Girls' School in the north. The girls' parents were able to obtain very high bride-wealths and many were betrothed at an earlier age than their sisters in the interior.

The bulk of a young man's bride-wealth for his first marriage comes, unless he is independently employed, from the stock of the uterine family to which he belongs, the allocation being made by his father. This is added to the groom's own 'navel-knot stock', and although there is sometimes a conflict of interest between a father who wishes to acquire another wife and a son who wants camels to marry his first wife, there are few fathers who do not meet the bulk of a son's first bride-wealth from the family estate. Other contributions come from wealthy elder agnates, elder brothers, real and classificatory father's brothers (*adeerro*, sg. *adeer*) within the dia-paying group. Sometimes, also, help may be given by the mother's brother (*abti*), this being characteristic of the special relationship of friendliness and indulgence which obtains between a man and his maternal uncle. Finally, even affinal kin may sometimes contribute. Thus in principle those people contribute to the bride-wealth who are concerned in the marriage which it establishes. And ideally when a Sultan, the head of a clan, marries, his clansmen as a whole pay his bride-wealth, at least in the first marriage after his coronation. Somali explain this as being an appropriate gesture of respect and a means whereby a Sultan's people contribute directly to the perpetuation of his title.

This ideal appears generally to have been fulfilled in the past when amongst some northern Somali clans (e.g. the Gadabuursi, 'Iise, and Majeerteen) Sultans had apparently greater power than they currently enjoy. Today I think it is seldom adhered to. For at the present time the office has little effective secular power attached to it, although it still retains a certain aura, partly connected with the fact that the clan-head is thought of to some extent as a mediator between his people and the clan founder, who is usually regarded as a saint in a Muslim sense. Nevertheless some northern Somali clan-heads still like to maintain that they do not "buy" wives like humbler folk, but are 'given' women in honour of their position.

Whatever its source, the bride-wealth is received by the girl's father, or if the latter is dead or not available, by her paternal uncle or elder brother. That portion of it which is not returned to the husband as dowry (*dibaad*) is mainly paid into the polygynous family estate and usually credited to that part of it which belongs to the uterine family of the bride. Some of it may be distributed more widely amongst close agnates within the dia-paying group, As the table shows, while livestock are the primary medium of payment, money and other articles may also be given in bride-wealth. The extent to which they are distributed amongst the receiving kin-group to some degree depends upon their nature. The most prized items of wealth - horses, which are tradi-

tional prestige wealth *par excellence* and rare today, and rifles - are usually kept by the head of the girl's family for himself. Money, like livestock other than horses, tends to be shared more readily among close kin.

Bride-wealth and dowry exchanges [18]

Yarad	Dibaad
1. 22 camels and 1 rifle	10 camels, 2 burden camels with equipment, and 1 rifle.
2. 20 camels	6 camels and 2 burden camels with equipment.
3. 40 camels and 1 rifle	20 camels and 3 laden burden camels.
4. 26 camels	12 camels and 2 laden burden camels.
5. 20 camels	3 camels and 3 laden burden camels. (A poor exchange).
6. 15 camels	5 camels and 2 burden camels.
7. 20 camels	10 camels and 2 laden burden camels.
8. 10 camels	2 laden burden camels. (A poor exchange).
9. 9 camels	2 laden burden camels.
10. 20 camels	6 camels and 2 laden burden camels. (A poor exchange).
11. 40 camels	20 camels and 4 laden burden camels.
12. 32 camels	15 camels and 3 laden burden camels.
13. 24 camels	12 camels and 2 laden burden camels.
14. 28 camels	13 camels and 3 laden burden camels.
15. 18 camels	9 camels and 2 laden burden camels.
16. 30 camels	15 camels and 4 laden burden camels.
17. 10 camels and 40 sheep and goats	4 camels, 1 laden burden camel, and 20 sheep and goats.
18. 30 camels and rifle	15 camels and 3 laden burden camels.
19. 40 camels and 7 cattle	20 camels, 4 laden burden camels, and 60 sheep and goats.

20. 40 camels and 6 cattle   20 camels and 4 laden burden camels.
21. 4 camels   - (Very poor marriage).
22. 20 camels and 5 cattle   7 camels and 3 laden burden camels.
23. 10 camels (elopement)   4 camels and 1 laden burden camel.
24. 3 camels   - (Very poor marriage).
25. 30 camels   15 camels and 4 laden burden camels.
26. 20 camels and 30 sheep and goats   10 camels and 2 laden burden camels.
27. 5 camels   - (Very poor marriage).
28. 12 camels and 600 Rs.19   5 camels and 2 laden burden camels.
29. 24 camels and 70 sheep and goats.   7 camels, 70 sheep and goats, and 2 laden burden camels.
30. 50 camels and 2 horses and 1 rifle.   30 camels, 4 laden burden camels,
31. 40 camels and 1 rifle and 30 sheep and goats.   20 camels, 3 laden burden camels,
32. 02 camels, 1 rifle, 600 Rs.   2 laden burden camels, and 100 sheep and goats.
33. 40 camels, 1 horse, and 20 cattle and 500 Rs.   25 camels, 5 laden burden camels, 10 cattle.
34. 24 camels   12 camels, and 2 laden burden camels.
35. 6 head of livestock (camels and cattle mixed)   2 head of livestock and 2 laden burden camels.
36. 13 head of livestock   5 head of livestock and 2 laden burden camels.
37. 4 head of livestock   2 laden burden camels.
38. 23 head of livestock   12 livestock inclusive of camels withequipment.
39. 40 head of livestock   10 camels, and 100 sheep and goats.
40. 10 head of livestock   70 sheep and goats.
41. 9 head of livestock   4 head of camels and cattle.
42. 15 head of livestock   7 head of camels and cattle.
43. 12 head of livestock   2 head of camels and cattle.
44. 10 head of livestock   3 laden burden camels.
45. 8 head of livestock   2 laden burden camels.
46. 3 head of livestock   24 Rs.
47. 25 head of livestock   7 camels and 70 sheep and goats.
48. 15 head of livestock   6 camels.

I have mentioned the dowry which the bride's kin have a moral obligation to give in return. In most cases the amount of dowry is proportionate to the value of the bride-wealth but rarely exceeds two thirds of it. Unlike the bride-wealth which is an agreed amount often negotiated after long discussion between the two families, the value of the dowry is essentially a matter for the girl's family to decide. It is not something over which the groom's kin can normally exert any direct control. Nevertheless, the amount of dowry returned is naturally influenced by the relations between the two kin groups, and is regarded partly as an index of the standing of the bride's family. A poor dowry in return for a generous bride-wealth reflects badly on the girl's family.

As the table shows, the dowry consists essentially of sheep and goats and of burden camels laden with the mats, skins, etc., from which the nomadic tent is constructed. It includes also such essential domestic equipment as water and milk vessels, basins, cooking pots, clothes, and very often food and ghee, especially a wooden container of *muqmad*, a sustaining delicacy made of finely chopped dried meat flavoured with garlic and onions and spice and mixed with dates. The dowry is thus designed to enable the couple to set themselves up as an independent stock-herding unit, although they usually move as part of a larger nomadic hamlet. If the groom is already rich in small stock (sheep and goats) more burden camels or milking camels, money, or other goods may be offered as dowry. Quite commonly, irrespective of the groom's wealth in sheep and goats, she-camels are given, and are frequently indeed chosen directly from those paid in bride-wealth. The entire dowry is primarily the property of the groom, although claims may be made to a few head of stock by those who have helped to pay the bride-wealth.

The marriage house is normally erected at the home of the bride, for although residence after marriage is mainly virilocal men often spend the first few months of marriage and sometimes even a year or two with their relatives by marriage.[20] The new tent is itself symbolic of marriage: it is called *aroos*, a word which also means bridegroom, and sometimes even marriage (although the more general expression is *guur*). In the bridal tent - unless the dowry is paid after the marriage has taken place - the bride and groom celebrate their wedding and the wife lives in it throughout her marriage.

There is considerable variation in the details of northern Somali weddings but in those that I have witnessed after the religious ceremony is over (see below) the bride was led to the tent by women of her lineage singing hymns such as 'Oh Prophet, light of God' and songs in praise of the girl's lineage. Then the groom was led to his bride by men singing more hymns seeking the blessing of the Prophet and of God for the couple. Traditionally, the man's first action on entering the bridal tent was to beat his wife ceremonially with a whip (*jeedal*) in order to 'drive the devil out of her' and also to establish his authority over her. After this, the groom kills a ram which is held by the bride and the way in which the slaughtered animal falls is carefully scrutinised, since from this the couple's future fortunes may be predicted. The couple then retire into the tent where they are brought milk and food. Sometimes the bride's mother, if it is her daughter's first marriage, then stands out-side the bridal chamber and addresses a short homily to the girl on her various tasks and duties as a wife.

When the mother withdraws the couple are left alone and the wedding festivities, which usually last seven days begin in earnest. During this time the couple hardly leave their house, especially not the bride, and their food is prepared by the wife's kin (unless the wedding takes place at the groom's home). The couple are expected to devote this period of seclusion to consummating their union. In the dancing and fes-tivities which proceed outside the tent the groom's kin sing songs in praise of his lineage, the bride's kin songs in praise of hers. The two par-ties may also insult each other. The wedding celebrations reach their cli-max on the seventh day when the Prophet's birthday service (*mawliid el nebbi*) is read and gifts and presents are brought to the couple. A cow or camel may be killed by the girl's kin and a concluding feast held. This marks the end of the new bride's seclusion in the marriage house.

The bridal tent and the other gifts made at the time of marriage do not complete the dowry transactions. Any gift made to the husband by the wife's kin, as for example when she periodically visits her natal home, during the marriage is regarded as dowry. Thus throughout the marriage there is usually a continuing exchange of wealth between the families and lineages concerned and this is considered the appropriate accompaniment to the marital relationship.

MARRIAGE AS A PERSONAL CONTRACT

These marriage transactions link families and lineages in a way which I shall examine more fully presently. They do not, in themselves, unite a man and woman in legal wedlock. The crucial marriage trans-action is the Islamic *mahar*,[21] a separate gift which is given by the hus-band to his bride, and is always very considerably less in value than bride-wealth. I shall refer to this gift as the woman's personal dower. The dower is agreed to in the presence of witnesses and before the sheikh or 'man of religion' (*wadaad*)[22] who obtains the formal consent of the par-ties to the union, pronounces them man and wife, and blesses them with a few verses from the Quran. It is this brief Muslim ceremony, including the man's public undertaking to give his wife a stipulated dower, which effects the marital union. Normally the dower contract takes place after the bride-wealth, or at least part of it, has been paid, and before the couple enter their new marriage house as man and wife. Without it no relationship between a man and woman is marriage, and children of a dowerless (*maharla'*) connection are inevitably bastards (sg. *gar'a*)[23] For the dower agreement gives a man full rights over a woman both as a partner and as a bearer of children.

In practice, however, the personal dower need not be paid at the time of its agreement in the marriage ceremony. Its actual payment to the wife may be postponed. Often indeed it is not paid until the marriage is terminated either by divorce, or by the death of the husband. In the latter case the widow claims her dower from her husband's estate. If the woman dies, her dower is divided between her agnatic kin and her children and husband. For example: As his second wife a man of the Dulbahante clan married a woman of the Hawiye, paying a bride-wealth of fifteen camels, and received two burden camels laden with the marriage tent and its accessories, and five she-camels. When this woman died she left sixty sheep and goats from her dower and these were divided between her children and father. While thus held in suspense, the personal dower is in effect a kind of safeguard against divorce, and as I discuss more fully presently, it is often in fact never paid and remains a nominal transaction. But it is nevertheless the dower agreement which is the critical transaction in marriage. When a couple elope (*waa la tegay*) bride wealth and dowry are dispensed with, at least initially. But a sheikh has to be approached to solemnise the union and to witness the dower contract between the couple. The amount of the dower is essentially a matter for the man and woman to agree to between themselves, although where they do not elope the girl's kin will attempt to see that its value is worthy of her person and of them as members of a lineage with a certain standing.

Thus the dower contract establishes the union of a man and woman in matrimony and gives the husband full rights to all children which his wife bears during their marriage, whoever begets them. Marriage can take place without bride-wealth but not without dower.

Marriage, however, is normally not merely a personal contract between two individuals, it also involves a wider relationship between their respective kin. The corporate character of marriage which is implied in the spread of bride-wealth and dowry contribution and distribution can be seen initially in the customs of widow inheritance and the sororate.[24]

WIDOW INHERITANCE AND SORORATIC MARRIAGE

Traditionally a man has a pre-emptive right to marry the widow of a brother or other close agnate of the same generation. Usually the widow is married by a brother or younger patrilineal cousin (*ina'deer*) of the deceased. A man calls his brother's wife or the wife of a patrilineal cousin *dumaal*, and the expression for widow inheritance is *waa la dumaalay*. This results in a new marriage in which children are born to the name, lineage, and estate of the new husband and not to the deceased. They are related to the issue of the previous marriage both as maternal half-siblings (*walaallo hooyo*, lit. "siblings on the mother's side") and as paternal cousins (*ilma'adeerro, sg.ina'adeer*).[25]

A new personal dower is contracted, but no betrothal gift since the widow is regarded as already betrothed to her late husband's lineage. A reduced bride-wealth may be offered, but is rarely sufficiently substantial to produce a further payment of dowry by the woman's agnatic kin.

Although Somali sometimes describe this gift as bride-wealth (*yarad*), it has a special significance quite distinct from normal bride-wealth. More specifically it is known as *haal dumaalleed* or as *faras dumaalleed*, expressions which reflect its real meaning. *Haal* is a general term for compensation paid in reparation for moral injury as distinct from compensation paid for physical injury (*qoomal*; and in the case of homicide, *mag*). It is the reparation claimed for any attack on the name and honour of a person or group. Thus *haal dumaalleed* means the compensation paid for widow inheritance. *Faras dumaalleed* means literally "horse for widow inheritance," and the horse in northern Somaliland represents prestige wealth *par excellence*, the most appropriate currency in which to pay damages for a serious moral injury. In actual fact horses are today rare, and I know of no case in which a horse was given to the kin of a widow by the man marrying her. But whatever the nature and value of the payment, which as I have said is usually small and not infrequently dispensed with altogether, its object is to honour the widow's kin and to effect the transition from sister-in-law to wife. This is in fact a very considerable transition since, between a man and his brother's or cousin's wife, there is respect and shame (*hishood*) and even avoidance. Thus the widow's marriage gift is in the nature of a *rite de passage*, and Somali acknowledging the magnitude of the change are fond of quoting the proverb "he who avoids his brother's wife (after marrying her) will not beget children" (*dumaal nin ka hishooday kama dalo*).

Since full bride-wealth is not paid in widow inheritance Somali regard the institution as a means of conserving what has already been obtained by bride-wealth, and, especially if young children are left by the deceased, of retaining their mother to look after them without temporarily removing them to another lineage. Moreover, if the widow leaves her late husband's group she has the right to take her personal dower with her and any property she may have inherited from him. By marrying her to a near kinsman of her former spouse this is avoided. And where the widow is an old woman and unlikely to find another husband elsewhere unless she is rich or desirable in some other way, the custom is regarded as being of direct benefit to her.

Similar considerations are equally clear in the sororate (*higsiisan*, lit. "the one given next"). Between a man and his wife's sister or cousin, also called *dumaal* (and in the north-west, *seeddi*), there is again respect and shame, and normally avoidance. When a wife for whom an honourable bride-wealth has been paid dies, the widowed husband is entitled to claim her younger sister. If a replacement for the deceased is not forthcoming a claim will be made by the widowed husband's lineage for a return of bride-wealth, or at least for a return of the bride-wealth stock which are still alive. Such claims devolve on the heirs. Thus in some cases, the sons of a deceased couple may even claim a return of those bride-wealth stock still living from their mother's brother or the latter's heirs.

When, however, a dead woman is replaced by a sister in sororatic marriage, a new dower is contracted but no betrothal payment is made and usually only a small gift which has much the same significance as the *haal dumaalleed* given when a man marries the widow of a kinsman. Amongst some clans the value of this gift varies according to whether the sister and the dead woman are of the same or different uterine families (*baho*). If the women are of different uterine families the amount paid is higher. I have mentioned that, as in widow inheritance, the sororatic marriage prestation is small where a generous bride-wealth was given in the previous marriage. Where, this is not the case, however, a man's right to a replacement for his dead wife is correspondingly weaker and a larger marriage gift will be required. Thus a man called Faarah eloped with a girl whose father was dead. Later her brothers approached him and demanded bride-wealth for their sister. Faarah agreed to give them seven camels. They accepted this but returned no dowry as the bride-wealth was so small. When the woman died in childbirth, Faarah asked her brothers to give him her sister. They were rich in stock and said they would give Faarah a replacement for his dead wife but he would have to pay a considerable bride-wealth, largely as an appeasement for his earlier elopement. Faarah paid thirty camels, 100 sheep and goats, and 100 rupees. This pleased his brothers-in-law who gave back the same number of camels as dowry as well as 3 burden camels laden with all the effects and trappings of the nomadic tent.

If the deceased wife leaves children, sororatic marriage gives rise to two separate uterine families where the children are full agnatic siblings (*walaallo aabbe*),[26] but of different mothers, of different uterine estates. The new wife takes over the flocks of the deceased and looks after the latter's children as well as her own. Her husband and his agnatic kin will do their utmost to see that the woman does not favour her own children unjustly at the expense of those left by her sister. Children call their mother's sister 'little mother' (*habaryar*) and Somali relate this terminological usage to the practice of the sororate, and to the fact that on their mother's death her position may be assumed by her sister.

Despite a man's customary right to a replacement for a deceased wife or to marry the widow of a close kinsman, in the north in the 1950s both the sororate and widow inheritance occurred rarely and formed a very small proportion of all marriages. Thus of 135 marriages recorded only 8 (6%.) were by widow inheritance, and 3 (2%.) by the sororate. To some extent this may be attributed to the effect of the Natives Betrothal and Marriage Ordinance of 1928 which, amongst other things, entitled a widowed or divorced woman 'to register personally before a District Commissioner her intention to marry contrary to tribal custom' and similarly enabled an unmarried woman to avoid being betrothed against her will.

The Significance of Bride-Wealth and Dowery

The preceding considerations show that although it is the Islamic dower agreement which effects a legal union between a man and woman, marriage is much more than a contract between individuals. Before examining the implications of this in the affinal and matrilateral relationships created by marriage, it will be convenient first to consider how Somali evaluate bride-wealth and dowry.

Between non-kinsmen Somali regard the exchange of gifts as the appropriate accompaniment to the creation of a social relationship and quote the proverb "the hand which rubs without oil achieves little" (*faro aan dufan lahayni wah magduugaan*). Thus the exchange of bride-wealth and dowry before and at the beginning of marriage is sometimes explained as the process by which the two sets of kin "come 'to know each other" and to esteem each other. More specifically, bride-wealth itself is seen as an appropriate, or indeed essential reward (*abaalgud*)[27] to the girl's parents for their expense and care in her up-bringing, similar to the "price of up-fostering" of early English Society (cf. Radcliffe-Brown, 1950, p. 4-8). It is part of the natural order of things in Somali eyes that, when a girl passes puberty, she should find her livelihood through marriage and that her father should receive a just return for his maintenance of her prior to marriage. At the same time, through marriage a man acquires a valuable economic asset, a woman who in return for being cared for will cook for her husband, manage his flocks, and produce children for him, above all sons to continue his lineage. This also has to be paid for, and is viewed as one of the purposes of bride-wealth.

Despite the fact that there is sometimes little net difference between the value of the bride-wealth paid and the amount of dowry received in return, Somali do not regard these transactions as cancelling each other out. Dowry does not minimize the importance of bride-wealth. While they are aware that by paying bride-wealth they not only receive a wife but often gain the means of establishing her as an economic unit as well, Somalis still consider the payment of bride-wealth as extremely important. It is shameful not to honor the bride's father with an appropriate gift and Somali find it hard to understand how in societies where no bride-wealth is paid (even when no dowry is returned) good relations can possibly be established between a man and his wife's father. Marriage without bride-wealth savors of the casual unions of the urban poor, almost of prostitution, despite the fact that it is the woman's personal dower and not bride-wealth which legalises marriage. An honourable bride-wealth and a correspondingly generous return are cause for pride. They imply a satisfactory transaction between people of substance and honor. Thus elopement, although sometimes resorted to, is generally regarded as dishonourable. In fact the vast majority of cases marriages which begin with elopement are later transformed into a proper union by the exchange of marriage gifts between the families. The following example is typical.

A young man called Ahmad was in love with a girl whose parents objected to him, partly on the grounds that he belonged to a small and poor lineage, and partly because they wanted a larger bride-price than he could offer. Faced with these difficulties, Ahmad persuaded the girl to elope with him. The couple ran off to a trading village in an area grazed by the youth's clan some hundred miles distant from the girl's father's hamlet (in discussing his marriage afterwards with me, the groom said that betrothal was "old-fashioned"). There the couple were married by a local sheikh in the presence of witnesses and the girl's dower was settled at ten camels. The couple then went to the nomadic hamlet of the groom's father where they were given the temporary use of a tent. Later the bride's father came to them and a bride-wealth of twenty-four camels (a mixture of young she-camels and of burden camels) was agreed to and paid. The girl's father, who had not anticipated achieving so favourable a settlement, was pleased and returned twelve of the younger bride-wealth camels on the spot as dowry. When the wife subsequently visited her parents she returned afterwards with a further gift of two laden burden camels which enabled the couple to set up house independently.

Most elopements seem to end in this way, with the acceptance of the situation by both sets of kin and some exchange of marriage gifts. Where no bride-wealth is paid no effective affinal relationship between lineages is established. As has been seen, in these circumstances no claim can be entertained for the automatic replacement of a dead wife unless some adjustment for the original elopement is made.

The Affinal and Matrilateral Relationships

All satisfactory matches require the exchange of wealth between families and lineages, and although the settlement of the woman's personal dower (*mahar*) gives a man full uxorial and genetricial rights over his wife (to paraphrase Bohannan, 1949), it is bride-wealth (*yarad*) and dowry (*dibaad*) which create and maintain an effective affinal relationship and, in the filial generation, the important matrilateral connection between their respective lineages. A man speaks of his wife's agnatic kin (*hidid*) as a group and the link between the individual families is generalized on both sides imposing rights and obligations on each. The implications of this in widow inheritance and the sororate have been discussed. In a wider context the affinal relationship implies general cooperation; but the relationship is one of formality and respect, even of reserve, different in quality and kind from the less formal and more binding ties between agnatic kin. One exists by virtue of marriage, the other by virtue of birth and with the frequency of divorce these stand for very different values in Somali eyes. Where the two ties come into conflict, it is inevitably the affinal relationship which—temporarily at least—is forgotten and the agnatic loyalty asserted. Agnatic allegiance underlies the structure of political units and can be upheld by direct coercive action. Affinal ties are not the basis of political cohesion, affines do not unite politically except when they are also agnates. Consequently while the affinal relationship has a strong moral force it cannot be directly maintained by punitive sanctions.

Yet as was stated earlier, affinal ties provide a valuable subsidiary basis of social intercourse. They offer a tie on the strength of which a person can claim hospitality and assistance, not merely as a protected guest (*magan*), but also as a relative who is entitled to honour and respect. Thus affinal ties may become important when a man is far from his own kin and yet needs support in the watering of his stock, or access to grazing held by non-agnates, or the loan of a burden camel, or in other ways. Equally, a man who has quarrelled with his kin, or whose kin are far distant from him, or for such other personal reasons as visiting his affines in the hope of receiving gifts, may join a hamlet containing his affines and for a time move with them. And in the first months of marriage it is common for a man to reside with his wife's kin. Thus, as a basis for co-operation in general sheep and goat herding movements, the affinal tie is by no means of negligible importance. It will be recalled that the sample of 57 nomadic hamlets discussed earlier contained 13 (23%.) hamlets in which affinally related heads of families were included.[28]

Moreover, as has been pointed out, affinal ties are similarly relied on to secure preference in employment and to some extent also in trade, in both these fields supplementing agnatic loyalties in much the same way as they do within the pastoral economy. In the interdenominational rivalry between the Muslim brotherhoods (*taariqas*) in Somaliland, religious leaders also make full use of affinal connections (as of other ties) to attract adherents. It is not without significance, for example, that Sayyid Mohamed 'Abdille Hassan (the so-called "Mad Mullah") who between 1900 and 1920 led a religious war against the Christian and "infidel" administrations as a leader of the Saalihiya Order, contracted in his lifetime more than a dozen marriages with widely scattered groups and used the affinal relationships so established to encourage people to join him. More recently, a campaign for adherents was launched by the Qaadiriya religious Order amongst the Dulbahante clan in the north-east where the rival Saalihiya *taariqa* is firmly entrenched. The main leader of this missionary enterprise was a Somali sheikh from Ethiopian territory with only very distant agnatic links with the Dulbahante. Having established a teaching centre of his Order in the region, the sheikh found it expedient to marry two local women, both the daughters of sympathizers, who had some contact with his *taariqa* in the past. One of the girls was said to have been given to the sheikh as a reward or tribute (*abaalgud*) in recognition of his piety and as a gift to obtain his blessing.

Thus while marriage does not join lineages in political union as new political entities, it does have economic importance and at least some political implications. As in other societies, the pastoralists like to marry where affinal ties will be of advantage to them, and although every marriage does not have this specific objective, they usually seek to spread their affinal ties as widely as possible.[29]

These conclusions are supported by other considerations. In peace-making and the settlement of disputes between hostile lineages, affines are regarded as ideal mediators and often sent on peace-making deputations because of their dual affiliation. Here they join with "men of religion," who, whatever their lineage, are regarded ideally as neutral in lineage politics.

In addition, though not so common today as in the past, feuds are sometimes composed not only with the transfer of livestock but also with a gift of a nubile girl. Here a girl is given as an additional compensation without a corresponding bride-wealth being sought, and explicitly for the purpose of re-establishing harmony and creating an affinal link. Thus a dia-paying treaty concluded by the four segments of the Hassan Ugaas lineage of the Dulbahante clan in 1947 and communicated to the local District Commissioner contains the following clause: "In the case of deliberate murder amongst the four Hassan Ugaas sections, the murderer shall be surrendered to the next of kin of the deceased (i.e., close agnates) for execution,[30] or pardon. If the kin of the deceased do not wish to exact vengeance in kind they shall be given a 'good girl' by the murderer's kin and fifty camels contributed jointly by all the Hassan Ugaas 'to encourage the family of the deceased'."[31]

The application of this procedure is seen in the following case. In the dry season two men of different dia-paying groups (A and B) quarrelled over precedence in watering their livestock at a well. In the ensuing fight one of the men who belonged to lineage A was killed and camels were seized by the administration from the second and stronger party B. One hundred head were given to the bereaved lineage. A few days later, however, the brother of the slain herdsman, dissatisfied with the settlement and spurred on by the desire for revenge, shot a man of lineage B. Elders of this lineage promptly went in strength to the elders of the group A and demanded reparation. This the latter agreed to, proffering 200 camels, a rifle, and a girl who was a close relation of the man of group A whom lineage B had previously killed. She was in fact a sister of the dead man's father. One hundred camels with the rifle and the girl were taken by the brother of the lineage B elder killed, and the remaining hundred were shared out amongst other members of the group. In this incident lineage B were entitled to claim higher damages than the statutory hundred camels, since the killing was in revenge for a death for which compensation had already been paid. However, the alacrity with which lineage A made this settlement, and their inclusion of a bride in it, is a measure of their weakness in numerical strength and political power in relation to their rivals.

Thus marriageable women offer a medium for adjusting social relationships, and in times of crisis of adding to the power of compensation paid in livestock to prevent further strife and to compose differences. Here women have an obvious advantage over livestock, since their transfer creates an affinal relationship and the issue of the union establish a matrilateral tie between the aggrieved lineage, of which they are members, and their mother's kin.

The continuing validity of these procedures was demonstrated in their utilization in the early 1990's in the major cycle of clan negociations, conducted by clan elders, which restored peace throughout Somaliland (North-West Somalia) in the aftermath of the collapse of General Siyad's military dictatorship.[32]

Affinal ties are thus to be regarded as providing a channel for negotiation between groups divided by fighting, and as a factor to some extent inhibiting unlimited hostilities. It is not to be imagined, however, that affinally connected lineages cannot fight. As I have said, where agnatic solidarity is mobilized to protect lineage interests and these conflict with affinal loyalties it is the latter which give way. Many of the lineages and clans which most frequently come into conflict through competition over access to grazing and water are heavily intermarried. Thus, for example, the Dulbahante (Daarood) and Habar Tol Ja'lo (Isaaq) clans of the eastern part of the ex-British Protectorate, who for the past few decades at least have been engaged in recurrent strife, frequently intermarry. Here it may be noticed that even during hostilities affinal relations can be of value since a man may be able to trade upon his relationship with his affines to secure military information. However, a person staying as a guest amongst affinal relatives with whom his own kin are at war cannot be certain of his safety and may be in danger. Yet even in battle a man will normally try to spare his wife's close kin and, if they are captured, treat them well.

So where agnatic ties are weak or non-existent, marriage is regarded positively as a means of establishing useful connections between groups. But where people are closely connected agnatically it is viewed negatively as a threat to existing social solidarity. Some dia-paying groups even include in their contracts specific punishments for internal marriage for this is not regarded as incest and is not subject to ritual sanctions. Thus a Dulbahante dia-paying contract which I recorded contains the following clause: "If a man of our group marries within the group he shall pay damages of 20 camels (in addition to any bride-wealth) to the girl's father," and the treaty concludes "We have made this contract because we do not want to have internal marriage." Again, the elders and Sultan of one small clan are recorded, around 1920, as having prohibited internal marriage because "they did not want trouble." Having become more numerous, marriage takes place within their clan as with other northern Somali clans.

PATTERNS OF EXOGAMY

The primary lineage is normally, and the dia-paying group always, exogamous, because these units are already so strongly united that marriage within them is considered to threaten their cohesion. Here, the smaller groups are, the greater their internal unity, the less their strength, and the more they marry externally. Thus in 89 marriages contracted by Dulbahante men, 55 (62%.) were with women of Dulbahante primary lineages other than those of their husbands; 30 (33.7%) with surrounding clans of other clan-families (with the Habar Yuunis, 10; Habar Tol Ja'lo, 18; and Hawiye, 3); and 3 (4.3%.) with other clans of the Daarood clan-family (Majeerteen, 2; Ogaadeen, 1).

This emphasis on the desirability of marrying outside the primary kinship group to extend ties of alliance is forcefully expressed in a well-known Somali poem addressed to a famous beauty:

Woman, the man who comes from next door,
Is not your equal,
He who travels through danger,
And desolate country, like a lion,
Is your equal!

That such exogamic preferences are not static aspects of culture or social organisation but, on the contrary, reflect wider socio-political circumstances (which may change over time) was poignantly illustrated in the prolonged blood-bath of inter-clan fighting which accompanied the collapse of the Somali state in 1991 (see chapter nine). Clan loyalties epitomized in the formation of clan militias, were intensified to an unprecedented degree and, in areas formerly characterized by clan heterogeneity, with people of different clans living together harmoniously and inter-marrying, marriage *outside* one's own clan became the exception rather than, as formerly, the rule. Indeed, in the devastated capital, Mogadishu, women who had married outside their own clan found themselves at a serious disadvantage, they and their children being disowned and left unprotected by both sets of kin. Insecurity required maximum clan solidarity, including now clan endogamy rather than exogamy. This new trend was further encouraged by the intensified contact with Arab society, and its preference for cousin marriage, through the experience of labour migration in the Gulf. The tension between this politically expedient practice and traditional cultural precepts was reflected in the popular view that such endogamous marriage amounted to a kind of incest akin to the mating of animals.

People who may legitimately marry are described as *gayaan;* and since the primary lineage is normally exogamous and has a span of from six to ten generations according to its size, agnatically related men and women have to be separated by at least this number of generations before they may marry. Marriage within this prohibited range, however, is not regarded as incestuous nor is it subject to ritual sanctions. The idea of incest has a limited range among the northern pastoralists. It applies to sexual relations between children and parents, between siblings whether they are of the same father and mother, of different mothers, or of different fathers but of the same mother. It also applies to relations between a man and his paternal aunt (*adeer*), and maternal aunt (*habar yar*, 'little mother'); and brother's daughter (*adeer*), and sister's daughter (*abti*). Equally, relations between a woman and her paternal uncle (*adeer*) and maternal uncle (*abti*), and brother's son (*adeer*), and sister's son (*abti*) would likewise be considered incestuous. Similarly, as has been seen, there is avoidance between men and women and the spouses (of opposite sex) of their siblings during their marriage.

In addition to the range of lineal kin within which marriage is prohibited and to those with whom marriage would be incest, the children of sisters (*habar wadaag*, 'mother together') are regarded as being too closely related to marry, although I have recorded a few such marriages. Marriage between a man and his mother's brother's daughter (*ina'abti* - 'child of mother's brother') sometimes occurs but is not a preferred union with a high incidence.

It will be seen that this degree of exogamy renders impossible the union of a man with his father's brother's daughter, the preferred marriage of the Arab Bedouin and that especially approved by Islam (see Dickson, 1951, pp. 122-3; Westermarck, 1914, p. 19 ff.). This patrilateral cousin marriage, however, is said to be practised to some limited extent by the Warsangeli clan of the east of the ex-British Protectorate and Majeerteen clan of Mijerteinia Province in the north-east. Amongst the clans dealt with here, this marriage is of such rare occurrence that it can be ignored.

Somali picture their lineage system expanding as they have extended their territory over the past ten centuries with increasing population, and there are sound historical grounds for accepting this view (*cf.* Lewis, 1960 (b)). Somali describe how, (corroborated by District Office records) as lineages expand and ramify over the generations, their segments begin to intermarry where before they did not because they were "too small in numbers." Thus, it is clear that the range of agnatic connection within which people do not marry is related to lineage size

and numerical strength. In addition, marriage is a means of lineage dif-
ferentiation and people who are so loosely linked agnatically that they
readily fight, use marriage to foster additional ties between them. Hence,
while within the dia-paying group and primary lineage, marriage is seen
as weakening an established cohesion, between primary lineages and
clans it is encouraged to spread social links — except as we have seen,
under conditions of conflict on an unprecedented scale.

Northern Somali society as a whole can thus be conceptualized as
consisting of a widely ramifying lineage system, based on agnatic descent,
and cross-knit by extensive and far-reaching affinal ties. These, though
they have no corporate political value in themselves, contribute much
to the total cohesion of society. Somali themselves see the position in
this way and the term for affines (*hidid*) is also used for the roots of a tree
or plant, for affinal ties are regarded as fulfilling much the same functions
as roots do in relation to the trees which they support; and segments in
the lineage system are often described as 'branches' (*laamo, sg.laan*).[33]

MATRILATERAL TIES

The bond between a man and his mother's brother (*abti*) is generalised to the respective lineages so that a man refers to his mother's
lineage as his *reer abti* ("people of the mother's brother"). This relationship is one of co-operation between the lineages concerned, an
extension of the individual relationship between mother's brother and
sister's son. In the domain of familial relationships the maternal uncle
is the favourite, proverbially spoiling his nephews and nieces. He may
contribute something to his nephew's bride-wealth, and when the latter has children the uncle may be called upon to bless them and be
given gifts in return. While there is no enjoined or even preferred marriage with the mother's brother's daughter, men sometimes marry from
their mother's lineage, thereby strengthening the matrilateral link
between the two lineages. On a personal basis, such marriages are seen
as the result of the frequent visits which children pay to their mother's
kin, where they meet and form friendships with their maternal cousins.
As in the case of the affinal connection, on the strength of his own personal matrilateral tie through his mother, or on the strength of the
matrilateral affiliation of a clansman, a man may claim support and
succour from those with whom he is not otherwise closely related. Thus
in the sample of nomadic hamlets mentioned earlier[34] the majority of
the smaller number (9%) which included family heads who were neither affines nor agnates were men matrilaterally linked to the hamlet
core of agnates.

On a more abstract plane of analysis the matrilateral connection is extremely important in lineage morphology. Marriage as we have seen serves to differentiate lineages, forging links between them. Through the matrilateral relationship in the filial generation a lineage is internally divided according to the agnatic affiliation of the wives of its common ancestor. As the polygynous family is divided into uterine groups (*baho*) according to the agnatic affiliation of a man's several wives, so in the lineage system as a whole, uterine cleavages supplement strictly agnatic segmentation in the definition of lineages. Lineages are defined primarily by reference to their apical agnatic ancestors, and secondarily according to the affiliation of their founders' mothers.

An example from the 'Ali Geri primary lineage of the Dulbahante clan may serve to illustrate this. This lineage is segmented as shown and had (in 1956) a male population of approximately 2,800. It will be seen that the lineage is divided in the generation of 'Ali Geri's sons into three uterine groups, the Bah Helaawe, Bah Helaan, and Bah Ogaadeen. The Bah Helaawe and Bah Helaan are the successive issue of 'Ali Geri's marriage to two sisters, both daughters of Lagmadoobe of the Bartirre clan. After the death of the first, 'Ali Geri took her sister Helaan in sororatic marriage. These two uterine groups are joined together as the Bah Lagmadoobe and form one dia-paying group. The remaining three lineages, the Hirsi, Subaan,[35] and Shoowe 'Ali Geri, each of which is an independent dia-paying group, derive from 'Ali Geri's three sons by a woman of the Ogaadeen clan and are grouped together in opposition to the Bah Lagmadoobe as the Bah Ogaadeen, which, though divided (in 1956) into three separate dia-paying groups, a few years earlier had been a single dia-paying group.

ALI GERI

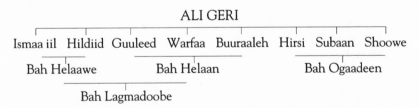

Ismaa iil Hildiid Guuleed Warfaa Buuraaleh Hirsi Subaan Shoowe

Bah Helaawe   Bah Helaan   Bah Ogaadeen

Bah Lagmadoobe

Similar uterine cleavages occur at all levels in the lineage system. Complementary filiation - to use Fortes' term - is a vital principle of lineage morphology and with contractual alliance is often the basis of lineage coalitions where the historically founded genealogical order of segmentation does not correspond to the man-power and political status of lineage segments (*cf*. Lewis, 1961 (a)). Sometimes, even, though rarely, matrilateral ties between apical lineage ancestors are used as the basis of alliances where no agnatic connection exists. This, for example, is often the case where groups claiming direct Arabian origin are accreted to local Somali lineages. Where, more generally, uterine alliances are struck within the field of agnation, no attempt is normally made to translate such matrilateral links into agnatic relationships. In general amongst the northern Somali, agnatic genealogies are not manipulated in this way. Agnation , culturally constructed as a fact of nature, is regarded as absolute and irrevocable, and in contemporary lineage relations fictional kinship, so common in other segmentary lineage societies, is comparatively rare. This, again, is consistent with the exclusiveness of the Somali patrilineage.

Thus matrilateral ties retain their own unique validity and with affinal ties are of primary importance in the total field of social relations, both in the sphere of personal or familial kin relations, and in the wider sphere of corporate relations. It is these links which marriage establishes, directly and in the filial generation, and this, it seems, is the significance of the considerable transfers of wealth between lineages. For marriage itself as a spouse-maintaining and child-rearing relationship is established by the dower contract alone. Yet, despite the importance of these wider links which marriage establishes, marriage itself is not regarded as a permanent union. In relation to the dynamic character of the nomadic economy and of grazing movements, the direction and boundaries of pastoral social relations are in a constant state of flux. Thus quite apart from domestic tensions between a married couple, they are also subject to the pressures of shifting external relations which only weaken the marital bond. Before, however, examining the frequency of divorce and the circumstances which most often lead to the disruption of individual marriages, it is necessary to consider the jural position of a man and wife in some detail.

The Husband-Wife Relationship

Marriage, as has been seen, is the union of a man and woman of different, and potentially hostile, lineages. Although a man may spend the first few months and sometimes even one or two years with his bride's kin as *inanlayaal*, in very few cases does he live permanently with them. Thus the woman leaves her kin to join her husband's group where she establishes a viable domestic unit, part of which she brings with her as dowry and part of which is contributed directly by her husband. Over the years, subject to the vicissitudes of pastoralism - stock disease, famine, and stock-looting - the flocks which she manages for her husband increase with the children she bears to him, and she and her husband become increasingly bound together in a nexus of common domestic economic interests. As she grows old and her children marry off, the family flock which she has built up is depleted by such demands as may be made upon it for the bride-wealths of her sons, and by her husband in contracting new marriages and drawing stock from her flock to set up new wives as independent domestic units.

In the same way, parts of her tent, usually the bridal house built for her by her kin when she married, may be taken to furnish new homes for her daughters, so that an old woman's tent (*buul*) is often a much depleted affair and tends to be neglected. If her husband predeceases her and all her daughters have married, although she still has her dower flock, she is now dependent on the support of others and usually lives with her married sons or daughters. During her marriage she is increasingly absorbed morally into her husband's group, especially through her sons, but as will be seen presently, she is never fully identified with it in a legal sense.

To a considerable extent marriage removes a woman from her father's moral authority and places her under that of her husband. Throughout her marriage she is expected to obey, honour, and respect her spouse, and to be particularly scrupulous in this regard in the early years of marriage. Immediately after the wedding her subordination to her husband is emphasised in the traditional beating which her husband is supposed to administer on the wedding night with a ceremonial whip (*jeedal*). In practice this instrument is rarely seen today, but is said to have been proudly carried by all newly married husbands in the past as a sign of their new marital authority. Other gestures of submission are expected by the husband. His bride should remove his sandals on the wedding night and in the early days of marriage. In contrast to their own exuberance, men even regard the pain which a bride experiences on her first nights of intercourse through the opening and enlargement of the infibulated vulva as a further expression of male virility and female submission.[36] In addition, the forced removal of a bride to her marriage tent by her husband's friends, which is reported to take place in some weddings, although I have not witnessed it, can be seen to emphasise the dominant role of the man and the subservient, even captive, status of the woman.[37]

Throughout her married life a wife is expected to sustain this ideal of male domination, at least publicly, whatever the affective character of the relationship between the couple. And this, an aspect of the general subordinate status of women, finds strong support in traditional Islam although it began to be challenged in the 1950s by many of the new elite and by some women as well.[38] In the vast majority of marriages both amongst the pastoralists and in towns, however, the traditional pattern still prevails. Thus publicly a woman must defer to her spouse -

whatever happens in private - cook for him but eat apart from him, and when they walk together in public walk behind her husband. The women of a hamlet may, however, publicly ridicule those of their menfolk who return ignominiously from an unsuccessful battle or raid. There tend to be strong sentiments of female solidarity.

A wife should also provide for her husband's sexual needs, bear children, especially sons, and care properly for these, as well as adequately performing her herding tasks with the sheep and goats which are exclusively her domain. Here the division of labour coincides with the subordinate status of women, for wealth[39] and substance are rated primarily in terms of camels whose care is the province of men. And although the sheep and goats are in law the property of the husband and family head, men like to affect a disinterest and scorn for the affairs of their flocks, even though in the dry seasons they are intimately concerned with their watering. The only camels with which women have any direct concern are the burden camels of the hamlet, and it is primarily their duty to see to the loading and unloading of these beasts with the parts of the nomadic tent and other domestic effects.

Despite, however, the acknowledgement in Somali law of the head of the family's final authority over his wives' flocks the family-head cannot arbitrarily interfere in their management. If he wishes to sell a beast or to kill a sheep for a feast or for some other occasion he may have to ask his wife's permission. Here as in other matters his actual power in relation to the flocks of his various wives depends often to a considerable extent on the age of his sons. A full-grown son often sticks up for his mother's and his uterine family's rights even to the extent of disputing with his father. Thus a man who has a disagreement with one of his wives may find her sons against him. Hence, though legally the head of the family exercises ultimate authority, his actual power is not absolute and is subject to constraints, especially through the loyalty which unmarried adult sons display towards their mother. However, men tend to convert profits, whether from the sale of sheep and goats, or hides and skins, or from money obtained from employment, into camels;[40] and women often complain that gains so invested would have been better spent on new clothes for them or their children. Since in principle women cannot own camels this removes wealth to a sphere where its control by the head of the family is less directly subject to the pressures of his wives.

In return for the benefits obtained from marriage, the husband must maintain his wife and her children and see that they are adequately provided for. Where he has more than one wife, each wife has a right to a just share of her husband's favours, and the husband is expected to eat and sleep with each wife in turn. This is especially enjoined by the

Shariah. In any case, a man will take care not to show publicly any strong dependence on a wife lest she be thought to dominate him. No husband wants it to be said of him that he needs his wife more than she needs him. Indeed men sometimes claim that they deliberately restrain their sexual desires to prevent their wives gaining too strong a hold over them. And, living as they do often very close to famine for many months of the year, and having to conserve all their mental and physical energies for the husbandry of the stock in the dry seasons, Somali seem to regard sexual intercourse as a gift to be used sparingly, and in fact the pastoralists sometimes say this directly.

PROCREATION AND IDENTITY

Traditionally, both men and women hold a plural theory of procreation which they see as requiring both divine and human contributions. Thus, in Somali, one says: "I begot children but God created them " (Anigaa dalay Ilaahay baase abuuray; the verb abuur, to create from nothing, is reserved for acts of God one of whose praise-names is Abuure (Creator), equivalent to the Arabic title al-Khaaliq.) More specifically, and in common with medieval European Hippocratic medical science, Northern Somalis believe that conception results from the meeting of male and female 'sperm' or sexual fluid (biyo, 'water'; or mani) in the woman's uterus (ilmogalen, literally 'gateway for children'). According to some sources, if the man climaxes before the woman, their child will take after his father in looks - and vice versa. More generally, contrary to the findings of Helander (1994) and Talle (in press) and to some extent to received anthropological wisdom, a child is believed to inherit both bone and blood from his father's kin, and flesh from his mother's side. This genetic division (which corresponds to the Arab pattern - cf. Mohamed, 1980, p.40) is reflected in the common phrase: bari iyo bawdo, maternally derived sustenance as evidenced in a fat bottom (considered an attractive feature in women) and paternally derived strong thighs. Blood (diig) is powerfully associated with agnatic descent, and the term diig is used interchangeably with mag, "blood-money," claimed by and paid to agnates who, in turn, are described equally as being of the same tol or diig.

Sexual intercourse[41] is most frequent in the spring after the rains when food is abundant, vitality is high, and less attention has to be given to the needs of the stock which in the dry seasons severely curtail the amount of time a husband can spend at leisure with his wife. Quite apart from its results, intercourse is valued in itself and a wife has a strong claim to a just share in her husband's sexuality, although the issue of marriage belong exclusively to the husband. All children born to the wife during her marriage are legally her husband's, and his rights in this respect are safeguarded on divorce since a divorced woman may not remarry until it is definitely established that she is not with child. Here Somali generally follow the Shafi'ite regulation that a divorced woman may not remarry until one hundred days (three menstrual periods) have elapsed from the date at which her marriage was terminated.

While marriage confers on the husband rights over a woman as wife and mother which cannot be alienated except with his consent,[42] it does not give the husband the power to transfer these rights to others. A man cannot accept bride-wealth for a wife and hand her over to another man without reference to her kin. Indeed, at law, a man is not fully responsible for his wife. In keeping with the strength of agnatic loyalties, a woman is never finally cut off from her natal kin, and, whatever the character of her affective relations with her husband and his kin, never completely identified with them. A married woman's position is thus similar to that of a protected relative living amongst non-agnates, or at least with people of a different dia-paying group or primary lineage. Throughout any marriage a woman retains firm ties, affective as well as jural, with her own siblings and agnates whom she visits regularly and who also visit her. To a considerable degree, if not entirely, a married woman retains the legal and political status of her birth. The actual division of responsibility in law between lineage of birth and lineage of marriage varies to some extent from clan-family to clan-family. In contrast to the position in some other societies, in Somaliland it is possible to discuss the distribution of legal responsibility quantitatively in terms of a married woman's blood-wealth.

Among the Isaaq clans, when a married woman is killed, whether or not she has borne children, her blood-wealth is shared between her own agnatic kin and those of her husband. Similarly, if a wife is guilty of murder, her own agnates and her husband's contribute jointly to the blood-wealth paid to the bereaved lineage. For smaller debts and damages incurred by his wife, however, a man is solely responsible up to a maximum amount which varies from dia-paying group to dia-paying group, but which is always very considerably less than a woman's full blood-wealth (50 camels). Amongst the northern Daarood and 'Iise clans, on the other hand, a married woman's kin are entirely responsible when she commits homicide, and conversely claim her blood-wealth in full if she is killed. In this situation I was told by the Dulbahante that while the husband might be able to claim a sister of his late wife as a replacement for her, he could in no circumstances claim her blood-wealth.

If a murdered woman leaves children, however, they are entitled to some share in her blood-wealth.[43] Smaller liabilities incurred by a wife are usually charged against her personal dower, or if her children are adult, paid by them, and in some cases even by the husband as amongst the Isaaq. For in general a husband is considered excessively mean and lacking in honour if he is not willing to accept responsibility for minor liabilities incurred by his spouse.

Further evidence of the joint distribution of jural responsibility for a married woman between her lineage of birth and her lineage of marriage is seen in the treatment of homicide within the polygynous family. Generally, amongst both the Isaaq and Daarood clans, if a woman murders her husband, her own agnates are held responsible for settling damages with her husband's kin. Here the children of the deceased normally receive the bulk of the blood-wealth. Such a killing has a particular piquancy for Somali since it represents so blatant a reversal of the moral and physical superiority of men over women. I quote one example. A "man of religion" of a small clan who are dispersed amongst the Dulbahante, had two wives, one a Dulbahante woman. Jealousy between the co-wives led to a quarrel between this wife and the husband which developed into a fight in which the husband lost his life. The case was complicated by the fact that there were few witnesses to the killing, and in the circumstances the woman's kin paid only a reduced blood-wealth to the children who were left fatherless.[44]

In the reverse case where a man murders his wife, full blood-wealth is claimed from his dia-paying group by his wife's kin. This again occurs rarely. Finally, if a woman kills one of her children, her kin are held responsible and required to pay blood-wealth to the husband and his lineage.

These facts show that marriage does not lead to the complete identification of a wife with her husband's lineage. Here it is to be noticed that there is a tendency for the legal responsibility of the husband's kin towards his wife to increase when her children become adult. Through her children a woman is more firmly bound to her husband's kin than through him.

The contrast between the divided agnatic loyalties of spouses, and the jural identity of agnates of the same dia-paying group, is thrown into relief when the situations described, where the wife is the victim or culprit in homicide, are compared with the treatment of parricide and fratricide. If a man kills his father, or a father his son, vengeance is impossible and blood-wealth cannot be paid to wipe out the crime, for as Somali say "Who will pay and who receive damages ?" Despite this, however, although both these crimes are regarded as particularly heinous, no ritual expiation is required. The position in fratricide is much the same. No ritual action is taken to cleanse the culprit and although the latter cannot pay compensation, usually the dia-paying group as a whole allots a number of livestock to the children of the deceased. Since all these acts are regarded as despicable, striking at the very roots of the ideal of close agnatic kinship, the culprit usually absconds and if he is caught may be surrendered to the administration for punishment.

Thus, in marriage, despite a woman's affective and economic absorption in her husband's family, her ties with her own kin are not severed. And although there is no ceremonial[45] representation of the division of rights and of the retention of part responsibility by a woman's kin when she marries, this can be measured in terms of responsibility for blood-wealth. On marriage, a woman's kin accepts continued responsibility for the more serious crimes she commits and for her life because they still regard her as a member of their dia-paying group. It can now be seen that the token marriage payment in widow inheritance[46] also acknowledges the continuing interest of a woman's kin in her after marriage.

In this patrilineal society the acquisition by a man of full uxorial and genetricial rights in a woman, by the dower contract and the establishment of an affinal relationship between the two sets of kin by the transfer of bridewealth and dowry, do not entail the complete adoption of the woman into her husband's lineage. A married woman (always known by her maiden name) retains her natal lineage affiliation and is still, after marriage, regarded as a member of that lineage. Throughout her married life, and in its initial years especially, a woman's brothers and other close male agnatic kin are very much concerned with her well-being. Indeed the anxiety which the pastoralists display in maintaining effective relations with their affines is to be understood not only in relation to economic and political considerations, but also to the continuing moral interest of a married woman's kin in her welfare and security. Here Somali apparently acknowledge the instability of marriage and frequency of divorce in their society. Although ideally a serious commitment and one affecting the interests not only of the individuals most concerned in it, but also of a wider range of kin on both sides, marriage is nevertheless an insecure relationship in comparison with the binding and irrevocable character of agnatic affiliation. And the ideas Somali have about the nature of marriage are reflected in the phrase *dahdin iyo dalasho*,[47] by which women distinguish between their relatives by marriage and their agnatic kin. The word *dahdin*, relatives by marriage, comes from the verb *dah*, to pause or stop in transit on a journey, and this is precisely how Somali view marriage.

Divorce

Divorce (*furriin*, "opening") amongst the northern pastoralists is both easy, especially for the husband, and frequent. Thus in a group of 101 marriages, 24 (i.e. 24%) ended in divorce; and in a sample of 77 marriages 16 were broken by death and 19 by divorce, giving a divorce rate of 32%.[48] Some further indication is seen in the records of Kadis' Courts whose jurisdiction in the administration of the Shafi'ite code of the Shariah is limited to matters of personal status. In 1956, out of 995 cases heard in five official Kadis' Courts, 699 (70.2%) were divorce cases and the majority of the remaining cases dealt with related matrimonial disputes - desertion by wife, custody of children, etc.

A man can at any time divorce his wife, having merely to pronounce the full Islamic divorce formula "I divorce thee three times" in the presence of witnesses, thereby dissolving his marriage. A wife's position is more difficult. While Somali follow the normal Shafi'ite rules on the dissolution of marriage by a Kadi where either party suffers from serious physical incapacity or disease, a wife can in no circumstances obtain a judicial separation or dissolution of marriage merely on the grounds of cruelty, despite the Quranic provisions for the treatment of such cases (cf. Anderson, 1954, p.52; Brown, 1956, p.10). If a wife fails to obtain proper maintenance (food, clothing, etc.) she can apply for the dissolution of her marriage at a Kadi's Court, but the position here is complex as there is so wide a range of criteria in regard to adequate maintenance, and by no means all such applications are successful (see Brown, op. cit., p. 11). In most cases, however, where a woman is determined on obtaining her freedom, conjugal relations become so strained that eventually the marriage is dissolved by mutual consent. In the last resort a woman can usually force her spouse to divorce her by deserting him, refusing to return, and if her kin persist in forcing her to rejoin her husband in order to hold on to their bride-wealth, threaten to become a prostitute. Hence, although a woman cannot herself directly divorce her husband, and is likely to encounter considerable difficulties in seeking a divorce, there are very few cases in which a woman does not eventually succeed in breaking off an intolerable union.

There are of course many sources of marital disharmony. Some of the more important which, unless outweighed by other considerations (sometimes quasi-political), eventually lead to divorce are: barrenness, jealousy (hinaase) and strife between co-wives (dangalo, "those whose interests cross"), misconduct - especially on the part of the wife - and general incompatibility. Sometimes, also, a high bride-wealth, which the husband and his kin accepted at the time of marriage and which was not at once paid in full, comes to be regarded as exorbitant and leads to friction between the families which may be resolved by divorce. Again, tension may develop when a husband spends his first months or longer at the home of his wife's kin and difficulties arise over the payment of the woman's dowry. Here the husband is in any case in a difficult position, and his relations with his wife's kin, particularly with her mother and father, formal and by no means easy.

Often an arranged match simply does not work out in practice and the woman shows her dislike of her husband by being slovenly in her marital and herding duties or is openly disrespectful. In other cases disagreement arises when a man marries a townswoman and later expects her to look after his flocks in the interior. Some women who are accustomed to town life and who consider themselves above the harsh life of the interior refuse to follow their husbands into the pastures. I have known cases where this was one of the main issues in marital conflict and led to divorce. These and other disputes are aggravated often by disharmony in the triangular relationship of a polygynous family. For although the first wife and her children enjoy a position of seniority, it is usually the most recently married and youngest wife who is most attractive to the husband. Neglected older wives whose company is rarely sought by the husband become uncooperative and difficult. A man for example may want a sheep from the flock of one of his senior wives whom he seldom visits and be told to go away and get what he wants from the younger wife with whom he spends his nights. Moreover, in northern Somaliland tensions between co-wives are not directly canalised through witchcraft and witchcraft accusations: they remain open conflicts which tend eventually to lead to lasting bitterness and hatred which can only be resolved by divorce.[49] To some extent men attempt to maintain harmony amongst their wives by according them at least openly parity of treatment, and where they tend to quarrel and rancour develops, to separate their tents and families and place them with different kin in different nomadic hamlets.

Taken as a whole, my records suggest that one of the commonest and most important contributory factors in the break-down of a marriage is infertility. In most cases the marriage histories of barren women reveal a series of short unions. Men, certainly, readily divorce a woman who after a few years of marriage has borne no children, unless other attributes compensate for her sterility. Sometimes even after years of marriage and after bearing many children old women are divorced after passing the menopause. But this is more rare. This, of course, reflects the ardent desire of Somalis for children, especially for sons, who bring strength and honour to a man and his lineage, for as Somali are fond of saying "when a son is born the clan extends" (*wiil dalaya ba ab durug*). One of the commonest petitions addressed by women at saints' shrines is that they may bear sons.

While a man may have clandestine relations with prostitutes when he visits a town to buy provisions or for other reasons, wives are expected to remain faithful to their husbands and misconduct by women[50] is regarded as more serious than a man's illegitimate relations. Rape, since the woman is not responsible, seldom leads to divorce. But most men divorce unfaithful wives as well as claiming compensation from their lovers.[51] Here the stock expression used by men in referring to a woman divorced for adultery is "she spoiled herself (*wey humaatey*), her womb, her person - everything." Only men who are very fond of a wife over-look unfaithfulness, and usually only when the matter can be kept dark and the husband not exposed to public shame.

External pressures also may add to matrimonial tension. Marital conflicts are sometimes aggravated by wider hostilities between the lineages of the spouses. Again, economic or quasi-political motives may tempt a man with already four wives to consider contracting a new match and thus dispose him to dispense with one of his existing spouses. But this is rare. And it is also perhaps as well to emphasise that the economic and political advantages of a specific affinal relationship some-times do not prevent men from divorcing women in the heat of the moment, however much they may regret their action afterwards.

Whatever factors lead to the dissolution of a marriage, divorce immediately raises the question of the wife's personal dower - if this has not already been paid. Since the dower in practice is seldom paid prior to divorce (or death) women tend to regard it as a divorce surety. But even on divorce, especially when the man is generally considered to be in the right - as in the case of desertion by the wife or misconduct, the stipulated dower is often never paid. Eager to escape from a partner who has become unbearable, many women readily forego their dower rights and are content merely to accept a letter signed by a sheikh or Kadi stat-ing that they are divorced and accordingly free to remarry after the statu-tory period of a hundred days has elapsed. In some cases, indeed where a very large dower has been agreed to, a woman anxious to secure her freedom chooses to demand her dower at a time when she knows her husband cannot, or will not, pay it.

Young women especially show great eagerness to leave a husband for whom they have no affection and to be free to remarry without trou-bling much about their dower. With the acceptance by Somali of the instability of marriage and the frequency of divorce, a divorced woman is unlikely to experience much difficulty in making a new match. Indeed, particularly for a secondary marriage, a divorced woman (*'armali*) may be at an advantage, for her bride-wealth is likely to be considerably less than that sought for a virgin. This reflects the fact that since such a high value is placed on virginity, divorced women, like widows (also called '*armali*), are correspondingly less valued as brides.[52] But although her first marriage thus devalues a woman, so to speak, from the point of view of any later unions she may contract, divorce, like widowhood, carries little stigma.[53]

CLAIMS TO BRIDE-WEALTH

While in theory, if very often not in practice, the dower must be given on divorce if it has not already been paid, the position with regard to the return of bride-wealth varies according to the husband's grounds for divorcing his wife. A man is entitled to divorce his wife if she commits adultery or if she persistently absconds. Here the amount of bride-wealth returned by her kin depends on the difference between the original amount paid and the dowry received, the proportion of the bride-wealth stock living, and whether or not children have been born, especially sons. Naturally where a large bride-wealth is thus in jeopardy every effort is made by the woman's kin to patch up a marriage which is in danger of coming asunder. It is in this sense that among the Somali there is sometimes a connection between the value of bride-wealth and the stability of a particular marriage. For even on the husband's side the amount of bride-wealth paid is related to the desirability of the match. the following case is typical.

A man who had been married for eight years, having had one previous wife whom he divorced, decided to marry again. A bride-wealth of thirty sheep and goats, ten camels, one rifle, and 600 Rupees (i.e. £45), and a personal dower of fifteen camels were agreed to. The first few months of marriage were spent with the wife's kin who provided the marriage tent and two burden camels for its transport (total value about £40). Later, the husband moved his new wife with this dowry to join his first and senior wife with her family of four children, and set up a nomadic hamlet consisting of the two women with their separate tents and flocks of sheep and goats. At once there was trouble. The new wife complained that she was being bullied by the senior wife (which as far as I could ascertain was untrue) and objected to her husband sharing his affections. She received scant sympathy and eventually ran away and tried to get a government Kadi to dissolve her marriage on the grounds of cruelty. She was of course unsuccessful, and was brought back to her husband by her brothers who admonished her and apologized for her behavior. After a few months she ran away again. She was caught by her brothers and beaten and returned to her husband. She was threatened that if she did not now stay with her husband in peace her kin would curse her and pray for her death. Her elder brother who had received the bridewealth, keeping the rifle for himself (her father was dead), was naturally anxious to prevent a divorce which would require his surrendering the rifle. Finally the woman, not deterred by the threat of being cursed, and allegedly in love with another man, again ran away. This time her kin admitted failure, but approached the husband and offered him a new girl and a further return of dowry if they could keep the rifle.[54] This was refused and the disgusted husband agreed to cut his losses and to accept a settlement of five camels and the return of his rifle. There were no children. The woman was formally divorced and given a letter indicating that she was free to remarry, but no dower was paid. The husband kept the marriage tent and burden camels which he had received as dowry.

Where a marriage is dissolved by a Kadi on the grounds of physical incapacity, or on account of the husband's refusal or inability to maintain his wife, there may be a partial return of bride-wealth according to the particular circumstances. But if the divorce is initiated by the husband without such obviously justified grounds as adultery or desertion on his wife's part, no claim can be made to a return of bride-wealth. Here it should be emphasised that claims for the return of bride-wealth are outside the jurisdiction of the Kadis' Courts whose concern is solely with the specifically Islamic personal dower (*mahar*). Claims for the payment or return of bride wealth may, however, be preferred in the Subordinate Courts which administer "native law and custom" but have no extensive criminal powers. But the majority of such cases are settled outside the official courts by negotiation, with the help of arbitrators between the families and lineages concerned. Here, as in the settlement of all disputes and claims, the size and power of lineages, as well as their relations at the time, are of significance.

It is now necessary to consider the question of the custody of the children of broken marriages. Here as in many other matters Somali practice parts company with Islamic Law. According to the Shafi'ite School of the Shariah, which Somali follow, a mother is entitled to keep her sons up to the age of seven, and then, if they so choose, up to the age of puberty: daughters may remain with their mother until puberty or marriage. However, Somali hold that the husband has an absolute right to the custody of all his children, irrespective of age or sex. This is less a reflection of the fact that as long as his children are in the custody of his divorced wife, maintenance will have to be paid, than of the inalienable right of a man to the possession of his legal children. In practice infants are normally allowed to go with their mother to be returned to the father after weaning. In no case can they assume the lineage affiliation of their mother. Sometimes the mother is allowed to hold on to her children, especially her daughters, for a longer period, but this may be at the cost of forfeiting her rights to maintenance by her former husband. Frequently children who have been separated from their mother, especially girls, run away from their father's home to visit their mother. And Somali fully recognise the strength of the natural bond of affection between a mother and her children. This, however, has to be accommodated to the patrilineal norms of Somali society.

Finally, it is necessary to mention the effects of divorce on the affinal and matrilateral relationships created by marriage. On divorce the affinal tie in its socio-economic implications is weakened. The affective content of the matrilateral tie of personal relations between the children and their mother and mother's brother, however, remains, and after several generations may be appealed to retrospectively as a justification for lineage alliances within the general field of agnation. Whether or not a lineage ancestor's parents were divorced, the mother's lineage name is used to differentiate lineages according to their uterine connections.

Conclusions: Marriage Variations
In Patrilineal Societies

We must now set the salient features of northern Somali marriage in the wider context of marriage in other patrilineal societies. As we have seen, the northern Somali marriage contract has both an individual and a corporate aspect and this distinction is reflected in the two sets of marriage payments. As a formal legal union in terms of which the husband acquires full rights over all his wife's children during their match, marriage is established by the performance of the dower contract before a man of religion or sheikh who pronounces the couple man and wife. It is this ceremony which defines legal marriage.

But ideally, and usually also in practice, marriage is in addition a union between lineages, and this wider alliance is established by the exchange of those gifts which I have referred to as bride-wealth and dowry. These marriage payments, which as a rule are considerably more substantial than the woman's personal dower, create the corporate affinal relationship which entails mutual support and collaboration between the two groups. But the character of this relationship is not such that future war and feud are impossible. Indeed the northern Somali tend to spread their affinal links widely, and to marry where their agnatic connections, if they have any, are so attenuated that friction is not unlikely. Conversely, within tightly integrated political units, marriage is strongly discouraged and, though not regarded as incestuous, treated as an offence against the unity of the group. The affinal relationship also entitles a husband to claim a replacement in the event of his wife's death, and permits the husband's agnatic kin to claim his widow in the event of his death. When these sororatic and widow inheritance unions take place only nominal marriage payments with special functions are made by the husband's lineage; full bride-wealth is not paid again.

Marriage transfers a woman from the economic support of her kin to the support of her spouse and his kin, at least insofar as the wife's subsistence is concerned. Although, however, the wife brings an often considerable dowry with her, and with the aid of her husband builds up a flock of sheep and goats for her sustenance and the sustenance of her children, she is not at law the owner of this property. Nor is there any other means whereby a married woman can acquire any considerable fund of property over which she can exercise sole rights of disposal. Except for small personal possessions, a wife's dower is her only outright property, and this she usually only obtains when her husband dies or divorces her. Even on divorce, the wife often resigns her rights to the stipulated dower and is content to leave her former husband with a letter showing that she is divorced and hence free to remarry. Thus often in practice the dower remains with the husband, who, on divorce, usually also keeps the woman's bridal house.

Hence, although a wife is dependent for subsistence on her husband and his kin, marriage gives her little more than use rights in her husband's home, similar to those which she enjoyed in her father's home before her marriage.[55] And whatever the character of the affective relationship between the spouses, a woman's legal status after marriage is still to a very considerable extent defined by her continuing attachment to her own agnatic kin. The husband and his lineage assume only partial responsibility for the legal person of the wife. Ultimately, the woman's own kin are more concerned than her husband's kin in any serious offence committed by or against her, and it is they who claim her bloodwealth if she is murdered. Thus at law a woman is only lightly attached by marriage to her spouse and his lineage, and her relationship with her own lineage is not effectively severed.

In these circumstances it seems not surprising that in northern Somaliland divorce should be common and marriage unstable. Indeed, the instability[56] of northern Somali marriage appears to be consistent not only with these factors and the local interpretation of Islam, but also with the exclusive force of agnatic descent and uncompromising identity of agnatic kinsmen in general. This strong emphasis on agnatic identity is seen in the rarity of genealogical fictions in contemporary political relations, and in the extensive use which is made of contractual alliances to adjust the fighting strengths of unequally balanced lineages without altering their genealogies. Since marriage frequently has political implications, it appears further that the instability of the marital union and of the affinal relationship accords well with the general fluidity of pastoral groupings and the shifting character of political alignments in northern Somaliland.[57]

Here then is a strongly patrilineal community where, although high marriage payments are made and a man gains full rights over his wife's children throughout their union, marriage and the affinal relationship are nevertheless unstable. Here I argue that the weakness of a woman's marital ties and the strength of her continuing attachment to her own kin are evidence of strong patriliny. Others, however, judge differently. They consider that in patrilineal societies where the wife is fully incorporated in her husband's group, agnation is stronger than in those societies like the Somali where this does not occur. This, however, is an unsatisfactory evaluation for it concentrates upon the position of the male members of the agnatic group and ignores the position in respect of female agnates. The truth is clearly that where marriage breaks a woman's ties with her own kin to the advantage of her husband's group, men and women cannot be subject to equal agnatic loyalties. In societies such as the Somali, on the other hand, where marriage does not sever a woman's ties with her own kin, men and women appear to be bound by agnation more or less equally.

Since among the Somali unstable marriage and the non-absorption of a woman in her husband's group occur together, the question arises as to whether or not there is any general or necessary correlation between these two traits in patrilineal societies. Or, to put the question differently, whether there is any correlation between the stability of marriage and the degree to which men and women are subject to unequal agnatic loyalties. On the face of it, this would seem likely since amongst the Somali as in several other patrilineal societies (e.g. the Soga, Fallers, 1957, p.121 ; the Tallensi, Fortes, 1949, p.90, etc.) the divided agnatic loyalties of the spouses undermine the cohesion of marriage and of the affinal link.

Gluckman's "Hypothesis"

To take this question further it is necessary to set our material in a wider perspective. From his stimulating comparison of Lozi and Zulu kinship and marriage, Gluckman (1950) reached the conclusion that marriage in patrilineal societies entails the complete and permanent transfer to the husband's group of rights in a wife's fertility. Gluckman suggested further that a general correlation exists between patriliny, high marriage payments, and stable marriage; and, conversely, between other forms of descent (particularly bilateral and matrilineal), low marriage payments, and unstable marriage. Although Gluckman does not specifically say so, his argument appears to imply that marriage in patrilineal societies is the converse of marriage in matrilineal societies, where rights in a woman's fertility are not transferred to the husband in marriage. However, Mitchell (1959) argues that such a permanent and absolute transfer of rights over a woman's fertility in marriage in patrilineal societies relates to the prolonged infancy of children. A child needs its mother, it is held, for several years before it can safely be separated from her. And normally the mother is pregnant again before this point is reached and will accordingly not be readily released by her husband's group (Mitchell, 1959, p.3).[58]

This reasoning, however, is not entirely convincing. The necessity for child and mother to remain together can easily be accommodated with divorce. Thus in the Somali case a divorced woman normally has the custody of her infants, at least until weaning. And following Islamic law, a divorced woman, or a widow, may not remarry until one hundred days have elapsed from the date of termination of her previous marriage. This provision is interpreted by Somali as being designed to ensure that the first husband's rights in his wife's fertility are fully protected.

Thus, while accepting the obvious fact that if descent is traced patrilineally, men must obtain rights over their wives' fertility in the sense of securing rights in the affiliation of their children, it is difficult to see why logically these rights must necessarily be held permanently. It is possible to imagine a patrilineal organisation where these 'genetricial rights' are, as it were, hired out to a succession of husbands without necessarily any thought of permanency. Indeed, the Somali approximate to this position, and so apparently do the Lakher people of Assam (Leach 1957, p.53), who, like the Somali, are characterised by unstable marriage. Hence, there is no conceivable reason why stable marriage should be a necessary condition of the transfer of genetricial rights from the wife's group to the husband's. One does not necessarily entail the other; and in fact, of course, marriage is not stable in all patrilineal societies.

Despite the impressive array of patrilineal peoples practising stable marriage, marshalled by Gluckman and thus supporting his hypothesis,[59] there are nevertheless a considerable number of other patrilineal societies where, although genetricial rights are transferred and generally high bride-wealths paid, marriage is unstable. In addition to the Somali, the following peoples on whose marital arrangements data is readily available may be quoted as falling within this category: the pastoral 'Afar of Djibouti (Albospeyre, 1959, pp.144-145); the pastoral Fulani

(Hopen, 1958, p.145 ff.; Stenning, 1959, pp.173-193); the Soga (Fallers, 1957); the Amba (Winter, 1955, p.26 ff.); the Tiv (L. and P. Bohannan, 1953, pp.76-78); the Tallensi (Fortes, 194-9, pp.84 ff.); the Birom (Gunn, 1953, p.89); some of the patrilineal Nuba tribes (Nadel,1947, pp.107-108,120-125, etc.); the Mambwe (Watson, 1958, p.114); the Thonga (Junod, 1927, i, p.198, and Gluckman, 1950, p.205); the pastoral Arab Bedouin (Murray, 1953, pp.225-226; Dickson, 1951, pp. 122-123, 143-145); the Moroccan tribes (Westermarck, 1914, pp.19, 328, etc.); the Spanish Saharan nomads (Caro Baroja, 1955, p.269); and outside Africa and Arabia to mention only two cases - the Fox Indians of America (Tax, 1955, p.273); and the Lakher of Assam (Leach, 1957, pp. 50-50).

Although selected from a limited range of sources, these examples, widely distributed geographically, and differing considerably in economic and political structure, provide good evidence that stable marriage is not invariably associated with patrilineal descent. Since in most cases, although marriage is unstable, considerable marriage payments are made, there is thus no demonstrable correlation between patrilineal descent as such, high bridewealth, and stable marriage. Nor, it should be added, is there any reason to doubt that the societies instanced are all in fact firmly patrilineal in descent and affiliation. The unstable character of their marital institutions cannot therefore be attributed to changes in the system of descent such as those which Barnes (1951) suggests account for the instability of marriage amongst the Ngoni of Zambia.[60]

Mitchell, (*op. cit.*, p. 7), however, recognizing the existence of patrilineal societies where marriage tends to be unstable, has attempted to account for this in terms of a distinction between marriages which transfer genetricial rights to the husband and his group, and those which transfer genetricial rights to the husband only. Thus in modern urban African conditions the nature of marriage and its stability are held to change concurrently with general structural changes attendant upon urbanization. In the case of peoples with agnatic descent, patrilineages shed some of their corporate functions and marriage confers genetricial rights on individuals rather than upon groups, marriage in these circumstances being unstable. This explanation, however, cannot satisfactorily apply to the particular patrilineal societies cited above. For although there are differences amongst them in the extent to which the husband is regarded as the legal father of all his wife's children, whoever begets them,[61] all these peoples appear to practise some form of leviratic and sororatic marriage. This shows that for them marriage is not merely an individual contract between a man and a woman, but also an alliance involving the transfer of genetricial rights between their lineages. Thus here, as in the Somali case, marriage implies some measure of corporate union whereby the wife is married to her husband's group as a whole; and yet marriage is unstable.

Thus neither in logic nor in reality are there grounds for assuming that marriage in patrilineal societies necessarily entails the permanent transfer of genetricial rights to the husband and his group. A man, and potentially his lineage also, can enjoy full rights over the affiliation of a woman's children without possessing permanent control of her fertility. Here the word *permanent* must be emphasised. Much of the confusion in the discussion of the stability of marriage in tribal societies seems to arise from a failure to distinguish between the acquisition of *full* gene-tricial rights and the *permanent* holding of these rights. In theory and often in practice these are entirely separate issues. If, however, marriage is defined as a contract which, amongst other things includes the trans-fer of genetricial rights, then clearly when these are permanently bestowed upon the husband and his group marriage must be stable. But there is no necessary correlation between the acquisition of genetricial rights and marriage stability.[62] It is merely tautological to state that in those patrilineal societies where genetricial rights are permanently held by a husband marriage is stable, whereas in other cases where they are not held permanently marriage is unstable. Thus preoccupation with the position in regard to the transfer of genetricial rights leads eventually to an impasse.

Further consideration of the patrilineal societies with unstable marriage which have been cited above suggests, however, that they share a common feature which may be of significance in this discussion. As with the Somali, amongst most of them (certainly the Amba, Soga, Fulani, Tallensi, Bedouin, and Lakher - the position in the other cases is not entirely clear) marriage does not incorporate a woman fully in her husband's group. Thus this is a feature shared by the Somali and a num-ber of other patrilineal societies with unstable marriage. The question now arises as to whether there is here a significant point of distinction between these patrilineal societies and those other patrilineal societies where marriage is stable. It would appear that this is in fact the case, for amongst the Nuer (Evans-Pritchard, 1945, 1951), the Zulu (Gluckman, *op.cit.*; Krige, 1950, pp.120-123), the Shona (Holleman, 1952, pp. 202-211), the Kgatla Tswana (Schapera, 1940, pp.93-116, 275-304), the 'old Ngoni' (Barnes, 1951), and the Kumam,[63] who are all characterized by stable marriage, a wife is firmly incorporated in her husband's group.

Thus, as was anticipated earlier in this chapter, it would seem that there is in fact some correlation between the extent to which a woman's ties with her own agnatic kin are dissolved by marriage to the advantage of her husband's group, and the stability of marriage. Whether or not this correlation holds in all patrilineal cases and in societies where descent is traced other than agnatically, would of course require a much more extensive survey than can be attempted here. Superficially, however, it would seem that this interpretation also applies to matrilineal societies where marriage is usually unstable and where after marriage a woman retains her own matrilineal affiliation and is not absorbed into her husband's group.

It will of course be evident that to speak, as I have done here, of the degree to which marriage incorporates a woman in her husband's group is to speak in vague terms. And to state the position more generally in terms of a distinction between patrilineal societies where men and women are bound more or less equally by agnation, and those where they are not, is even more imprecise. Ideally, however, the position can be examined in the light of what (and to what extent) legal responsibilities are shouldered by the husband's group in respect of a wife, and what responsibilities by the wife's own kin. As I have shown, amongst the Somali the distribution of legal responsibility in respect of a wife between the two lineages involved can be assessed directly and even quantitatively. For here it is the wife's kin rather than the husband's who are involved when her blood-wealth is at stake and it is they who are concerned in all other serious issues in which she is implicated. In contrast, the husband's responsibility only extends to minor matters. In such patrilineal societies with stable marriage as the Nuer[64] and Kgatla,[65] however, where a woman is firmly integrated in her husband's group, it is the latter who are responsible at law for the person and possessions of the wife.[66]

Thus, accepting the inevitable limitations of such a cursory review of so complicated a problem as this, it appears that in patrilineal societies, and perhaps generally, there is a correlation between the stability of marriage and the degree to which marriage removes a woman from the legal charge of her own kin and places her in the legal care of her husband's group. In patrilineal societies, where men and women are subject to similar agnatic allegiances and where a wife retains much of her pre-marital legal status, marriage seems to be unstable.[67] Conversely, where the wife relinquishes her pre-marital legal status and is incorporated in her husband's group, men and women here being subject to dissimilar agnatic loyalties, marriage is stable.[68] These differences in marriage stability correspond to variations in the structural implications of agnatic descent in different types of patrilineal societies.

Notes

1. *Survey of Rural Somaliland*, Save the Children, 1992.
2. Save the Children estimated that agro-pastoralists formed a third of the population: other estimates suggest that agro-pastoralists represent a quarter or less.
3. The political implications of clan-family allegiance are, however, seen in modern politics, *c.f.* Lewis 1958; 1988, p.166 *ff* and below, chapters seven, eight, and nine.
4. As a social unit the hamlet is called *reer*, and in its physical aspects as a structure of huts and fences is known as *guri*. In an extended sense the term *reer* is applied to any group of agnates and means lineage.
5. The organisation of a typical grazing encampment is shown in Lewis 1962(a).
6. In 1992, most men seemed to be armed with Kalashnikovs and clan militias often possessed machine guns, rockets, and other powerful weapons.
7. For comparative figures on the cultivators of North-western Somaliland, see Lewis, 1982, p.143.
8. From his research in 1971 and 1972, Abdi Gaileh Mirreh (1978) estimated 70 head of sheep and goats as the minimum size of flock.
9. As far as I know the term *bah* is only used in this context. I have not heard it used for womb, for which the usual word is *mahal*. Its derivative *boho* is sometimes used to refer to a coalition of lineages on a putative uterine basis.
10. Camels represent the epitome of livestock wealth (*nool*), are the measure for other forms of wealth, and are a major focus of Somali oral tradition and culture. As the proverb says, "Everything equal in value to a camel can be considered a camel". For further details see M.A. Rirash, "Camel herding and its affects on Somali literature," *Northeast-African Studies*, 10, 2-3, 1980; see also A.A. Abokor, 1987.
11. Since 1928, there has been legislation making it possible, if not always easy, for a girl to evade an enforced match. This trend was further encouraged by the provisions of the "family law" introduced during the socialist period of Siyad's military rule.
12. *C.f.* Lewis, 1969.
13. Amongst the younger generation of the towns, however, short lyrical poems called *belwo* (literally, a trifle), became popular in the 40s and 50s. Traditional Somali verse forms do sometimes take love as their theme, but handle it with great delicacy and much circumlocution.
14. Girls are infibulated about the age of puberty - between eleven and thirteen years of age - but sometimes earlier, the vulva being scarified and then drawn together and held until its sides have knit together but for a small orifice. This is done usually by a woman who belongs to a specialist occupational group of low status. A portion of the clitoris is also excised to make the girl clean (*halaal*) in a Muslim sense. The operation is usually performed individually and without much ceremonial. The object is to prepare a girl for marriage and to safeguard her virginity until that time. The excision of part of the clitoris may be made separately at a more tender age. See de Villeneuve, 1937; Raqiya H. Dualeh Abdalla, 1982.

15. The betrothed girl is referred to as *doonantahay* lit. "wanted."
16. From the man who has stolen his bride the fiancé is also entitled to claim compensation. This reparation for injured pride is usually valued at a few camels.
17. In towns, houses are so expensive that their cost is likely to be contributed to by the groom's family as part of the *yarad* as well as by the bride's, or indeed may be entirely provided by the groom's family. In the event of divorce it remains the property of husband and his kin.
18. Information collected in 1955-57.
19. The value of the rupee was one shilling fifty cents (East African). The East African currency entirely replaced the former Indian one, although the latter was still used in reckoning in the 1950s.

Numbers 1-34 refer to rich nomadic camel-herders, mainly Dulbahante.
Numbers 35-48 refer to the 'Iise camel nomads.

20. A man residing with his wife's people is called *inanlayaal* literally, "living with the girl." The couple's removal from the bride's home may sometimes be delayed by the husband's inability to pay the full amount of bridewealth at the time of marriage. It may also happen that the girl's father is waiting until his flocks have increased sufficiently to allow him to make an appropriate gift to the son-in-law. Or, again, it may be the preparation of the new bridal tent by the woman's kin which delays the departure of the bridal couple. In any case, the son-in-law participates in the daily tasks of the hamlet, his camels remaining with his own kin. Uxorilocal residence while sometimes providing a refuge from a man's own kin - if there has been a violent breach - is a common source of friction in marriage. See below.
21. This is now the essential element in the Muslim marriage contract; but *mahar* in the Pre-Islamic period was apparently a form of bride-wealth comparable to the Somali *yarad*. See *Encyclopedia of Islam*, iii, pp 137-8.
22. The Somali term *wadaad* is synonymous with the Arabic sheikh which is also used. In practice, however, the term sheikh is usually reserved for a man of religion whose knowledge of Arabic, the Quran, and Islamic Law is considerably more profound than that of a *wadaad* often hardly able to write Arabic and having only a restricted knowledge of religion.
23. A woman's husband has the right to claim any children his wife produces during their marriage whoever begets them. Children borne out of wedlock by divorced women, or prostitutes, take the affiliation of the man who begets them. Where the father is unknown the mother invents a genealogy for her children: they never take her affiliation. Even abandoned infants brought to a hospital for care are provided with a genealogy. In the interior adopted foundlings take the genealogy of those who adopt them.
24. Thus Somali speak not only of individual men marrying women, but also of their lineages marrying. For example, in reply to the question "who married your daughter?" Somali often give the name of the lineage of the woman's husband.
25. Literally. "child of paternal uncle."
26. Whatever the relationship between their fathers. children whose mothers are sisters are referred to as *habar wadaag* ("mother together").

27. This term also describes the gestures of tribute sometimes made to clan-heads (Sultans).

28. See above.

29. See below

30. I have not heard of a summary execution of a man, and this expression, I think, means no more than that the murderer would be surrendered to the administration.

31. The fact that blood-wealth here is valued at fifty camels does not represent a deduction for bride-wealth. Within the Hassan Ugaas as within other dia-paying groups blood-compensation is less than that paid externally. This reduction reflects the internal solidarity of the dia-paying group. See Lewis, 1959, p. 285.

32. See F. A. Farah, 1993.

33. Somali are fond of using the imagery of tree growth to describe kinship relationships. Thus, for example, very distant kinship relationship is described as *qaraabe qansah* from *qansah* an acacia with long roots. In the west of northern Somaliland the term *ga'al* is also used for affines but does not also mean a root.

34. See above.

35. For the genealogy of a man of this lineage see above p. 21.

36. Men sometimes boast that their virility is such that they can, unaided, force an opening in the infibulated vulva. Generally, however, the bride's mother, or if the marriage is celebrated at the husband's home, his mother, opens the vulva with a small knife. This is said to be something that a mother readily does for her daughter as she wishes to make everything "smooth" for the couple. Sometimes, however, the incision is made by a woman of the despised occupational group who, amongst other things, specialise in infibulation. There is no doubt that in the early weeks of a first marriage most women experience much pain (Cf R.H.D. Abdalla, 1982; Talle, in press).

37. Cerulli who reports this amongst the Majeerteen argues from it to a former state of marriage by capture (Cerulli, 1919, p.73). But as far as I know, there is no sound evidence to suggest that marriage by capture was ever a general process in northern Somaliland.

38. See for instance the interesting correspondence in *The Somaliland News* (Hargeisa), nos. 75, 82, 85, 89 and 93. These issues provide the theme of a number of modern Somali plays. See e.g. Mahammad Dahir Afrax, *Maana faay*, Mogadishu 1981; Mahammad Hassan Isman, *Adeegto*, Mogadishu 1979.

39. The commonest word for wealth in northern Somali is *hoolo*, literally livestock.

40. Or use the increase of their stock as bride-wealth for marrying another wife. While women weave mats and make utensils which they sell to their own personal profit thereby acquiring a small fund of "pin money," the money gained from the sale of milk and ghee (clarified butter usually made from sheep or goats' milk) in towns accrues to the family as a whole and the husband may direct the manner in which it is spent.

41. Although the private parts are ritually washed before and after intercourse, sexual intercourse has little ritual significance. I know of no occasion where it is performed as a rite. The pragmatic way in which Somalis regard it is seen

in the explanation given for sexual abstinence on the eve of a battle. Men abstain from intercourse on these occasions, I was told, because sexual intercourse is exhausting and tired men who are not fully alert cannot be relied upon to give a good account of themselves in fighting. Negatively, however. intercourse has some ritual implications. Thus a newly-born child - especially in the first forty days of its life during which its parents abstain from intercourse - must not be exposed to the gaze of strange women who, if they had committed adultery or had intercourse without washing, might cause it to fall ill. It may be further noted that abstention is practised during a woman's monthly periods and in the last months of pregnancy. After birth amongst most of the northern Somali, with the exception of some of the 'Iise clan in the west, relations are resumed forty days later according to Islamic practice. The 'Iise claim to adhere to the older Somali custom according to which a man avoids sexual relations with his wife until the child is weaned, usually at about the age of two years.

42. Thus, of course, a married woman's kin cannot marry her to someone else while her first marriage lasts. In a case in which this occurred, the outraged husband (who was absent at the time), claimed fifty camels from his wife's kin in a Subordinate Court as the price of his affronted honour and was awarded half that number.

43. Cerulli, 1919. p. 62, basing his evidence on texts, describes a much fuller absorption of women on marriage into their husbands' kin group amongst the Majeerteen.

44. For another example of compensation being claimed from the kin of a woman who had caused her husband's death, see Drake-Brockman, 1912, pp. 154-155.

45. Unlike the patrilineal Coorgs of India (see Srinivas, 1952, pp. 127-135) where the re-distribution of rights in marriage is represented symbolically by twelve pebbles ("pieces of gold") of which eleven are given to the husband's family and one retained by the Wife's kin.

46. See above, p. 43.

47. This is the counterpart for women of the expression *tol iyo hidid* (agnates and affines) used by men.

48. i.e., the number of marriages ended in divorce, expressed as a percentage of all marriages, except those ended by death. These are uncompleted marriages of varying ages with the information from the husbands only. They include marriages of only a few years' duration, but since a marriage may break-up after only a year or two's duration this seems to give a fairly general indication although, of course, it is a small number from which to generalize. *Cf.* Barnes, 1949, pp. 44 ff.

49. Married women, however, are frequently prone to certain spirit possession afflictions which require costly treatment and enable a woman to obtain gifts from her husband. Often these seem to compensate women for their hard lot. But men regard them as female malingering and repeated affliction usually ends in divorce (see Lewis, 1969). In this connection it should be mentioned that witchcraft and sorcery play a very small part in Somali life and mystical modes of aggression or retaliation are only found in a very restricted field of

social relations where for one reason or another fighting is impossible or inappropriate. The vast majority of disputes lead to open conflict, not to conflict through the medium of witchcraft or sorcery. And in general it is only the weak and politically helpless, and those who practise as men of religion (sheikhs), who are held to possess mystical powers harmful to man. Moreover, misfortunes and sickness are not ultimately ascribed to the action of witchcraft; God is the ultimate focus of causation in Somali eyes, and awards and punishments may not be experienced in this life but in heaven.

50. Adultery is called *gogoldaaf*, literally "passing the bed."

51. Amongst the Dulbahante the usual rate of compensation was 100 Rs in the 1950s.

52. In order to achieve technical virginity, however, some divorced women resort to the device of having themselves re-infibulated before seeking a new partner. Such deceptions are only likely to work where the divorced woman seeks a partner far from her former husband's people.

53. Divorce has however certain disadvantageous ritual implications. Ideally a claimant for the office of clan-head should be the son of an un-divorced woman, and even sometimes of a father who has never divorced a wife.

54. In 1957 a rifle was valued at approximately 500 rupees (£37) By the 1990s, almost every pastoralist had a kalashnikov (valued at approximately US $300), and a rifle had ceased to be prestige wealth.

55. Before marriage women enjoy ample use rights in their father's estate, but in the division of the estate on the death of the father have, in comparison with male siblings, very limited rights. especially in regard to livestock. It is particularly unusual for women to inherit camels.

56. Here, as elsewhere in this chapter, by the instability of marriage I mean the extent to which the formal legal marriage union is broken by divorce. We are dealing with formal jural positions - marriage and its dissolution by divorce - not with informal positions such as separation without divorce.

57. I have expressly excluded from this account those northern Somali who in the west have recently turned to cultivation and have established stable cultivating villages. In this area of social change which is discussed in my A *Pastoral Democracy* (Chapter IV) there is a wider field of community of interest in relation to the maintenance of communal water-holes, agricultural collaboration, community development, and the like. To a considerable extent this is independent of agnatic connection and stems directly from common local interests. Here, through a person's attachment to his agricultural holding, local elders exert more widespread authority than their counterparts do among the pastoralists. Moreover, disputes less readily lead to fighting and administrative intervention: negotiation is effective over a wider field than among the pastoralists. The whole pattern of social relationships in this area is thus apparently more permanent and stable, and certainly much less fluid and shifting than in the pastoral society. And, apparently in harmony with these distinctive features, marriage is here more stable than among the pastoralists. At least the cultivators seem to place greater emphasis on marriage stability and the few figures which I was able to collect indicate that divorce is less common than with the pastoral nomads.

58. Much the same argument has also been advanced by Gluckman (1959, pp. 74-75). See also Mitchell, 1963 and Colson, 1978.

59. It is only fair to add that Professor Gluckman recognised that there appeared to be exceptions to his hypothesis; e.g. the Thonga, Pondo, and Bedouin are cited by Gluckman as apparently having unstable marriage and thus not conforming to his hypothesis.

60. Stenning (1959, p. 190 ff.), however, attempts to correlate the instability of contemporary Fulani marriage with structural changes, but nevertheless considers that the Fulani are still today strongly patrilineal; so that, whatever the position may have been in the past, the present situation is that unstable marriage and strong agnation occur together amongst the Fulani.

61. i.e. a distinction between the physical father or *genitor* and the legal father or *pater*. Thus among the Soga illegitimate children belong to the lineage of the man who begets them (the *genitor*, not to the legal father, the man married to their mother. (Fallers, *op. cit.*p. 120).

62. By the same token, the literature overconcentrates on the distinction between uxorial and genetricial rights, ignoring the question of the bride's legal status independently of these. Thus Parkin (1980) unconvincingly suggests that a "total and unambiguous transfer to...the husband's group of the woman's roles as mother and wife and the 'negation of her roles as daughter and sister in her natal group" is associated with "the absence of terminological distinction between uxorial and childbirth payments."

63. J. van Velsen, personal communication.

64. See Howell, 1954, pp. 57-58.

65. See Schapera, 1940, pp. 103-104.

66. I have been unable to substantiate this fully from the literature on all the patrilineal societies cited above as possessing stable marriage. Accounts of tribal marriage seem often to be surprisingly deficient on this point.

67. Fortes, 1959, p. 210, seems to take the same view although he states the correlation more generally, for he writes:
"...divorce is correlated with the degree to which a person has jural status that is independent of his or her status as a spouse. For a woman the significant factor is the degree to which she retains her status as a daughter and sister after marriage, for this determines her claims on support as well as her jural status outside the conjugal relationship."

68. *Cf.* also Ackerman, 1963.

Chapter III

A PATRILINEAL KINSHIP PUZZLE

It is quite a few years since Needham (1971) and Schneider (1972; 198) independently pronounced the demise of "kinship" and of "kinship theory". The survival of the subject in anthropological discourse suggests however, that neither of these weighty authorities has been any more successful than the military regime in the Somali Democratic Republic in its campaigns to eradicate kinship which, whatever its shortcomings, is evidently an extraordinarily persistent phenomenon in the cultures traditionally studied by anthropologists.

The Problem

Although, of course, my involvement in Somali culture over the last forty years has been intermittent, such prolonged exposure to an "other culture" might be thought to have administered a sufficiently strong dose of "secondary ethnocentricity" (Herskovits's phrase) to eliminate any capacity to perceive further puzzles or experience surprises. Not so, as I discovered in the course of an interview a few years ago (in Somali) on Djibouti television. What, my interviewer inquired, was the most surprising feature of Somali custom I had encountered? My unguarded answer was the strange practice, as it seemed to me, by which a father called his children 'father' and a mother, similarly, addressed her children as 'mother'.

The interviewer was very polite. But people who had watched the program stopped me afterwards in the streets of Djibouti, asking what was odd about this. It was evidently quite pointless invoking the authority of Meyer Fortes, who had reacted with disbelief when I had reported these aspects of Somali kinship to him. To Somalis this was a perfectly rational, natural practice and my astonished reaction simply demonstrated how stupid and ethnocentric I was! In what follows, I attempt to

make sense of these aspects of terminology in the wider context of
Somali kinship. This usage is, in fact, not unique to Somali. How widespread it is in other cultures and kinship systems seems, however, in the
present state of information, hard to determine. This appears to be a further symptom of the paucity in studies of kinship terminology of detailed,
systematic data on how kinship terms are actually used in daily social
interaction - a "Malinowskian" requirement laid down by McLennan
(1886) almost a century ago and more recently reiterated in different
contexts by Firth (1970), Goody(1972), Reining (1972) and Irvine
(1974) among others.

Close kinship

The northern Somali pastoralists, with whom we are primarily
concerned,[1] are natural relativists. They divide their social universe into
"those who are close" (*sokeeye, or higto*),[2] and "those who are distant"
(*shisheeye*): the precise reference of these terms varies according to the
social context. More generically and absolutely, Somalis distinguish
between agnatic kin (*tol*) -the epitome of closeness - and affines (*hidid-*
who, as we shall see, may also be distant agnates.

The notion of binding together which is present here is also specifically implicated in the concept *tol*, agnation, which is traditionally the
cornerstone of Somali social relations, providing the individual's primary
group identity and loyalty - or more accurately, as others and I have
demonstrated (Cerulli, 1918, 1959; Colucci, 1924; Lewis, 1961 (1982)
etc.) - an elastic range of solidarity. In conformity with this socio-political import, in its verbal form *tol* means to bind together, to sew, etc.
Thus, as the phrase has it, *tol waa tolane*, "agnates are bound together"
and a large number of the proverbs in which Somalis so delight dwell
on the "irreducible" solidarity of those so related by common patrilineal descent. In harmony with my own ethnographic data, Keenadiid's
authorative Somali dictionary gives *qolo, qabiilo*,[3] and *reer*, all words
meaning "tribe," "clan" or "group" as synonyms for *tol*, which he also
translates as "nation." In this vein, the term *tolayn* has been coined (or
applied) to translate "Nationalisation." Here the bounds of agnatic identity are widely stretched.

More commonly this agnatic identity is concentrated and embodied in the genealogies (*abtirsiinyo; abtiris*) "reckoning of descent (*ab*)
which children learn from the cradle. These are most emphatically *not*
implicit *etic* anthropological artefacts elucidated by the Rivers mode of
kinship study. They are *emic* cultural phenomena and any description
and analysis of Somali culture which ignored them would be gravely

flawed. Somalis, thus, would have no hesitation in endorsing Scheffler's view that "kin classification is reckoned genealogically" (Scheffler, 1972, 115). Socio-political closeness or distance is moreover, very accurately titrated genealogically in terms of the "number of generations counted apart" as Somalis say; or, what amounts to the same thing, in terms of the "point at which genealogies converge." There is thus, literally, a genealogical tracing and reckoning of kinship and I have collected thousands of genealogies from individuals. Typically these are traced by ego, patrilineally, through twenty or thirty named generations to one of the eponymous founders of one of the six main descent groups (or, as I have called them previously, "clan-families") into which the Somali nation is divided. The ultimate sections of these genealogies usually reach out to the Prophet's line of Qoraysh in Arabia (and in some cases go back as far as Noah!), thus anchoring Somali adherence to Islam in the most respectable origins (cf.Lewis, 1961, 144ff; 1962, 35-48 etc.).

Segmentary Lineage

These family trees (whose segments are often referred to by terms which in other contexts denote tree branches (cf. Lewis 1961, p.144) are, of course, the basis of the Somali segmentary lineage political system which has been analyzed extensively elsewhere (see e.g. Lewis 1959; 1961; 1965 etc; said Samatar, 1982). The standard question, posed to a stranger in order to decide how to place him and so react to him, is "whom are you (descended) from?", segmentary genealogical distance being, as already indicated, a primary criterion in defining socio-political identity. In this native calculus, all groups are, of course, relative and the terms for segmentary divisions (jilib - 'joint' etc.) tend to be used at various levels of segmentary division, rather than being specific to any particular level. In a Whorfian fashion, the presence of inclusive and exclusive first person plurals in standard Somali grammar ("we" including all those present; "we" excluding some of those present), is in harmony with the extreme fluidity and flexibility of segmentary alignments (I do not, of course, imply a causal nexus here: I simply point out a correspondence). Specific groups are normally designated eponymously by attaching the word reer("descendants," "people" of) to the name of an apical ancestor at any point in the genealogies: e.g. Reer Mohamed etc. The smallest unit to which reference can thus be made is the domestic family or more accurately, the children of a particular man.

If tol is the generic word for agnation and reer the commonest word for descent group or lineage, agnatic unity is typically mobilized at the level of what, following local usage, I have called a "dia paying group".

As explained above (chapter two) this is normally an exogamous group with a genealogical depth of up to six generations. Somali nomads generally endorse the "we marry our enemies" policy, or to put the same thing as they usually do themselves, "we do not marry our friends (i.e. close agnatic kin)." Unity at this level of agnation is cemented by an explicit contractual treaty (*heer*), according to which these close patrilineal kin are bound to pay and receive blood-money (Arabic *diya:* Somali *mag*) in concert. Policy decisions are made in general assemblies where all adult men participate.

Somalis would be amused and possibly irritated by those anthropologists who, with naive assurance, assert that lineages do not exist/even conceptually (see e.g. Kuper, 1982). Their lineages are very real and, as I have documented extensively elsewhere (Lewis 1972, 1979, 1988, etc.) pervade the political life of the contemporary state of Somalia. Relegated to the past by a linguistic conceit in the heady nationalist days of the late 1950's and early 1960's, when, in public, people spoke no longer of lineages but literally, of 'exs' (ex-lineages), lineages were officially eliminated and symbolically buried in state-orchestrated rituals in the early 1970's. Since then, the Somali head of state made a regular practice of publicly condemning these divisive forces (which his opponents accused him of encouraging).

Affines and matrilateral kin

Although they may actually also be distant patrilineal kin, affines (*hidid*) are clearly distinguished, conceptually and in behaviour, from agnates (*tol*). Relations between affines are, as we have seen, those of formal friendship and correct behaviour. They are not insignificant. More weight, however, is attached to the matrilateral ties ("complimentary filiation") resulting from marriage. As in so many other patrilineal systems, the mother's brother (*abti*) is an extremely important relative and the warm familiarity associated with him is generalised to include his agnatic kin who are known as reer abti (literally "MB's people"). I may tease my maternal uncle with impunity and expect to be spoilt by him. He should join my agnates in contributing to my marriage payments for a bride. If my wife bears a son, I should give a present to the child's MB (my wife's brother) in exchange for his blessing. Ideally, the mother's brother performs the ceremony (*gardaadin*) signifying the end of a baby's forty days of seclusion after its birth. The child (the sister's son) is proudly perched on the mother's brother's shoulders, with its legs set astride for the first time since its birth. The auspicious mystical power of the mother's brother is balanced by the force of his curse which, as the proverb has it, can "pierce the strongest defence" *(il abti alool bey ka dustaa)*. On his death, I should also contribute to the expense of my MB's burial. We shall come in a moment to the intriguing derivation of the kinship term for MB.

First, we need to consider the various sibling relationships which derive from the practice of polygyny, widow inheritance, and the sororate. The closest collateral kin are full siblings sharing the same father *and* mother *(walaalo isku aabbe iyo isku hooyo)* - literally "siblings of the same father and mother"). There is no separate term for brother or sister and when these terms are used in address, no way of knowing the sex of the sibling so addressed. Such siblings are distinguished linguistically and in behavior from children of the same father by different wives. These latter half-siblings - with their normally separate domestic flock of sheep and goats and house - are known as "siblings of the same father but different mother" *(walaalo is ku aabbe ah, kala hooyo ah na)*. Children by the same man of wives who are sisters (usually as a consequence of sororatic marriage on the death of the first wife) stand in the same relationship and are also *habar wadaag*[4] - literally 'mother-sharing'. Somalis specifically links this term with the common term *habar* for mother and for mother's sister *habar yar* (literally 'little mother'). In a more general sense *habar* also means woman.

A slightly more complex situation results from widow inheritance *(waa la dumaalay)*. In line with Sapir (1916) and others who have sought connections between kinship terminology and leviratic marriage, we should note here that *dumaashi* is the reference term for both my brother's wife and my wife's sister. (In common with other Somali words formed by adding the suffix *aal* to a root, we may hypothesise that *dumaal* is derived from the verb *dum* to collapse, and has the sense of "understudying or substituting in case of collapse.") As we have already seen, there is marked avoidance behavior between a man and these relatives, who should be treated with great respect *before*[5] they are available for marriage. While the collective aspects of the Somali marriage contract (see chapter two) give a husband an entitlement to a replacement bride in the event of his wife's death and to marry his brother's widow (which is seen as a duty), in the latter case a gift of honour - called the *"dumaal horse"* - should be made to the latter's agnatic kin. In this event, of course, avoidance and restraint are no longer appropriate and a number of proverbs refer to the fact that an untimely continuation of avoidance will undermine the leviratic husband's ability to sire offspring by his new spouse. If the inherited widow does bear children there will be three sets of siblings. Two share the same mother, but are by different fathers (who are brothers); two share the same father but are of different mothers. The last are agnatic half-siblings, the former more distant 'true' patrilineal cousins who happen also to be maternal siblings (*walaalo hooyo*).

Let me emphasise again that matrilateral filiation is important not only at this domestic family level but also in the lineage system as a whole. Uterine identity is both a point of cleavage and of convergence in inter-lineage relations. The pivotal role of complementary filiation is thus an important feature of Somali kinship at the macro-political as well as micro-domestic levels. So, for example, one of the principle components in the inner circle of the power-structure of the (1969-1991) military regime in the Somali Democratic Republic derived from the relationship between the lineage of the Head of State and that of his mother's brother (also a distant clansman). The latter (the Ogaadeen) are the dominant Somali lineage in eastern Ethiopia (ethnically 'Western Somalia') and hence exert a major influence on Somali foreign policy as well as having held certain key positions within the army (*cf.* Lewis 1979,1980a,1980b). Most of Somalia's huge refugee population (0.75 million) came from this Ogaadeen region - following the Ogaadeen war of 1977/8 with Ethiopia.

Kinship terminology

We now turn to examine how, and to what extent, kin terms register the patterns of relationship we have discussed (see appendix I). In contrast to many other similar patrilineal systems, in northern Somali (except by courtesy or metaphorically), the term sibling *walaal)* is only applied to refer to, or strictly address, those who are, as qualified above, actually siblings (full or half). Agnatic parallel cousins (*ilma' adeero*, literally "children of father's brother") are *not* assimilated terminologically to siblings. They are, on the contrary, clearly distinguished and their degree of cousinage stated specifically according to the precise genealogical connection involved (in Somali "true, second, third, etc. cousins") depending on the number of generations counted to a common apical ancestor.

The terms of reference and address for FB (*adeer*) is quite distinct from that for F (*aabbe*) which, in turn, has no connection with the term of reference or address for MB (*abti*). Following Lowie (1928) and Kirchoff (1932), this means that standard Somali here corresponds to the so-called bifurcate collateral type: F ≠ FB ≠ MB. In the case of first ascending generation female kin, however, the pattern is bifurcate merging: M = MZ ("little M") ≠ FZ (*eeddo*).

As might be anticipated from the earlier discussion, the term *abti*

(MB) is used reciprocally between MB and ZS as a term of address. This term is linguistically especially interesting. It evidently derives from the root *ab*, origins, ancestry (especially agnatic as in *abtirsiinyo* above), following the etymological pattern indicated in appendix 2. Structurally, in relation to these parallels, it conveys the sense of person or persons involved in the action or state described by the root (here *ab*). MB is thus seen here as the person most directly involved in the generation and reproduction of his ZC. This is reflected in the *gardaadin* ritual, referred to above (p. 84), in which an infant's forty day seclusion period is terminated by the MB. The MB thus, as it were, finally ushers his ZC into the wider circle of life. This seems to be a cultural view very close, if not identical, to that implied in Fortes's concept of complementary filiation.

Although, as we have seen, ego regards his mother's kin as a distinct category referred to as "MB's people" (*reer abti*), the kin term *abti* is notitself employed regardless of generation within this group. It specifically designates mother's brothers, and their patrilineal cousins of the *same* generation (MBFC etc.). I refer to and address my MBC (and other matrilateral kin of equivalent generation) as "child of MB" (*ina'abti*). As with *abti*, this is a self-reciprocal term: the latter addresses me using exactly the same term. Generational distinctions are thus registered terminologically in the kin terms used to refer to, and address uterine (matrilateral) kin so that, despite the powerful emphasis on agnatic lineage, the Omaha pattern is not found here.[6]

The same generational distinction in reference and address is made within ego's own patrilineage in the terminology applied to agnates of ego's own and his father's generations. The term for my FB is *adeer* and for FBC *ina'adeer* literally child of FB). Beyond this, all patrilineal kin of the same generation (counting back the same number of generations to a common ancestor) refer to and address each other reciprocally as FBC (*ina'adeer*). This term (or, *adeer*, FB) is also that generally employed in polite address to a stranger whose attention one wishes to attract (less commonly and more persuasively, one might use the expression "brother" - *walaal*[7]). Because of its kinship and lineage connotations, at the height of its campaign to stamp out "tribalism," the military regime in Somalia sought to replace this kin term (*ina'adeer*) in general salutation by the word *jaalle*, "comrade" or "mate" (*cf* chapter seven). As the former Head of State proclaimed (somewhat optimistically) in a speech on 29 April 1971, marking the end of the nation-wide campaign against tribalism: "We have replaced Tribalism with Socialism, my cousin with my compatriot, and fear with courage". Although the term *jaalle* still enjoyed a certain official currency on the radio and in written documents, its salience in everyday speech seems to have declined since the mid 1970's with a reversion to the traditional *ina'adeer*. Whether directly linked or not, this revisionist trend at least corresponds to the marked revival of lineage factionalism which had reached acute proportions by the late 1980s in the Somali Republic.

As we have seen, the term for FB is *adeer*, which is used reciprocally as a term of address by a man or woman and his or her father's brothers (FZ is referred to and addressed as *eeddo*; the referential term for BC means literally "child to whom I am FB"). This usage is extended to agnatic descendants with genealogies going back to a common ancestor, but differing in genealogical depth by one ancestor. Similarly, a man or woman addresses his or her FF as *awow* and vice versa, and this usage is generalized to reciprocally address agnates separated by two or more generations in descent from a common ancestor. There is, however, a separate term of reference and address for FM - *ayeeyo*. This applies equally to matrilateral kin (see appendix 1)): FF = MF = SS = DS etc; FM = MM = SD = DD etc. and also = WFM. These terms are used in reference unilaterally to refer to the senior generation, FF, FFF, FM, FFM, etc. The corresponding reference terms applied to the junior SS, SD categories make this completely clear since *I* (male speaking) *refer* to my SS as "boy to whom I am FF (*awow*)" and address him as *awow*. Since, as has been stressed, Somalis explicitly trace out genealogical connections, moving from closest to more remote agnates, all these wider usages should obviously be regarded as "extensions" (cf. Scheffler and Lounsbury, 1971; Scheffler 1972, etc; Shapiro, 1982).

Self-reciprocals

The presence of self-reciprocal vocative terms of address for MB and ZS and for FF and SC is, of course, no surprise in this strongly patrilineal system. The same holds true of self-reciprocal terms for members of the same generation (FBC). More striking and more interesting theoretically is the fact that self-reciprocal terms of address should also apply to kin of *successive* (proximate) generations, between for example ego and his FB and BC.

This cross-generational familiarity, as it were, is of course in harmony with the highly egalitarian ethos of Somali culture where people are normally addressed directly, and with little formality, by their personal names (and/or nicknames). So, for example, even such grand personages as the head of the Somali police force - before the military *coup* of 1969 - was regularly addressed directly by his first name by street urchins in Mogadishu and took no offence. (In contrast, the military tyrant, General Mohamed Siyad Barre, whose personal nickname is "Big

Mouth" banned such references to himself as being disrespectful.) At the same time, however egalitarian, Somali culture and institutions also certainly accord precedence to seniority by age. The first born (*'urad*) enjoys privileged rights to inheritance and status and the "elders" (*odayaal*) are the leaders of opinion and policy at all levels of lineage activity. (In this vein, the dictator Siyad was widely referred to familiarly as "the old man," *oday-gii*.)

Thus, as has been noted elsewhere (Ayoub, 1964; Scheffler, 1977; Serzisko, 1983) in such "bi-polar" terms (as they have sometimes been called), what is happening is that a term whose primary reference is to the *senior* (and not the junior) member of the kin dyad is being employed reciprocally in address. In Somali this comes out most clearly in relation to the puzzle with which we began: the self-reciprocity of the terms of address F/C and M/C. This intriguing usage is dramatically illustrated for a non-Somali speaker, when a Somali mother is heard in England or America addressing her *child* as 'mummy' (*cf.* Arvanites, 1983). These usages which are similar to those reported in Lebanese Arabic by Ayoub (1964) have, as far as I can see, little in common with the practice reported (by Scheffler, 1977, 247) for certain Australian Aboriginal languages where a man is said to address his adult son as "father" and his adult daughter as "father's sister." A closer parallel would seem to be the reciprocal use reported by Malinowski (1929) among the matrilineal Trobriand Islanders of the term *kada* between mother's brother and sister's child.

As implied above, this traditional Somali self-reciprocating use of the terms F/C (*aabbe* and M/C (*hooyo*) continues in the modern urban setting, and occurs frequently also in contemporary novels and plays written in Somali by Somali authors. When one cannot see both the speakers involved, as for example when overhearing telephone conversations, the ambiguity of these terms makes it impossible for the observer to know whether a parent or child is being addressed. That the terms primarily connote the parent who is the senior party can be easily demonstrated. First of all, these terms which can be used to address and refer to the parents are *not* used in reference to the children (child =*inan* in Somali). Similarly, while I politely address my WM as "mother", she replies by politely calling me "son": she does not reciprocate the term M/C (*hooyo*).

More generally, these parental self-reciprocals are employed in extended metaphorical use to mean parent and *not* child. So, for instance, the great Somali poet and national hero, Sayyid Mohamed Abdille Hassan, who led a *jihad* against the European colonisers between 1900 and 1920, built up a personality cult in which his followers were

encouraged to call him "father" (*aabbe*) as a sign of respect and veneration (see Samatar, 1982, 112). In the same style, shortly after the 1969
military *coup* in Somalia, and in line with similar tendencies in other
Third World states, President Siyad assumed the lofty title of "Father"
(*aabbe*) of the nation whose "mother" (*hooyo*) was the "glorious revolution" (cf. Lewis, 1988, 210). These themes are embodied in the vigor-
ously disseminated "marching song", 'Victory Leader Siyaad,' employed
especially by the "Victory Pioneers" or Peoples' Vigilantes (the
Guulwaddayaal), in mobilizing popular support for national campaigns
and "crash programs". The suggestion that this metaphoric use of the
term 'father' implies that the Head of State should also have reciprocally
addressed his people as *aabbe* evoked merriment. The point, here, is
underlined by the fact that General Siyad himself often familiarly
greeted children at revolutionary youth centers with the familiar "*aabbe*".
There were also many subversive political jokes about independent-
minded, northern Somali clan elders asking President Siyad how he
could possibly have been their "father" (*aabbe*) when his name did not
figure in their genealogies.

My initial puzzle has, I hope, almost disappeared. When we set the
parent-child self-reciprocal terms of address in the wider context of
Somali kinship terminology we find that, far from being unique, they
conform to a general cultural pattern. The general pattern is that patrilineal and matrilateral kin in proximate (as well as alternate) generations
address each other reciprocally by the term of reference for the senior
relative. Within the semantic range of these kinship terms, the core-
meaning is referential but in a context restricted to direct, dyadic
address, they are employed reciprocally (*cf.* Serzisko, 1983). Affinal kinship terms, in contrast, are not used as vocative self-reciprocals. They are
formal terms, whose employment in directly addressing an affinal relative, is considered impolite. Such an affinal relative is normally addressed
directly by his (her) personal name.

These distinctions in the use of Somali kinship terms are in broad
accord with the moral value and socio-political significance of kinship
as opposed to affinity discussed earlier. Within the domains of agnation
and complimentary filiation, the familiarity and closeness implied in
the cross-generational reciprocal terms of address is achieved by assim-
ilating a junior to a senior rather in the same vein as in the English public school/Oxbridge use of the term "Sir" (used by a superior to address
an inferior as well as vice versa). In the case of the Somali parent/child
self-reciprocals, the child is honoured by being addressed as a parent: it
is not the father who is child of the man. The possible linkage between
these kinship usages and the egalitarian character of northern pastoral

Somali society might seem to be confirmed by the *absence* of self-reciprocal parent/child terminology in the more hierarchical circumstances of agro-pastoral northern Somali society. However, the presence of similar parent/child reciprocals in such obviously hierarchical circumstances as those of the Central African Lozi (Prins, 1980) or Iran (Spooner, 1965) casts doubt on any simple, cross-culturally valid correlation of this kind.

More generally, this use of senior kinship referential terms to apply to juniors is in line with similar usages reported patchily elsewhere (*cf.* Ayoub, 1962; Spooner, 1965 Scheffler, 1977; Prins, 1980). The whole point, here, surely is that these honorific, familiar vocative reciprocal usages depend for their validity and piquancy on the prior existence of the plan for the use of *non-reciprocal* reference terms. In Somali, any relationship can always be specified exactly in terms of agnatic and/or affinal genealogical connections and a father may even designate his own son by direct reference to his own name; if he is called Mohamed, he can refer to his son (in the latter's presence) as "son of Mohamed." Thus, at least amongst the Somali it might be argued that their system of referential kin terms is equally important not only in itself but also in providing the basis for appropriate vocative terms of address.

Although the terms are first defined on the genealogical grid, however, their vocative use and range is not immediately self-evident and cannot, therefore, be directly deduced from the reference terms themselves. To that extent reference terminologies - whatever their semantic structure may be presumed to disclose of the "native calculus" - are manifestly incomplete and partial. The extraordinarily neglected issue of how (when they are utilised in this way) reference terms are actually employed in address[8] - and hence of the linkage between modes of reference and address - constitutes one of the major challenges facing kinship studies today.

APPENDIX 1

Terms of Reference

AWOW	FF, FFB, FFF, etc. MF, MFB, MFF	G^{+2}
AYEEYO *(MO'OOYO)	FM, FMZ, FFM, etc. MM, MFZ, MFM	

AABBE	F	G^{+1}
ADEER	FB	
EEDDO	FZ	
HOOYO (HABAR)	M MZ	
ABTI	MB	
SODDOG SODDOH	WF, WFB WM, WBW	

WALAAL	B, Z	G^{0}
INA'ADEER INA'EEDDO INA'ABTI	FBC FZC MBC	
HABAR WADAAG AFO SAYDDI	MZC W WB, WZ, ZH	
DUMAASHI OORIO WALAAL	BW, WZ, FBSH WZH	

INAN	C	G^{-1}

(* Used in N.W. Somalia)

APPENDIX 2

(Words whose derivation follows the same pattern as *abti*: i.e. addition *ti* to root)

KAR	to be able	KARTI	ability
GAL	to enter	GALTI	recent immigrants
MAR	to travel	MARTI	guest
HAR	to remain behind	HARTI	those left behind
QAH	to run away from danger	QAHOOTI	refugees
KULAN	to meet	KULANTI	meeting
AF	mouth 'note verbale'.	AFTI	referendum, opinion,
DUQ	old man, elder	DUQAYTI	elders
HAARAAN	forbidden, unclean thing	HAARAANTI	forbidden actions
HEER BEEG	law to measure	HEERBEEGTI HEER	judges, experts in those who assess law.

Notes

1. Most of my data was collected originally in 1955-1957 when, three years before independence, I carried out fieldwork in northern Somalia financed by the Colonial Social Science Research Council (see Lewis 1977). Frequent subsequent visits, of regrettably short duration in the north, have enabled me to check and up-date some of my original field material. It has also been scrutinized by a considerable number of Western trained Somali linguists, historians and social scientists to whose work I increasingly turn for guidance. All kinship terms discussed here have been cross-checked by reference to the excellent Somali dictionary (in Somali) compiled by the Italian-trained Somali linguist, Dr. Yaasiin Keenadiid. As usual, I also owe much to the patient co-operation and guidance of my friend and colleague Professor B. W. Andrzejewski who possesses an encyclopaedic knowledge of the Somali language. Earlier versions were presented at the Second International Congress of Somali Studies, Hamburg, 1983, and at the Malinowski centennial conference of the Association of Social Anthropologists of the Commonwealth convened at the London School of Economics in April 1984 by Joanna Overing. For helpful comments I am grateful to participants at both conferences as well as to Jonathan Benthall, to Edmund Leach who drew my attention to the Trobriand parallels, and to

Warren Shapiro.

2. Other, slightly less common terms, probably of Arabic derivation, denoting close kinship ties include: *'asabo, qaraabo,* and *'ashiiro.*

3. * From Arabic

4. *Wadaag* is a general qualifying expression meaning 'sharing' and is used in the modern Somali term *hanti-wadaag* literally 'wealth-sharing' used for socialism and communism.

5. The second (replacement sister) wife is known as *higsiisan* -'the one given next'.

6. It was, of course, largely Radcliffe-Brown (1950) who initiated the examination of African kinship terminologies in this classical (American) style. In her admirably elegant study on Haya kinship, Priscilla Reining (1972, 94) correctly noted that the absence of Omaha features in Somali (and other strongly patrilineal African systems), casts serious doubt on the linkage generally posited between Omaha type terminology and lineage.

7. In southern Somalia, especially amongst the partly agricultural Digil and Rahanwin, the FBC is commonly referred to as B (*walaal*).

8. I take it for granted (cf. M. Bloch, 1971) that all kinship terms are apt to be used "tactically." The distinction between reference terms and vocative terms of address is not that the latter are uniquely tactical. Reference terms are also used tactically.

Chapter IV

MYTH AND HISTORY IN SOMALI GENEALOGIES[1]

Genealogies and History

Few anthropologists, I think, would question that the use of oral tradition as a historical source in tribal studies requires a knowledge of the part tradition plays in the society in which it occurs. Most would agree that oral tradition does not have a universal validity — it is not equally "true" or equally "false" in all traditional societies.[2] Rather its historical content, where unequivocal historical evidence is lacking, has to be evaluated in the light of the contemporary social situations to which it is related. Since Malinowski, many anthropologists have tended to the view that traditions about the past express the reality of the present more than they record what actually happened in the past. Legends about the past, indeed, have often been described as "charters" validating the present by attributing a respectable antiquity to its origins.[3]

Here of course one would expect that traditions relating to important aspects of present social conditions, such, for example, as present political structure, would be less neutral and more biased than those relating to less significant aspects of contemporary society. From this standpoint one would also expect to find, as to a certain extent one does, that different types of traditional society have different types of "charters" — different kinds of pseudo-histories legitimizing their present social and political constitution. Thus, for example, whatever their ultimate historical validity, the traditions of the so-called Hamitic "conquest states" of East Africa seem at least in general accordance with their present political constitution and class structure.[4] In other less centralized and less hierarchical tribal confederations or tribal groupings there are often as many traditional political histories as there are chiefs; and where each chief claims precedence over his rivals no means, in the absence of other sources of historical knowledge, of deciding which traditions are most authentic.[5] In these examples, traditional political histories relate to primacy of settlement in an area of conquest or to political power, and sometimes, though not always, to both at once. In other less hierarchical and more egalitarian tribal societies without strongly developed chiefly institutions, similar correspondences between oral traditions and contemporary social structure can often be demonstrated.

In this chapter I shall deal only with one type of oral tradition; that crystallization of the past which takes the form of a genealogy. Few historians would, I imagine, accept a genealogy as an entirely neutral historical document unaffected by the social milieu in which it is conserved. And in tribal societies without chiefs, where the basic social and political groups are kinship groups or lineages, anthropologists have been particularly sceptical of the historical content of genealogies. Thus Bohannan in describing the political organization of the Tiv of West Africa, a society of this type whose social groups are lineages, shows how genealogies are deliberately manipulated to represent not the past, but the present balance of political relationships. Bohannan indeed characterizes Tiv genealogies as a "charter," as she puts it, "at once a validation and mnemonic device for present social relationships."[6] The experience of most anthropologists who have studied such segmentary lineage systems corroborates this view of the way in which in this type of society genealogies are manipulated in accordance with the balance of political power.[7] Thus, in general, recent studies by social anthropologists support the interpretation of MacMichael, the authority on the Arab tribes of the Sudan, that tribal genealogies are historically true only in the sense that a parable is true.[8]

The social organization of the northern Somali, whose genealogies I examine in this chapter, belongs morphologically to the class of segmentary lineage systems and should therefore be expected to exhibit similar genealogical processes to those outlined above. I shall try to show, however, that in distinction to most other similar cases Somali genealogies are not manipulated in this sense and can be regarded only partly as a charter. I hope that this examination may serve to emphasize the importance, for those who use genealogies as chronologies, of an understanding of the contemporary significance of genealogies in the society whose history is under study.

Genealogies and Political Identity

As we have seen (chapter 2) the Somali nation is divided by patrilineal descent into a vast system of kinship groups or lineages which unite and divide politically according to the context of opposition or competition on any given occasion. It is here that contract (*heer*) is important as an instrument of political cohesion since it is through contract that different spheres of agnatic connection are mobilized as occasion requires. While the system as a whole is stable, its component parts — by allegiance to which the political and legal status of the individual is defined — are highly unstable. On one occasion a man acts with other patrilineal kinsmen as a member of a determinate lineage, while on another his political loyalties lie with a more or less inclusive range of kin at a different point on the genealogical scale. For, the genealogical system which encompasses the whole society, represents political and jural affiliation as well as constituting to some extent a historical or quasi-historical record.

Within this system of shifting genealogical attachment the most stable units are those we have called "dia-paying groups." But although the dia-paying group is the most stable and indeed fundamental political unit in northern Somali society, its identity and exclusiveness do not prevent the formation of wider lineage alliances by new contracts when need arises. In the political manoeuvres and re-alignments between dia-paying groups within the clan, which are part of the very substance of daily life in Somalia, the interaction between the principles of lineage and contractual allegiance is such that at every level of grouping concerted political unity requires contractual alliance. Patrilineal affiliation implies social cohesion and political unity: but it is a contract which calls this into effect and translates political tendencies into political practice. And it is precisely the way in which the Somali pastoralists utilize contractual unity as a basis for political solidarity, over and above lineage ties, which distinguishes their social system from those of other uncentralized polities based on lineage ties. I stress this distinction because, as I shall presently argue, the use Somali make of political contracts — contracts of government in a loose sense — is consistent with the way in which the historical content of their genealogies differs from that of other, otherwise similar societies.

It will now be clear that a Somali genealogy is not only a family tree conserving the historical origins of a group. In the sphere of politics its significance lies in the fact that it represents the political affiliations of individuals and groups. By reference to his ancestors, a man's relations with others are defined — or at least circumscribed, for their full definition depends also on contract. And it is through his genealogy of birth that the individual is placed in society. As Somali themselves loosely put it, a person's address in Europe is his pedigree in Somaliland.

If this is the political significance of northern Somali genealogies, the question at once arises as to how changes in political alignments and relations affect genealogies. Are Somali genealogies "charters" in the sense that they mirror existing political alignments and have to be adjusted when the balance of power between groups changes? The answer to this is in the negative, and here the lineage organization of the Somali differs from that of other similarly composed tribal societies. When two Somali kinship groups combine together against aggressors as a new political entity they do not normally adjust their genealogies. The new political relationship is not validated genealogically. Instead, political alliance is achieved by a formal contract entered into by the lineages concerned, in which the terms of the new union are expressed in detail. This usually takes the form of an agreement according to which the parties concerned accept joint responsibility in homicide and ancillary matters. Such treaties are at once legal and political in character. They set forth in detail the respects in which the new political entity will act as a corporate group in relation to others, and they define what actions within the group will be regarded as dangerous to its solidarity and consequently made subject to punitive sanctions.

At all levels of grouping, even that of the relatively stable dia-paying group, such treaties are in no sense permanent. They are made to meet a specific situation or set of situations and have to be amended or broken when new circumstances arise. Subsequent events may render an existing alliance no longer attractive or advantageous to some or all of its members and it may become necessary to terminate the agreement. Where this occurs by unilateral action and not by general agreement, the seceding party has to make financial reparation to the other members of the alliance.

Such alignments and re-alignments between and even within dia-paying groups are a constant feature of Somali pastoral politics. What is significant here is that while they generally take place within the framework of patrilineal connection they do not normally involve genealogical adjustments. To northern Somali the genealogy, which every child learns by heart at a tender age and which often goes back as many as twenty or thirty generations to the clan-family ancestor, is permanent and unchanging. The patrilineal solidarity which it represents is regarded as absolute and perpetually binding. In this context, Somali speak of patrilineal affiliation as having the strength of iron in contrast to weaker kinship ties which like thread can easily be snapped. As we have noted, they also compare their agnatic loyalties to the testicles, a particularly apposite allusion since Somali express the fighting power of their lineages in terms of the number of penises they possess. Thus, for the northern Somali it is the contractual alliances which are constantly changing, and the range of patrilineal connection recognized as politically binding: the genealogies remain unchanged, conserving a wide framework for future mobilization.

Demographic Factors

Do Somali genealogies then represent an accurate historical record? This question raises a complicated problem of interpretation which can best be approached from a consideration of the growth and expansion of lineages over the generations.

Somali discuss the expansion of lineages and lineage segmentation in terms of the birth of sons, for as they say, "when a son is born the patrilineal line extends." Each child takes his father's first name as his own surname and is given a new first name. Thus, for example, Mohamed has a son Jama, whose full name is then Jama Mohamed; and when he in turn has a son Ahmad, the latter's full name is Ahmad Jama and his genealogy to his grandfather Ahmad Jama Mohamed. In this way the genealogies are built up as with population increase lineages expand over the generations. At as young an age as five or six years, children are capable of reciting their full genealogy to their clan-family ancestor, and they are taught this by their mother - who may belong to another clan. Knowledge of the complete genealogical tree of any large group, however, is restricted to old men and elders for whom such information has direct political importance.

Wherever an ancestor begets two or more sons, the genealogies bifurcate, providing points of division (and of unity in the ascending generation) in subsequent lineage relations. But not all men can have the same number of sons, nor do the descendants of the latter multiply at the same rate. In addition, natural hazards - disease, famine, and war -affect different families and lineages unequally. Thus, natural increase over the generations does not proceed regularly and leads to the development of an unequally balanced array of descent groups, for all lineages do not expand at the same pace. Some lineages even die out and are lost to the genealogical record or are only recalled with difficulty. Thus Somali lineage proliferation, as a consequence of population growth, is irregular and can be represented as shown:

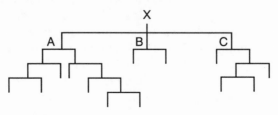

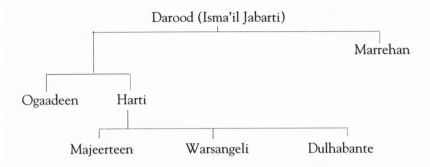

Somali are keenly aware of the uneven and often unbalanced character of lineage growth. In any genealogy they distinguish between "short branches" (*laan gaab*) and "long branches" (*laan deer*), terms which are also applied to plant and tree growth. Just as Somali genealogies are not merely records of the past growth and development of families but have political implications, so these terms also have a political connotation. Somali assume, and an extensive examination of clan genealogies shows, that there is a correlation between the strength in man-power of a group and its genealogical span. Large lineages, with many members which are said to have multiplied more rapidly over the generations than weaker lineages, have longer and more widely ramified genealogies than the former.[9]

Before considering what this correlation between numerical strength and genealogical depth implies in regard to the historical content of Somali genealogies it may be worth pointing out how this correspondence resembles a fairly general phenomenon in hierarchical tribal societies. In most cases in such societies the genealogies of chiefs are longer than those of commoners.[10] In Somalia, however, where there is no formal hierarchy of chiefly offices and political status depends on numerical strength, it is not the genealogies of clan-heads which are longer than those of other individuals, but the genealogies of numerically large lineages which are longer than those of smaller and weaker groups.

The question at once arises as to how this equation between genealogical span and numerical strength affects the historical content of genealogies. Whether a lineage is small or large, whatever its political status, its continued existence requires reproduction through an approximately similar number of generations. If representatives of two lineages of unequal strength trace descent from a common ancestor by a widely divergent number of generations it is difficult to explain this except on the assumption that in the case of the smaller group some names in its genealogy have been lost. It is hard to see how a difference in genealogical span of, for example, ten generations between collateral lineages can be accounted for except on this basis. For while some families evidently multiply more rapidly than others, unequal development could hardly account for the very wide discrepancies which often occur between the genealogical spans of collateral lineages. Thus it appears that genealogies, which represent merely the linear continuation of a line and do not proliferate in new collateral branches at each generation, are foreshortened or "telescoped." Names which are not significant points of bifurcation thus seem to drop out of the genealogical record and are forgotten.

Unfortunately, there are no sufficiently early written records of Somali genealogies to satisfactorily test this interpretation. Early references to Somali clans (the first occurs in the thirteenth century,[11] and later evidence comes from a sixteenth-century document[12]) do not furnish detailed genealogies. Their use of lineage names, however, is in keeping with the assumed numerical expansion of the Somali population and corresponding genealogical proliferation which underlies my argument. Moreover, the same process of genealogical elision has been shown to occur in other tribal societies,[13] and is, in my view, the only reasonable explanation. Somali, of course, with their immense pride in their pedigrees, reject the idea that it is possible for their ancestors' names to be forgotten. Yet if such an elision did not occur it would be difficult to understand how the correlation between genealogical span and numerical strength, and political status, could arise. In addition, the interpretation proposed is supported by the fact that if there is ever uncertainty or confusion in remembering the names of ancestors or their genealogical order, it is always in the *upper* portions of genealogies and usually when their descendants are few and politically insignificant.[14] Moreover, in tracing the genealogical structure of a lineage, Somali invariably follow through first the proliferation of the largest and most important segments and then return to describe the genealogies of smaller collateral segments. Here priority is given to lineage strength, not to order of birth.

All this suggests that for chronological purposes the longest available genealogies should be used in preference to shorter genealogies to an ancestor whose approximate date one wishes to establish.[15] This might be obvious to an anthropologist familiar with societies of this kind, but it is doubtful if a historian would have been able to deduce this without some knowledge of the part genealogies play in Somali society.

As I have said, there is at present unfortunately no absolute method of testing the chronological validity of even these "long branch" genealogies. However, the longest genealogies of which I have knowledge linking living people with the eponymous founders of the Isaaq and Daarood clan-families in northern Somaliland have a span of twenty-four and thirty generations respectively. Taking each named generation as representing thirty years, a somewhat arbitrary estimate, but one which I believe is close to reality, this would place the lifetime of Sheikh Daarood at about nine hundred years ago and that of Sheikh Isaaq at about seven hundred and twenty years ago. Thus, according to this reckoning Sheikh Daarood lived in the eleventh century, and Sheikh Isaaq in the thirteenth. In fact this tally compares very well with the dates given in oral tradition, for according to this source Daarood lived in the tenth-eleventh centuries, and Sheikh Isaaq in the twelfth-thirteenth centuries.

I hasten to say that as far as I am aware Somali do not base their dating of the lives of these two sheikhs on a genealogical reckoning such as that made here. So that at least the genealogical chronology, based on the longest genealogies available, agrees fairly well with the dates conserved in oral tradition which are handed down from generation to generation and amended to keep pace with the passage of years by sheikhs who act as the custodians of Daarood and Isaaq's main shrines. While stressing the tentative character of these dates, it should be observed that they correspond fairly well with what can be reconstructed from other sources of the early history of the Somali and their clan movements.[16]

The Arab connection: literacy

As has been seen, although "short branch" genealogies seem to be telescoped and to convey a distorted historical record, this appears to be less true of "long branch" genealogies. And since, as was shown earlier, Somali genealogies are not generally automatically manipulated to keep pace with re-adjustments in the balance of political power as they are in many other similar societies, they are not in this sense merely mythical charters.

Yet, at another genealogical level, Somali genealogies would seem to bear very little relationship to reality and to be justly described as "charters." I refer now to the apices of clan-family genealogies where descent is traced to noble Arabian families, and particularly to those closely connected with the Prophet. Thus to return to Sheikhs Daarood and Isaaq; each is traditionally described as an Arabian immigrant of noble family. Daarood is claimed to be the son of Ismaa'iil Jabarti, a well-known Arabian saint whose tomb is in the Yemen. He is said to have left Arabia and crossed the sea to Somaliland where he settled first at the port of Bosaso (other variants of the tale give other ports) on the north-eastern Somali coast. Here according to the traditional accounts he was discovered and at once recognized as a person of noble birth and welcomed as an honoured guest. This reception was accorded to him by the Dir Somali who at that time occupied much of north-eastern Somaliland and the Sheikh eventually married a woman of this clan. In addition to the wealth of oral tradition describing the Sheikh's arrival and settlement among the Dir, and the multiplication of his descendants and their expansion at the expense of their Dir hosts,[17] there are a number of written hagiologies in circulation, some of which have been published in Egypt,[18] describing the Sheikh's life and works and glorifying his pedigree. It is these written compilations, particularly, which insist on his connection with the Yemenite saint Ismaa'iil Jabarti. Since, however, the latter died in 1403 these records are chronologically at variance with the burden of oral tradition and with the dates arrived at by genealogical calculation. For this and other reasons the connection seems to be completely fictitious.[19]

Again, and even more fancifully from a historical point of view, Daarood clansmen sometimes claim a direct lineal connection with the Mahri and Omani Arabs and those of the province of Asir through their eponymous ancestor. They phrase this genealogically and speak of Daarood Ismaa'iil, Mahri Ismaa'iil, 'Asiir Ismaa'iil, and Suuri Ismaa'iil as brothers. This, of course, is genealogically completely invalid. It represents the expression in genealogical terms of the trading connection of centuries' standing between the Daarood of the north-eastern Somali coast and the peoples of southern Arabia and the Gulf of Oman.[20]

Similar traditions are conserved by the Isaaq in regard to their ancestor Sheikh Isaaq. His descendants trace their ancestor's pedigree to 'Ali, the son of Abuu Taalib,[21] who married the Prophet's daughter Faatima. Stories similar to those which attach to Sheikh Daarood describe Sheikh Isaaq's arrival from Arabia at the ancient Somali port of Zeila in the northwest of the ex-Protectorate and near the border with Djibouti. From this ancient settlement which is first mentioned by Arab writers in the ninth century, the Sheikh embarked on a series of travels throughout Somaliland and parts of Ethiopia, and eventually settled at the ancient port of Mait[22] in Erigavo District where his splendid domed tomb stands today and is the scene of frequent pilgrimages. Again, as with Sheikh Daarood, there are a number of published hagiologies in Arabic which describe not only the Sheikh's movements and life and works in Somaliland but also his peregrinations in Arabia before his arrival among the Somali. These works contain a mass of unlikely circumstantial detail and repeatedly insist on the validity of Sheikh Isaaq's pedigree, a feature which itself suggests that the genealogy is suspect.

As in the case of Sheikh Daarood, the names in the Arabian sections of the genealogy are also unconvincing since they represent those current at the time of the Prophet rather than, as one would expect if the genealogies were historically genuine, medieval local Arab names. And although in this case there is little divergence between the dates recorded in the hagiologies and those conserved in oral tradition, there are again strong grounds for doubting the authenticity of the genealogical claims made.[23]

Thus it seems that the traditions surrounding the origins and advent from Arabia of Sheikhs Daarood and Isaaq have the character of myths rather than of history, even although there is every reason to believe that one aspect of Somaliland's long contact with Arabia has been the settlement over the centuries of parties of Arab immigrants. In this respect the Daarood and Isaaq legends represent historical fact. But quite apart from this, their real significance in Somali culture lies in the fact that they validate, in a traditional Somali idiom, the Muslim basis of Somali culture. In this sense and at this generational level, where descent is traced outside Somalia to Arabia, Somali genealogies are charters supporting Somali religion and culture; and they also express the identity and exclusiveness of particular Somali groups. Sceptical Somali see these traditions in this light; and point to the way in which Daarood clansmen mock Isaaq claims to Arabian origin, as Isaaq also question Daarood pretensions. Thus while the Isaaq regard themselves as a separate clan-family tracing their agnatic origins directly to Arabia and only acknowledge a connection by marriage with the Dir, other Somali regard them as of full Dir affiliation. It would appear that the Isaaq have Arabicized their genealogy as a means of acquiring prestige and in keeping with their growing strength and separate identity as an independent group numbering some 400,000 souls (in 1958).

A comparable process is apparently in progress with the 'Iise (Dir) clan who occupy the extreme western part of northern Somaliland. Traditionally this clan belongs like its immediate eastern neighbour the Gadabuursi to the Dir clan-family and traces its Arabian connections through Dir to 'Aqiil Abuu Taalib.[24] By the 1960s, however, it had become the practice to regard the clan founder as a sheikh or even saint in much the same way as the eponyms of the Daarood and Isaaq are regarded by their descendants, and no doubt partly at least in response to their claims. Thus, although as far as I know, no printed hagiologies in honour of the 'Iise ancestor have yet appeared, a number of hymns (*qasiidas*) have been composed for him and there is a shrine (*maqaam*) where he is said to have appeared miraculously in Djibouti. What is said to be his actual grave lies close to that of Sheikh Isaaq several hundred miles to the east of the territory now occupied by the 'Iise,[25] so that the growing Muslim cult of the clan ancestor centers on his local shrine in Djibouti.

A similar process of Islamization of a traditional ancestor cult[26] is apparently taking place amongst the Gadabuursi. This clan which traditionally is of Dir descent, at least according to learned Gadabuursi sheikhs and historians[27] and to the general opinion of other Somali, is in close contact with the Isaaq and many of its members state that their founder, 'Ali Samarroon, is a brother of Sheikh Isaaq. As with the 'Iise, the grave attributed to the Gadabuursi clan ancestor lies close to that of Sheikh Isaaq in Erigavo District. Again the clan founder is coming to be regarded as a Muslim saint with a growing though yet small collection of praise hymns and a local shrine situated at Tukali between Borama and Jigjiga in Ethiopia.

I have quoted these examples because they illustrate, at least in my opinion, a process of myth-making in its early stages which has already proceeded much further amongst the Daarood and Isaaq. Thus at the point where Somali trace descent from Arabia outside their own society, a strong mythical component enters into the genealogies which is not present at lower generational levels. Here the genealogies become charters for the Islamic foundations upon which Somali culture is built, and they also serve to express in religious terms the political prestige and exclusiveness of large autonomous lineages. At the same time, although the particular genealogical claims they make seem completely untenable, they nevertheless record a tradition which is true — that of long historical contact between Somaliland and Arabia.

Far from discouraging the mythologizing processes, writing in the Arabic sacred script encourages them. This interpretation is also consistent with the overlapping and to some extent contradictory claims to Arab origin made at different levels in the Somali "national" genealogy. Thus, the genealogies tracing descent to Arab ancestors at the level of Sheikhs Daarood and Isaaq are in conflict with apparently earlier Arabicized traditions linking these two groups as also of common Arab origin. What is evidently happening here is that as groups develop in size, independence, and power they tend to establish their own, independent traditions of Arab origin. This process seems to have operated piecemeal over the centuries with, however, remarkable consistency in the validating idiom - the claim to Arab origins.

Thus, to conclude, an examination of Somali genealogies suggests (if there were more unequivocal historical evidence available it might be possible to say *proves*) that in contemporary political relations, contract is used to regularize inequalities in political status without usually resorting to genealogical manipulation. Over the generations, however, through the correlation which Somali see between genealogical span and numerical strength, the pedigrees of small groups are telescoped or foreshortened more than those of large and powerful lineages. To this extent within Somalia, genealogies preserve a distorted record. At a higher genealogical level again, where before it would have been inappropriate to speak of Somali genealogies as "charters," it now becomes necessary to do so, since the links which are traced between Arabia and the ancestors of clan families, and in some cases of clans, are fictitious and serve to explain the strong attachment of Somali to Islam.

These considerations demonstrate that even in the same society a particular type of oral tradition — in this case the genealogy — does not necessarily have a uniform social meaning or a uniform historical validity. Not only in different tribal societies is oral tradition a medium of varying historical accuracy but even in a particular tribal society one type of oral tradition may vary in its authenticity, according to the structural level at which it occurs.[28] In addition, the presence of literacy is no guarantee of truth: if anything writing makes genealogical forgery less rather than more difficult. This may perhaps serve to emphasize the complexity of the problem of decoding the historical content of tribal traditions and point to the necessity of evaluating oral tradition always in relation to its significance in the social matrix in which it occurs.[29]

The Clans Descended from Sheikh Ishaaq

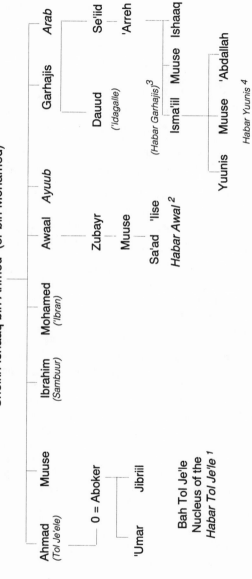

'Ali Abu Taalib

Sheikh Ishaaq bin Ahmed (or bin Mohamed)

(see notes page 108)

Notes to chart page 107

1. Habar Tol Je'le, or as they are commonly known Habar Tol Ja'lo, currently shortened to Habar Ja'lo, originally comprised the descendents of Abokor through his marrlage wlth a aaughter of Ahmad (Tol Je'le, 'he who loves his *tol*') but is extended to embrace the weaker collaterals - Tol Ja'lo (from the male issue of Ahmad); Sambuur; and the 'Ibraan. The Habar Tol Ja'lo thus include all the Habar Habuussheed, i.e. the descendents of Sheikh Isaaq's Ethiopian wife. Thus the Habar tol Ja'lo (or Habar Ja'lo) are a uterine bah alliance.

2. Habar Awal, a uterine bah group formerly including the Ayuub, named after the mother of Awal, the flrst-born, (*'Uraad*) and more prolific of the two brothers Awal and Ayuub. The ayuub have now however increased sufficiently in strength to break away at least to some extent from the descenaents of Awal who still however are called Habar Awal. Awal and Ayuub are commonly supposed to be of the same mother, but more authoritative opinion holds that while Ayuub's mother was of the Magaadleh (Dir) clan, a wife qiven in sororate (*higsiisan*) to Sh. Ishaaq after the death of his flrst Magaadleh wife, the mother of Garhalis and Arab, Awal was in fact begotten by a shariif woman who died before she could suckle him. Ayuub's mother then brought up Awal.

3. Garha is and Arab are both born of Sh. Ishaaq's first Magaadleh wife. The descendents of Garhajis, Dauud (eponym of the 'Iidaqale), and Se'iid (ancestor of the Habar Yuunis clan), are know collectively as Habar Garhajis, a *bah* alliance which sometimes includes also the Arab clan. The Habar Yuunis for example will sometimes allY with the 'Iidagale as Habar Garhajis in opposltion to the Habar Awal.

4. Habar Yuunis is the joint name for the clan comprised by all the descendents of 'Arreh Se'iid, and is therefore a bah uterine alliance. Yuunis, the first-born son of Isma'iil, Isma'iil's descendents being the most numerous, had given his name (although his descendents are not the most numerous of the three brothers, Yuunis, Muuse, and 'Abdullah) to this federation.

5. As indicated above, Habar Magaadeleh is the uterine group comprising all the descendents of Sh. Ishaaq who are not the issue of his Ethiopian wife (Habar Habuusheed) in opposition to the latter. This cleavage is that stressed when there is a friction between the Habar Ja'lo clan and the Habar Yuunis. In this context, the Habar Yuunis sometimes taunt the Habar Ja'lo for not being Somalis at all, but Ethiopians.

   These uterine divisions in a large polygynous family illustrate the principles of uterine cleavage which we have discussed above (p.

6. Although the Sh.'s genealogy roclaims him to be *Ashraaf* in descent he is said not to have called himself *shariif* at the time of his arrival in Somaliland because he was fleeing from persecution of the *ashraaf* in Arabia. He is sometimes also called *'Sayyid'* and while, Somali Sheikhs know the historical distinction between *sayyid* and *shariif*, in practice the two words are often used synonymously. Cf. an analogous use in Southern Arabia, R.B. Serjeant, 1956 p.4.

- - - lndicates small clans wno are not stronq enough to exist entirely independently of their more powerful collaterals.

Notes

1. Based on a paper originally contributed to *Historians in Tropical Africa*. *The Proceedings of the Leverhulme African Inter-Collegiate Conference in History*, held at the University College of Rhodesia and Nyasaland, Salisbury, September 1960.

2. It is difficult to agree with G. P. Murdock's sweeping strictures on the 'completely undependable' character of oral tradition beyond the direct recollection of living informants or his extraordinary statement that only in a few cases can some reliance be placed on oral tradition where it is automatically corrected in order 'to validate social status or land claims'. (Murdock, 1959, 43.)

3. See, for example, I. G. Cunnison, 1951; 1959, and J. van Velsen, 1959.

4. For a convenient discussion of these East African 'conquest states' and their historical traditions, see A. I. Richards, 1960.

5. This, for example, is true of the Lakeside Tonga of Malawi (van Velsen, op. cit.), and of the Nsenga of Zambia (R. J. Apthorpe, 1960).

6. L. Bohannan, 1952.

7. This view is expressed as a generalization applicable to all lineage societies by Fortes, 1953. For criticism of its validity, see Lewis, 1960.

8. H. A. MacMichael, 1922, 1, 131.

9. See Lewis, 1961 (a).

10. An interesting exception here are the Luvale of Northern Rhodesia (Zambia). In this case while commoners may have genealogies of between nine and twenty generations in depth, those of chiefs rarely exceed nine generations in their span. White argues that this is consistent with historical data which indicate that Luvale chiefs are of relatively recent arrival, and never established a political ascendancy which might have led them to seek support for their political supremacy by claiming lengthy pedigrees. (White, 1960, 43, 44.)

11. The first mention of the Hawiye Somali is by the Arab geographer al-Idrisi, and the Hawiye are also mentioned by Ibn Said writing in 1274 (see Cerulli, 1957, 92-4).

12. Shihab ad-Din's *Futuh al-Habasha* ('History of the Conquest of Ethiopia') written between 1540 and 1560, the main Muslim account of the sixteenth-century conquest of Ethiopia by the Muslim armies of Imam Ahmad Ibrahim al-Ghazi (1506-43) in which Somali participated. See my article "The Somali Conquest of the Horn of Africa," *Journal of African History*, no. 2, 1960.

13. See, for example, Evans-Pritchard, 1940, 198-200; Cunnison, 1960, 110-14.

14. Contrast the position described amongst the Bedouin of Cyrenaica where genealogical elision (and manipulation) take place at a lower genealogical level. See Peters, 1960.

15. It might of course be argued that the genealogies of large groups have been extended to emphasize their political status at the expense of smaller groups. In the light of what is known of Somali history I do not think that this interpretation is tenable. If anything, all genealogies — those of long and short

branch lineages — are shorter than the picture of Somali demographic history which emerges from other sources would suggest they should be.

16. See my "The Galla in Northern Somaliland." *Rassegna di Studi Etiopici*, 1959, XV, 21-38; and "The Somali Conquest of the Horn of Africa," op. cit.

17. What can be reconstructed of this Daarood expansion is discussed in my "The Galla in Northern Somaliland," op. cit. 32-6. Sheikh Daarood's grave, a rough stone structure, lies in utterly desolate country some twelve miles to the south-east of the village of Hadaftimo in Erigavo District of the ex-Protectorate, some two miles from the Hadaftimo-Buran road.

18. An example popular amongst the northern Daarood in 1957 is the *Manaqib as-Shaikh bin Ibrahim al-Jabarti*, Cairo, 1945, written by Sheikh Ahmad bin Husen bin Mahammad.

19. Thus, for example, Shihab ad-Din's *Futuh* describes the Harti division of the Daarood as a large clan in the sixteenth century. Today the Harti are a very large congeries of clans within the Daarood clan-family and Harti is represented genealogically as Daarood's great grandson, probably as a result of some elision. It seems very hard to credit that if Daarood had in fact lived in the fifteenth century the descendants of his great grandson Harti could possibly have multiplied to the extent of a large clan in so short a time. There is thus every reason to reject the lineal connection between the clan-family ancestor of the Daarood and Sheikh Ismaa'iil Jabarti, the Yemeni saint, as unfounded.

20. There are also a number of Arab immigrant communities of various provenance and in varying degrees of absorption living in Somaliland. Thus, for example, there are a number of Mahri groups settled amongst the Majeerteen Daarood of northern Somalia (cf. Cerulli, 1957, 109-10). A study of South Arabian manuscripts indicates that the Somali have in fact had for many centuries considerable trading contacts with Arabia (R. B. Serjeant, personal communication).

21. Daarood and the other Somali clan-families, on the other hand, trace descent from 'Ali's brother 'Aqiil Abuu Taalib.

22. The ancient town of Mait, today in ruins, lies some little distance to the west of the contemporary port of Mait and close to Sheikh Isaaq's tomb. Traditionally the old town was built (probably upon earlier foundations) by Sheikh Isaaq and his followers. It is mentioned on several occasions in the sixteenth-century *Futuh* and is also marked on early maps. Tradition indicates that the port played an important part in Somali history and the ruined site urgently requires full professional archaeological attention. See Chittick, 1976.

23. Thus none of the Arab connexions described in the traditions appear to be corroborated from Arab sources on southern Arabia. Here I am particularly grateful to Professor R. B. Serjeant for critical evaluations of the legends. C.f. also Hersi, 1977, pp 121 ff.

24. See above.

25. The location of the graves of the 'Iise and Gadabuursi clan founders in the east of northern Somaliland agrees with the traditional history of clan movement from east to west, see Lewis, 1959 (b), 28-36.

26. On the general question of the translation of the local Somali ancestor cult into a Muslim idiom, see Lewis, 1955-6. See also Hersi, 1977, for a very careful historical analysis reaching the same conclusions.
27. This, for example, is the version of Gadabuursi origins given in a manuscript history written by Sheikh Abdarahman Sheikh Nur which I hope to publish elsewhere.
28. This is, of course, quite apart from the twists in interpretation of tradition given by different individuals or interest-groups at the same structural level.
29. Cf. Vansina, 1965; Henige, 1974.

Chapter V

LINEAGE CONTINUITY AND COMMERCE IN NORTHERN SOMALILAND

Lineage, Ecology and Historical Trade

There are few corporate activities and few collective interests among the northern Somali which do not involve their segmentary lineage orgabization. In this chapter I discuss some of the ways in which trade and lineage affiliation are entwined.

For centuries the northern Somali coast has been linked commercially with its Abyssinian hinterland, and with Arabia and the East. From about the tenth century and probably earlier, Muslim Arab and Persian settlers developed a string of commercial coastal centers, in part probably a legacy from classical times, exporting slaves and ivory from the Abyssinian hinterland, and locally produced skins, hides, precious gums, ghee, and ostrich feathers. It was of course from the export of myrrh and frankincense that the Somali coast was most widely known in early times. But although Somaliland is still a main source of these precious gums,[1] the export of hides and skins and livestock on the hoof, chiefly to the Gulf, makes a far more important contribution to the northern Somali economy.[2]

The most important of these early northern coastal towns was Zeila, part of the wider Muslim state of Ifaat, of which it was the chief port, and with a mixed Arab, /Afar,[3] and Somali population. From as early as the thirteenth century, Muslim Ifaat and Christian Abyssinia struggled for political control of the western part of the Horn of Africa. In the second half of the sixteenth century, however, when the Muslim threat to Ethiopia was at last eliminated and Ifaat disintegrated, Zeila's prosperity declined. Yet the town still remained the main gateway to the outside world for the caravan routes from the hinterland; and in the early days of British colonization at the end of the last century, recovered briefly something of its past prosperity. This was soon lost, however, by the development of the French port of Djibouti and the construction of the railway between Djibouti and the Ethiopian capital. Zeila quickly ceased to be the chief port for the hinterland and declined rapidly. Today the old city is little more than an empty shell, a desolate place of crumbling and ruined mosques and tombs; and the ancient city population — the Reer Seyla — with its distinctive culture, is broken and dispersed.

Berbera, about which less is known from early times, but which is probably of similar antiquity, is now the main port of Somaliland. As will presently be seen, Berbera is more typical of northern Somali trade centers than Zeila, for unlike the latter, the town has not produced a distinct city population separate in culture and character from the surrounding Somali.

Prior to the coming of steam vessels, these and the other smaller northern ports were open to foreign traffic only during the North-East Monsoon which blows from about October to March. It was and still is only at this time of year that dhows visit the northern coasts; the South-West Monsoon winds close the coast to traffic. In the past, caravans descended from the interior, from Harar[4] in the west and from the Ogaden to the south, to trade local produce for the goods brought by the Arabian and Indian traders from the Persian Gulf and from further afield. Thus travellers in the nineteenth century describe Berbera during the South-West Monsoon period as a poverty-stricken collection of miserable huts with a population of some 8,000 people, but in the fair season as a prosperous center containing as many as 40,000 people; and this seasonal fluctuation is still evident today. When Burton witnessed this commerce, in 1855, the local produce brought to the ports was traded for coarse cotton cloth in pieces of seventy-five, sixty-six, sixty-two, and forty-eight yards; for black and indigo-dyed calicos in lengths of sixteen yards; for fillets for married women's hair; for iron and steel in small bars; for lead and zinc; beads of various sorts; and dates and rice. But money which is the chief medium of exchange today was also in use then, for Burton notes a preference for payment in dollars and rupees (Burton 1943: 289).

The segmentary nature of Somali society with its many lineages often at war, and with no central authority to which common appeal could be made, had its repercussions in the organization of the caravan trade. To reach the coast in safety a caravan had to have protection on its journey among many different and often hostile clans. This was achieved by an institutionalized form of safe-conduct. The leader of the caravan of laden burden camels entered into a relationship of protection with those amongst whom he passed on his way to the coast. A patron was selected for his probity, status, and above all in a society where force is all important, for the strength of his lineage. The position of protector is called *abbaan*, and the *abbaan*[5] is given gifts in return for his services. Having agreed to act in this capacity, the patron is responsible for the security of the caravan under his protection, for its goods and for the lives of those with it. Attacks on a protected caravan are attacks on the patron and his lineage whose honour and "name", as Somali put it, can only be upheld by prompt retaliatory action. It is the duty of the patron and his agnates to obtain reparation for any injuries inflicted on the caravan and to hand over the just amount of compensation to the injured lineage.

It is not to be imagined of course that all caravan protectors fulfilled their obligations with scrupulous honesty;[6] but here, quite apart from the danger of incurring the enmity of the caravan owner's lineage, a potent sanction was the bitter verses sometimes made by deceived caravan owners to vilify their protectors. These, if skilfully composed, might sweep through the country, and blacken a lineage's reputation.

Some idea of the complexities of the inter-relations set up through this patron-protege relationship may be gained by considering the position of the Dulbahante clan in the east of Somaliland. From the territory regularly grazed by the livestock of this land-locked clan, two main routes led to Berbera. One lay through the village of Bohotle, to Burao, and then through Sheikh to Berbera, a total distance of some 300 miles. This route was traversed by caravans of sometimes as many as several hundred burden camels laden with precious gums, *ye'eb* nuts[7] ostrich feathers, and ghee; and driving sheep and goats and camels and horses for sale in Berbera and for export. At Bohotle the caravans came under the protection of the Habar Tol Ja'lo clan; at Burao the Habar Yuunis assumed responsibility; at Sheikh the Habar Awal/Iise Muuse; and finally at Berbera itself, the Habar Awal Sa'ad Muuse. Another shorter route traversed the Sarar Plain, through which the Habar Tol Ja'lo conducted Dulbahante caravans as far as Berbera, where their patronage was exchanged for that of the Habar Awal. Thus in their access to the port of Berbera, the Dulbahante relied upon patronage relationships with the Habar Tol Ja'lo, Habar Yuunis, and Habar Awal, three clans with whom the Dulbahante marry and fight over access to grazing.

Today, the caravan trade is largely in decline. Except on short journeys and in particularly difficult country, trucks have replaced burden camels in trade. And although clan and lineage fighting still regularly threaten the security of the traveller, the presence of a neutral colonial administration diminished the need for the traditional trade patronage relationship. In this context Somali observed that all, the weak as well as the strong, were under the common protection of the government which was the *abbaan* of all. Here the proverb "the weak have found the European as protector" was often quoted. But the institution still persisted in other spheres of trade which I mention presently. (For its return under conditions of maximum insecurity caused by the collapse of the Somali state see chapter 9).

External Trade and Local Mareketing in Towns

Today, the main exports of northern Somaliland are livestock, hides and skins, and gums and ghee. Within the country there is little regional diversification of production; except in the case of sorghum (consumed internally and not exported), which is grown in bulk as a cash crop[8] only in the relatively fertile areas of high rainfall (above 12 inches annually) in the west and Hararghe Province of Ethiopia. The production of salt, however, is largely limited to the Zeila-Djibouti area (marine salt being the chief export of the Republic of Djibouti). Other less important regional specializations occur in the manufacture of fibre mats, the finer varieties of which are made from palm fronds on the eastern coasts; and the carving of stone censers which is limited to central Somalia. Another local product cultivated mainly in Ethiopia and thence distributed by truck in the west and center of northern Somaliland (and also exported by air to Aden) is the stimulant leaves of the *qaat* plant (*Catha edulis*)[9] Most other local Somali products are common throughout the area.

The main imports today are foodstuffs and manufactured goods.[10] In the first category, sugar, tea, dates, oils, rice, and millets are the chief commodities; and in the second various household utensils including transistors. These are carried, today mainly by truck, into the towns and villages of the interior which are in turn collecting points for local produce for export through the ports.

With the exception of the farming villages in the west and of a few religious settlements (sg. *tariiqa*)[11] all northern Somali places of settlement are essentially trade centers. Here imported goods are sold by local merchants and a few expatriate Arabs and Indians, hides and skins and livestock purchased largely for eventual export, and a few local products sold for local consumption — milk, ghee, meat and, in the west, grain. The distribution of these market centers varies with the nature of the terrain and with the local economy. In the predominantly pastoral and sparsely populated[12] areas of the center and east of Somaliland, market centers are often as many as forty miles apart. But in the more densely populated sorghum growing areas of the west, especially in Hargeisa and Borama Districts, they are less widely spaced. Here grain to a large extent replaces livestock and animal produce as the mainstay of marketing.

These market centers vary in size, complexity, and permanence, according to local circumstances. Trade follows the pastoralists in their movements; and the most ephemeral and simplest of trade centers, sometimes boasting no more than a single shop housed in a rough branch and leaf shelter, spring up wherever people are concentrated for any length of time. Thus, especially in the dry seasons when milk, the staple diet of the pastoralist, is scarce, and when men turn to dates, rice and tea and sugar,[13] traders move out into the pastures to set up temporary shops. This is usually accomplished nowadays by truck, or in less accessible areas by a train of burden camels laden with imported provisions which are sold to the pastoralists for money, or exchanged for hides and skins. It is particularly at this time of year that sheep and goats are killed for meat, and their skins to some extent constitute a dry season currency[14] in the trade between merchant and nomad. They are certainly used as often as money at this time of year. Not all debts with traders, however, are discharged at once, and to a lesser extent young lambs and kids are often employed by the pastoralists in the wet seasons to close outstanding debts carried forward from the preceding dry season. Thus, while money is widely employed in the trade of the interior, many commercial transactions are still conducted through the medium of livestock or hides and skins. And skins are a particularly desirable currency from the point of view of the merchant.

Small traders draw a draft or borrow money from a kinsman and use this initial capital to purchase skins. These are then dispatched from the interior by truck to a larger commercial center where they are purchased by a wholesale exporter. The latter loads the truck with such commodities as sugar, dates, tea, rice, and grain and a few items of hardware, razor blades, cigarettes, and cloth, etc., and returns these to the merchant in the interior who retails them at local prices. Much of the itinerant trader's takings are again in skins, and these are again sent back by truck to the town merchant. In this way, small traders with little equipment beyond a pair of scales, follow the pastoral movements of their clansmen and often make quite substantial profits. Few know sufficient Arabic to keep accounts and the majority keep no written record of their transactions.

At regularly frequented seasonal waterholes and wells, permanent trade settlements of a few nomadic huts and mud-and-wattle stores grow up. These are the oases of northern Somaliland. The extent to which their prosperity and permanence depends upon the prevailing patterns of pastoral movements is seen in the frequency with which villages are abandoned and new centers established over the years. Here the principal cause of drift and migration is lack of water; and the ever-changing routes of the dust tracks which serve as roads are a constant witness to the transitory character of settlement in a pre-dominantly nomadic society.

Apart from the ancient ports of the northern coast, few of the present towns with stone buildings are more than eighty years old, and all have developed from modest settlements of a few nomadic huts. The policy of the Protectorate government was to declare as gazetted townships those larger settlements which had maintained fairly constant populations over the years. These then became subject to the provisions of the Township Ordinance (Cap. 84 of the Laws) and became centers of educational, social and economic and political advancement. Buildings had to conform to the requirements of the Town Planning ordinance (Cap. 83 of the Laws), and the building sites for residential or commercial purposes were usually granted on a ninety-nine year lease. Schools were built partly from government funds, and partly by local subscription; police were provided; medical facilities; a community center equipped with a radio and some reading facilities; and eventually in the larger centers local government councils with fiscal authority were set up. The larger townships were also provided with a Kadi's and Subordinate Court, the first administering Islamic law in matters of personal status, and the second customary law and township rules. Subordinate Courts had very limited criminal jurisdiction and usually did not handle cases which concerned lineages rather than individuals. In the main centers taxes were levied on industrial, and trading sites, and a form of octroi known locally as *zariba* dues was levied on livestock and grain brought to the center for trade.

A good example of a smaller gazetted township is the village of Sheikh in the hills south of Berbera. The population occupying mud-and-wattle and stone houses in the main part of the township numbered some 500 souls in 1955. The village which owes much of its commerce to the fact that Sheikh was formerly the headquarters in the Protectorate of the Education Department,[15] lies to the west of the main Burao-Berbera road, and the 120 permanent houses and shops built of stone or mud-and-wattle are arranged in six parallel lines, bisected by a main street, and intersected laterally by six smaller streets. The township has a small police station, a medical dispensary, a Kadi's Court, an elementary school and two mosques. There is a government meat market behind the town and also a small open market place where grain, charcoal, eggs, milk, and other local produce are sold. To the southwest of the main center lies a miserable collection of small nomadic tents (sg. *buul*)[16] mainly occupied by old women, mostly widows; when not living with their sons in the interior, they eke out a modest livelihood by selling wood and charcoal, water, and grain.

Sheikh lies within the spheres of interest of two clans, the Habar Awal and the Habar Yuunis, the first of which is numerically dominant. Some eighty-three householders and shopkeepers were Habar Awal or Habar Awal affiliated, and mainly of the Deereyahan lineage; the remaining thirty-seven were Habar Yuunis, mainly of the Muuse 'Abdalla lineage or members of other clans attached to them.[17] Some twenty-four shops and eight "coffee-shops," where only tea is drunk,[18] were in the hands of the Habar Awal; and eleven shops and two coffee shops were in the control of the Habar Yuunis. The adjacent schools supplied some employment and the majority of traders were general merchants, some of whom were also engaged in the export of hides and skins. There were several truck owners who hired vehicles for trade and other purposes, several shoemakers and blacksmiths, and a few tailors. But whatever local employment was followed, the majority of the inhabitants of the township also possessed livestock in the interior in the charge of their clansmen. While most of these townsmen depend for their day-to-day livelihood on their urban occupation, their flocks of sheep and goats and herds of camels in the interior represent at once a source of capital and an earnest of their continued participation in the social and political life of their kin in the pastures. For as I shall presently show there are strong economic and political ties between town and rural society.

The largest towns of northern Somaliland owe their size, prosperity, and permanence to their selection as District headquarters. In these administrative centers there is a greater diversification of trade and, prior to the civil war in the 1990s, wider opportunities for employment in government service. The export of livestock and of animal produce still remains, however, the mainstay of the economy, but except in the commercial port of Djibouti (in Djibouti), few local industries have yet developed to offer any substantial employment of labour, skilled or unskilled. All these towns remain essentially the focal points for the redistribution of imported goods and for the buying and selling of livestock and livestock produce. The main centers are Hargeisa, capital of Somaliland with a population of about the same size as Berbera; and Burao with a population only slightly less. The other District headquarters — Borama, Las Anod, and Erigavo — have populations of only a few thousand inhabitants each. Most agencies have their head offices in Berbera and Hargeisa and these two towns are generally the main commercial centers.

All these towns had elected local government councils and all enjoyed similar social services which were naturally most advanced in the larger towns, Hargeisa, Burao, and Berbera. The local broadcasting service, Radio Somali, is based in Hargeisa.

I have spoken of all these centers, irrespective of their size and commercial diversification, as markets since they owe their existence primarily to trade and to the exchange of goods and services. In Somaliland there are no markets outside centers of settlement. All these trade centers consist of a core of stone and mud-and-wattle shops and coffee shops and, in the larger centers, of an open market place. Shops are concerned mainly with the sale of imported goods, while the open marketplace deals mainly with local produce and is dominated by women. Women bring in milk and ghee daily from the surrounding countryside and sell it in the market. They also sell woven bark containers, mats, rope and string, charcoal and grain, and some poultry, eggs, vegetables and fruit.[19] In the interests of public health, government meat markets where women sell mutton and goat's meat have been erected in most of the larger centers. The market place itself has no formal organization, and indeed spills over into a succession of stalls, where bread and meat pastries and other goods are sold, set up at convenient points along the streets within a town. The shops themselves also overflow into the streets, in as much as many of the general merchants have a tailor with a sewing machine sitting outside their premises.

The stalls where cooked foods and bread are sold are manned by men, who also serve at the counters inside shops, and work the sewing machines mainly engaged in shirt-making. The market place itself is usually devoid of formal stalls and most of the vendors squat on the ground, often on a mat, displaying their wares. Sometimes simple shelters are erected to shade the vendor and his customers from the heat of the sun. Finally, in another corner and usually some distance from the central shopping area, there is the livestock market where stock are bought and sold for local use and for export.

There are no special market days; and little variation except in quantity and quality in the goods offered for sale on different days. But the supply of milk and meat is to some extent influenced by the seasons. Except on the Muslim Friday (which begins on Thursday evening and lasts until midday on Friday) when all trade and commerce stop,[20] the market resounds with the noise of trade and barter and the shops and coffee-shops are busy.

Thus new trade settlements provide the primary source of livelihood of a relatively small class of entrepreneurs and merchants of whom the majority were by the 1960s Somali. Similarly widows domiciled in the towns manage to eke out a modest living by selling such local produce as mats, rope, poultry, eggs, fruit, vegetables, water, and charcoal. For the majority of the population, the pastoralists of the interior, they provide a market for surplus livestock and livestock produce, or for stock or stock produce which must be sold to gain cash. Except for gums, hides and skins, and much of the livestock sold, these products are all consumed locally, and the market is in this instance acting as a center for redistribution. The money thus obtained, along with that gained by women from the sale of their manufactures and poultry, etc., is used to purchase rice and grain, tea, sugar, dates, clothes and other necessities, and a few luxuries, such as cigarettes, *qaat* and an expanding range of household equipment. These transactions thus supply the pastoralist with what he now regards as essentials and additional foodstuffs which in the dry season especially help to alleviate his hard lot. With wages obtained from salaried employment, and remittances from migrant labour, they are also the means by which the pastoralist in the interior participates in the wider cash economy.

The nomad's involvement in the world economic system began to increase markedly in the late 1960's - as world livestock prices rose substantially and the volume of exports to the Gulf States grew correspondingly.[21] In Somaliland itself, the trucking of livestock from internal markets such as Hargeisa to the port of Berbera was also developed about this time (Samatar et al, 1988). The volume and value of livestock exports from the north (with sheep the key commodity) rose dramatically in the 1970's and peaked in 1981/82, according to IMF figures. The subsequent decline in exports reflected a Saudi Arabian curtailment of imports on the grounds of an alleged outbreak of rinderpest in Somalia and, in more recent years, the economic chaos consequent on civil war in the north. The pastoralist producers, protected by their kinship marketing links, seem to have benefitted substantially from the soaring value of their sales, although, of course, the price they have had to pay for imported consumer goods has also increased markedly. Abdullahi (1990) records that the difference between the rural pastoralist's selling price and the market export price seldom exceeded 10% to 15% (the latter applying where long transportation distances were involved). Clearly, the export traders made particularly handsome profits but, overall, during the last boom years at least, primary producers also seem to have benefited. Jamal (1981 and 1988) estimates that producer cash incomes increased five-fold between 1970 and 1978 while the general cost of living doubled. Samatar (1989), however, argues that while producer livestock prices matched inflation in the boom 1970s years, in the 1980s livestock prices stagnated while the costs of imported foods soared.

What is indisputable in the 1970s and 1980s is the marked inflow of currency (local and foreign) and imported goods to the north. This was further fuelled by remittances to nomadic kinsmen from Somali migrants working in the Gulf States. This "muscle-drain," as Somalis call it, assumed phenomenal proportions in the 1970s and 1980s. Some estimates put the number of migrant workers in the Gulf States at over 200,000 (1981); however, one of the few empirically based sample surveys of migrants carried out by a Somali firm in 1984 produced a figure of only 67,000 (SomConsult, 1985), the majority being from northern Somaliland. Although the value of remittances cannot be accurately measured, seemingly realistic estimates indicate that they tended to amount annually to two or three times the Somali Republic's export earnings! The money remitted remained largely outside the official banking system and was distributed along kinship lines. Migration was crucial in providing local Somali merchants and traders with access to hard currency for buying foreign goods.

Under the notorious *franco valuta* system introduced by the military regime in 1976 to counteract the scarcity of foreign exchange, importers who obtained foreign currency privately outside Somalia were granted import licenses (cf. Miller, 1981). As the number of migrants increased with the oil boom in the Gulf, Somali traders began to collect hard currency from migrant workers, using this to purchase commodities for sale in Somalia. The equivalent in Somali currency, or goods, was then handed over to the migrants' families and kinsmen by the merchant, of course the rate of exchange had to be agreed upon by the migrant providing the hard currency and he relied on kinship ties for honoring the transaction. Migrants and merchants also used the available hard currency to purchase and import building materials and vehicles. These were used in the north not only to develop urban housing and shops, but also small reservoirs (*barkad*) for private livestock watering in areas of the north, reducing nomadic mobility and the range of grazing movements and thus encouraging partial sedentarisation and the formation of small rural trading posts (*tuulo*). At the same time the outflow of able-bodied workers to the Gulf left some pastoral families short of manpower for herding tasks, prompting men with few livestock to work as hired herders (*qowsaar*) for better-off kinsmen (cf. Swift, 1979). They were paid in cash and kind (with livestock), and by the 1980's had not developed into a distinct servile class.

Lineage Continuity in Urban Economy

To understand the degree to which clanship[22] dominates trade in northern Somaliland, it is first necessary to consider the structural relation of the market center to the interior, of the urban to the rural community. Most modern towns of consequence are of recent formation. And in the economic, social, and political life of their inhabitants they represent an extension, or outgrowth, of the pastoral way of life. Djibouti with its unusual economic development is exceptional; and the only other northern Somali town which has evolved a distinct structure of its own — though for different reasons — is the ancient port of Zeila, now in ruins. The people of this city formed a separate political community with loyalties not so much to their lineages of origin as to their city of domicile. And even in 1957, despite their reduced numbers, they were still recognized in the Protectorate legislation as a special category, a community distinct from, and independent of, Somali clanship.

With its much more recent origins Djibouti has not evolved a distinct town society; but its great heterogeneity and considerable industrial development give it a character which is not shared by most northern Somali towns. Typically these have little civic identity. They are not independent fastnesses in a nomadic society; and their inhabitants have little sense of civic consciousness beyond that which depends upon lineage allegiance. This means that where a market center contains the inhabitants of a particular lineage its members are politically united as clansmen, but apart from this they have little sense of residential solidarity. In the larger centers occupied by people of several structurally remote lineages, or even clans, the community as a whole derives little sense of unity from its residential identity and is not an independent political unit.

Town and country are thus not polar extremes; but, on the contrary, closely associated. Indeed, one of the most significant aspects of modern urban developments in northern Somaliland is the structural continuity between urban and rural area. A pastoralist who goes to take up residence and employment in a town does not sever his economic and political ties with his pastoral kinsmen; nor does he adopt radically new social relationships in the urban community. This community is structured along the same lineage and contractual channels as the pastoral social system of which it is essentially a continuation. A man's lineage affiliation is as important in town life as in the pastures, in determining with whom he will associate and in what capacity. It is true, of course, that in proportion to the greater degree of lineage and clan diversification in towns, the range of genealogical connection recognized as socially significant is extended. Thus two men of the same clan, but of lineages which in the pastoral society are often opposed, see themselves as sharing common interests in opposition to townsmen of other clans. So, in towns there is often a significant shift in the range of agnation which affects social intercourse, but social relations remain for the most part dependent upon the segmentary lineage structure of pastoral society.

It is thus not surprising that in towns people tend to preserve the same patterns of settlement which they adopt in the pastures. The desire to match lineage affiliation with area of residence — so that one's neighbours are also one's clansmen —is still strong. This is most evident in some of the smaller settlements where town planning has not upset lineage patterns of grouping. But, even in the larger centers, the tendency towards the assumption of residential patterns which conform to lineage ties is marked, particularly in the clusters of nomadic tents, occupied often mainly by only transitory settlers, which lie round the peripheries of large towns some distance from the more permanent core of stone and mud houses. For example, in Las Anod (the administrative headquarters of the Dulbahante clan in the east of Somaliland), the area of the town composed of nomadic huts is divided into two distinct quarters along the lines of lineage cleavage. One sector is dominated by the Faarah Garaad segment and the other by the opposed Mahamuud Garaad, these being the two main segments of the clan, each divided into a hierarchy of smaller lineages.

And even in the permanent centers of towns where town-planning rules have prevented a complete congruence between area of settlement and lineage, when a lineage fight occurs, those concerned desert their houses and attempt to gather together in separate areas as far removed from their enemies as possible. Disputes between individuals readily take on a corporate character according to their structural distance in the lineage system in exactly the same way as in the interior. Indeed, many clan and lineage campaigns stem from town brawls between individuals of opposed lineages, and in the ensuing strife the center of conflict veers from town to rural area and back again as occasion offers. Pastoral lineage affairs are in any case often largely directed from the towns, where elders frequently live (at least during the dry seasons) and often own town property. Permanent townsmen equally have one foot with their clansmen in the pastures, and the economic links of clansmen are not severed because one lives in a town while another moves with the camels, in which both share common interests. The closest economic link between the two spheres arises when, as often happens, a group of brothers decide to form in effect a company sharing their profits, some going to work in the towns or in government service, while the others stay behind with their joint livestock.

At the same time, the pastoral dia-paying system is not replaced by some other organization in the towns. Merchants and others who live permanently in towns are still a party to the dia-paying contracts of their clansmen, and indeed the realms in which dia-paying solidarity operates are widened in modern conditions. Thus, although it was agreed some time ago in Somaliland that fatal traffic accidents and other accidents in town life should not give cause for claims for bloodwealth other than on an individual basis, collective responsibility is often in fact recognized. Death in a motor accident often gives rise to negotiations between the dia-paying groups concerned and, if compensation is not paid, a feud may develop. In one case where a man was killed by a truck driven by a man of another clan, bloodwealth was claimed; but, when it had not been paid some months after the accident, the aggrieved lineage retaliated by murdering a clansman of the guilty driver. Such cases, however, are more usually settled amicably outside the courts.

All this indicates the continuing force of traditional lineage allegiances in urban life. And in keeping with this, commerce is very closely bound up with lineage politics. Wherever possible, business is brought to agnates. A man prefers to take his custom to the shop of a clansman where he can expect generous credit, whereas a stranger would expect him to pay cash. Thus, in towns, a merchant relies for his customers largely upon those of his clan or lineage who live nearby.

The Arab legacy in trade (see below) is reflected in, amongst other things, the adoption by Somalis of the originally Arabic word *dilaal* for "broker," urban-based kinsmen through whose offices the nomadic producer markets his livestock. The *dilaal*, who has to compete with other brokers for trade from pastoralists selling livestock, deducts his commission on a per capita basis from the price realized, most of which is passed on to the herdsman. More generally, the organization of commerce follows the lineage structure. Each lineage in a market center regards certain shops as lying within its sphere of interest, and this applies equally to the coffee shops in which men spend so much of their time. In principle, every lineage of any size has at least one coffee shop, just as it has at least one member who is a general merchant or trader. Thus, in the township of Sheikh discussed above, the number of shops and coffee shops owned and patronized by the two locally dominant lineages is roughly in proportion to their numerical strengths. The coffee shop is of particular importance as an institution since it is the main center of gossip and often of lineage policy-making.

This division of commerce by lineage affiliation has further important repercussions. Lineages are constantly competing for the grant of trading licenses, just as they are continuously engaged in competition for appointments in government departments, in the police and administration, and indeed in all spheres. And here rivalry is as acute as it is in pastoral and also modern politics. It is typical of the lineage character of Somali trading interests that a peace settlement, reached at one stage in a long train of conflict between two clans contending for access to water and pasturage, should include a clause defining the trading rights of each in the disputed area. Monopolistic-like rights in trade concerning the economic prosperity of a lineage are an important consideration in politics in the interior as well as in towns.

Somali regard the extension of their corporate lineage interests into the spheres of trade and commerce as partly a natural continuation of the collective economic interests of agnates. More especially, this is considered necessary to safeguard the interests, economic as well as political, of the individual merchant. And quite apart from the fact that a man's prosperity is counted a direct gain to his clansmen, a trader expects the protection as well as the patronage of his dia-paying kinsmen as a matter of social right.

Foreign Merchants

It will be evident that trade and commerce are based on the agnatic system, which is the foundation of collective interests in general among the northern Somali. It follows from this that the foreign trader has somehow to be fitted into this exclusive system. It is here that the institution of trade patronage, which was mentioned earlier in connection with the caravan trade, is applied. The Indian and Arabian merchants, who once largely monopolized at least the export trade but of whom there were in 1957 only a few hundred in Somaliland,[23] were brought into the Somali lineage structure, though not completely, by being attached as clients to Somali lineages.

Each foreign trader appointed a Somali *abbaan* to protect his general interests, preferably a man of high personal status and of a strong and respected lineage. The *abbaan*, who was often paid a regular wage and sometimes received a share in profits, acted as an agent, broker or general assistant. And in all Arabian and Indian stores Somali *abbaans* were to be seen often acting as little more than caretakers, or doorkeepers, responsible to their clients for maintaining order amongst Somali customers. They and their lineages were also entrusted with the general security of their client. The latter, however, was not required to contribute to, and did not share in, the financial and legal obligations of the Somali lineage to which he was attached. The client did not participate directly in payment of bloodwealth, and the remunerations which the *abbaan* received were considered to exonerate the client from this responsibility.

The institution also operates in relation to those who practice the specialist (and in Somali eyes) degrading crafts of leatherworking, metalworking, pottery, and hair-cutting. These trades are despised by Somali and are followed by three groups of bondsmen, known collectively as *sab*, and traditionally attached to Somali lineages in a servile status. These are the Midgo (sg. Midgaan), traditionally hunters, leatherworkers, and barbers; the Tumaallo (sg. Tumaal), mainly blacksmiths; and the Yibro (sg. Yibir), who traditionally perform menial tasks and are above all feared as magicians. These *sab* bondsmen formed a very small proportion of the total population. Each of the three groups is divided into a number of small, nonlocalized, lineages segmented on the Somali pattern. Somali do not intermarry with *sab*, who marry among themselves, and traditionally *sab* individuals and families are attached to specific Somali patrons (*abbaans*) upon whom they are economically dependent, especially for bridewealth and blood-compensation.[24]

This is the traditional pattern of symbiosis between the numerically dominant and "aristocratic" Somali pastoralists and their sab dependents who differ physically little if at all from their patrons (Goldsmith and Lewis 1958). Today, however, *sab* are increasingly finding work in the towns, and many have left their traditional protectors to seek urban employment. Thus most large centers contain small Midgaan and Tumaal communities, the former mainly employed as barbers, and the latter largely blacksmiths and motor mechanics, living in their own part of the town. Somali regard the *sab* quarter as the least desirable residential area. At the same time, with this partial emancipation which the development of townships and urban industry, however minimal, is fostering, there is a movement among the *sab* to set up their own independent dia-paying groups on an equal footing with Somali.

Despite these indications of an increasing degree of autonomy, however, the traditional bonds of association between *sab* and Somali are reflected in urban patterns of commerce. For here, Somali tend to patronize those *sab* with whom their lineages have a traditional relation of protection. At the same time, when conflict flares up between rival Somali lineages in a town, there is a strong tendency for the local *sab* community to split up according to its traditional lines of allegiance. These are instances of the continuing importance of traditional lines of cleavage in modern Somali society, a topic to which I return presently.

Wealth and Social Organization

I have stressed some of the consequences in trade and commerce of the economic identity of agnates, an identity which is strongest and most clearly seen in the structure of the dia-paying group. In the pastoral situation, apart from collective solidarity in effecting reparation, members of a dia-paying group help each other in time of want as much as in time of war and in general tasks, such as the watering of the camels which are part of the collective wealth of the group. Men borrow most frequently from clansmen, and the obligatory Muslim alms (seko)[25] are frequently distributed amongst poor agnates. These are indications of what clanship entails in sharing resources and profits. Here the ethic of reciprocity and of mutuality is paramount, and the rich trader is expected to assist his poorer kinsmen. Those who are absent on business, or in employment in a town or overseas, are expected to send regular remittances to their clansmen in the interior.[26] These many kinship commitments increase with the individual's wealth.

The Somali for wealth is hoolo, which means primarily wealth in livestock. After horses, which are today rare, camels are the most prized possession, one of the familiar themes of poetry and song, and rivalry over them is a constant source of strife and loss of life. Ideally, it is in camels that bloodwealth and bridewealth are reckoned, and the exchange relation between a man's life and worldly goods is phrased in terms of camels. Today, however, money, with which Somali have a long familiarity,[27] is to some extent substituted for livestock in these transactions, the 1958 value of bloodwealth being 100 camels each valued at 45 Rs (i.e. 67 Shs. 50 cents East African).[28] According to the market value of camels, however, a good young camel might fetch as much as 100 Rs, and fifty camels, whose market value is 90 Rs each (or twice the standard bloodwealth rate), could be paid in lieu of the 100 statutory beasts. Indeed, the quantity of camels required is now unimportant provided their total value is that of full bloodwealth. And money is frequently substituted today as part, or even the whole, of the statutory 100 camels.

Somali value money partly because they regard it as an independent form of wealth, and partly because it can be converted into more desirable kinds of wealth, such as livestock.

Most travellers who have recorded their impressions of Somali character have noted the acute commercial sense of the Somali, and have described the pastoralists as mercenary and avaricious. Somali certainly seek to profit from financial transactions and would endorse the view that money talks, that wealth is power, and as such is highly desirable. Thus even in so egalitarian a society, it is proverbial that the rich elder commands ready support for his proposals while a poor man's words carry little weight. And Somali are very much alive to the exploitable resources of another. Some conception of their commercial attitudes may perhaps be gained from a conversation which I once overheard amongst typical pastoralists in the interior. The merits of the French people were being discussed, and the view was put forward that since their currency was known to be unstable they must be of little account as a nation. This was in the 1950s!

But it would of course be quite wrong to imagine that Somali consider money to be capable of buying everything they value. Although riches, if wisely spent, bring renown and influence, pride, dignity, and "name" are in the end more highly valued. A man, however poor, will readily reject a wage that he considers entirely disproportionate to his labours; he will withdraw from a transaction which has become repugnant to him with his dignity intact, if little the richer.

Above all, loyalty to one's kin is ultimately more important than the possession of wealth, even wealth of direct prestige value. Somali are also well aware of the conflict which frequently exists between the desire for personal gain and the responsibilities of clanship. Here idealists quote the decision of one elder faced with this dilemma expressed in words which are now proverbial: "Between wealth and clanship, I chose clanship."[29] In a society where war and feud are still almost daily events, clanship in the last analysis is often more important than wealth. Ultimately a person's security depends upon the strength and goodwill of his clansmen, particularly of his dia-paying group, not on the amount of his worldly goods. Thus the ethics of clanship are, in the last analysis, more precious than those of prestige founded on wealth; and honour, more valuable than profit.

Conclusion

In this chapter I have traced some of the effects in trade and commerce of the segmentary lineage structure of northern Somali society. I have argued that the economic and political continuity between the urban and rural society carries the bonds of agnatic solidarity into town life and commerce. It would, however, be contrary to the facts to maintain that the traditional pastoral social structure is exactly reproduced in town society. Today markets which are the traditional centers of pastoral politics are also the foci of social change in its widest sense. It is the new towns that most clearly show the effects of rudimentary industrial development, of modern economic and social change, and of education. It is, moreover, primarily through the towns that the inspiration of African nationalism elsewhere and of modernism in general impinges on the traditional pastoral social system.

In response to these new influences, and to constitutional developments in French and British Somaliland and in Somalia, and to what were regarded as the imperialist policies of Ethiopia, there was in 1957 in northern Somaliland a growing national awareness and a growing desire to replace clan by national patriotism. Merchants who lived permanently in towns showed reluctance in continuing to meet their financial obligations towards their dia-paying kinsmen; and in the better policed and more orderly conditions of urban society they felt less need for the support of their dia-paying group. One economic correlate of this was a tendency to bank monetary profits rather than to convert them entirely into livestock wealth. Thus, there was an increasing desire on the part of the townsman to divest himself of those collective obligations which traditionally bound him to his clansmen. At the same time, new patterns of social relationships were developing where people were thrown together by occupation and residence. Equally there was a growing, if yet minimal, sense of class in place of clan not only among government officials and nationalist politicians but also between tradesmen. This new modernist movement which found support and encouragement in the universalistic values of Islam was sufficient to stimulate strong nationalist ideals and aspirations. But since the traditional economic and social order had not been radically changed, pastoral values persisted. Commerce no less than modern politics (Lewis 1958, 1959a, 1988, chapters 8 and 9) continued to bear the stamp of agnation, kinship constituting a perennial source of security.

Notes

1   On the gum trade see Drake-Brockman 1912 : 239-61. See also Ahmad Yusuf Farah, in press.

2.   The total value of domestic imports from the Protectorate in 1957 was £1,355,418, to which livestock and skins contributed £1,275,571. Of the remaining amount, £53,980 was realized through the export of gums. Since then the trade has soared : in 1987 Saudi Arabia imported over 1 million Somali sheep valued at US$55 million. For detailed export figures, 1978-1988, see Elmi, 1991.

3.   A closely related Hamitic people living in Djibouti and Ethiopia.

4.   Traditionally three caravans left from Harar to cross the Plains to Berbera each year. The earliest set out from the old city in the Abyssinian highlands in early January and carried coffee, ghee, gums and other local produce to be exchanged for cottons, silks, shawls, and tobacco. Another left Harar in

February, but the main one, bearing slaves and ivory and livestock, only reached the coast at the end of the season. The arrival of this last Caravan in April 1855 is described in Burton, 1943 p. 228.

5. This word may be derived from *ab* or *aabbe*, father, agnation, with the sense of one who stands in *loco parentis*.

6. For comments on the unreliability and treachery of many caravan protectors, see Burton 1943 : 275-6; Ferrandi 1903 : 226-330.

7. The fruit of *Cordeauxia edulis*, which is eaten.

8. No figures were available for the total production in 1957. But since the total acreage was estimated to be about 140,000 acres, and the average acre yield about 800 lbs of grain, the total production was probably in the region of 50,000 tons. It was considered that a slight increase in the area cultivated would make the region self-sufficient in grain.

9. *Qaat* conserves its stimulant powers only when the leaf is fresh and for this reason was not chewed in the east of Somaliland which is too far distant from the centre of production for the leaf to arrive in a fresh condition. More recently, *qaat* is also imported by air from Kenya, especially into southern Somalia. See Cassanelli, 1986.

10. In 1957 the values of these in British Somaliland were £1,240,957 and £1,031,402 respectively.

11. There are about a dozen such autonomous religious settlements, in some areas engaged in sorghum cultivation. These belong to the various Muslim Orders which Somali follow. On this aspect of Somali Islam, see Lewis, 1955/56.

12. The overall population density in Somaliland in 1957 was about 10 per square mile. No figures are available for the western regions.

13. Somali tea (*shaah*) is a potent and sustaining beverage with the consistency of soup, made by brewing tea leaves, sugar, milk, and a little water. It is very highly sugared and nutritious. A man will often do a day's work on a mug of tea drunk in the early morning, waiting until the evening before eating rice or grain.

14. In 1957 the local value of a sheepskin was between three and four shillings (East Africa).

15. Close to the township there was (in 1957) a vocational training school, an intermediate school and a new secondary school. To the north-west lies the religious settlement (*tariiqa*) of Sheikh which I do not describe here.

16. This is the typical hut of a widow, smaller than the nomadic tent (*aqal*) of a married couple.

17. These included several Arab immigrants from the Hadramaut, local Somali of other clans, and *sab* bondsmen whom I discuss below.

18. Before the introduction of tea from the East, coffee which is grown in Ethiopia, is said to have been widely favoured in northern Somaliland. Today, however, tea is the universal beverage, although Somali invariably refer to their teashops as "coffee-shops."

19. The proceeds from the sale of livestock produce accrue to the family as a whole. Mats and other utensils made by women are sold for their own personal profit.

20. For Somali, Friday is the day of repetition. A gift received on Friday is likely to indicate that more will be received; but a payment made on Friday is likely to mean that more will have to be expended.

21. It is difficult to generalise about the number of head of livestock sold in relation to herd size since so many factors are involved. However, under favourable conditions, rather than extreme drought, from a flock of 100 sheep and goats it would not be unusual to cull 30 head (mostly sheep) in a year. From a herd of cattle, 10 might be sold, while from a camel herd of the same size, only 5 might be sold, or killed for consumption. Except in severe drought, the animals sold are mainly females. Camel production is much less commercialised than that of sheep and goats, being subject to stronger social constraints.

22. I use "clanship" here to refer to lineage solidarity at all levels of lineage segmentation.

23. In Djibouti, however, there is a substantial Arab community.

24. Traditionally *sab* have no voice in the councils of their patrons, but this discriminatory rule is disappearing today. This institution was extensively utilized by General Mohamed Siyad Barre in his military dictatorship - see chapter 7. Siyad's longest serving Minister of Defence and Vice President was a Tumaal placeman.

25. An annual contribution to the poor from a man's current wealth.

26. As has been pointed out, there are few opportunities for local employment except government service, and trade.

27. Coins dating from the fifteenth century have been found in the ruined sites of early Muslim trade centres in northern Somaliland. See Curle, 1937.

28. In other parts of Somaliland the value of bloodwealth varies and the monetary value of a bloodwealth camel has increased considerably since the 1920's. At one time, the rate was 20 Rs. It is important to note that these conventional evaluations refer only to blood compensation. There is no standard rate of bridewealth which ranges between two or three and fifty camels or their equivalent in other currency — cattle, horses, money, rifles and arms, etc. A dowry of often as much as two thirds of the value of the bridewealth is paid in return to the husband by his wife's kin. In the early 1990s, a camel was worth approximately US $20. Full blood-waelth was running at more than 100 camels, each valued at at least $100.

29. *Tol iyo fardo, tol baan doortay. Fardo* is literally horses, prestige wealth *par excellence*.

Chapter VI

FROM NOMADISM TO CULTIVATION:

The Expansion of Political Solidarity in Southern Somalia

The Problem and its Setting

The southern cultivating Somali, with whose social structure this chapter is concerned, derive, to a very considerable extent, from immigrant waves of northern nomadic pastoral Somali who have settled on the land and adopted cultivation in the most fertile region of southern Somalia. As well as adopting many new elements of culture, in the process these northern settlers have become absorbed in the distinctive social structure of the south, which differs in a number of important respects from that characteristic of the northern pastoralists. These differences, I shall argue, follow from the contrasting economic and historical circumstances of these two great divisions of the Somali nation. The particular southern structural features for which I shall thus try to account are: the formation of large, stable politico-legal groups in the south; the associated development of a hierarchical, though far from strongly centralized authority system; and the widespread adoption of foreign clients in group formation. These are all characteristics that are either rare or absent in northern pastoral Somali social structure (cf. Lewis 1961a), and which seem to be closely interrelated in southern Somali social organization.

Although the influence of some of the factors which I discuss can already be seen among neighbouring northern Somali who have recently adopted some cultivation in the vicinity of the Shebelle River (e.g. some Hawiye clans), I shall confine my argument here to the southern cultivating Somali proper. By this useful but arbitrary designation I mean those tribes of the Rahanwiin and Digil clan-families which inhabit the vast wedge of fertile land, almost 200,000 square kilometres in extent, running from the Juba River in the south to the Shebelle in the north-west and bounded to the east by the Indian Ocean. This region, which contains the principal agricultural resources of Somalia and includes the plantation banana-farming industry along the rivers, provides two forms of traditional cultivation: dry-farming on the upland soils of the hinterland (known as *adaableh*) and wet-farming in the irrigated rich alluvial soils (*doobay* and *doollo*) of the river basins. The principal traditional crop in the former areas is sorghum millets, while in the better-watered conditions of the latter maize takes precedence. At the same time, there are large wide areas of plain with a lighter red soil (*dooi*) which, though unfit for cultivation supply excellent pasturage.

These conditions give rise to striking variations in modes of livelihood and degrees of settlement and encourage a degree of economic diversity which is fully paralleled in the ethnic and tribal heterogeneity of the region. The present Digil and Rahanwiin populations are in large measure the outcome of a long, disjointed series of migrations and expansionary movements by Somali nomads from the north and north-west, their conflicts and agreements with earlier Oromo and Bantu communities, and the blending of these elements in a variety of patterns of mutual accommodation (cf. Colucci 1924: 55). In no other part of the Somali culture area is there evidence of such admixture and diversity.[1]

Southern Somali Social Organization

In this historical setting which spans some three or four centuries in time (cf. Lewis 1960), the Digil and Rahanwiin clans are largely but not exclusively cultivators. Some groups live in sedentary cultivating villages and though often keeping cattle and small stock, have no nomadic patrimony, while others participate in both the cultivating and nomadic economies. Others again are solely pastoralists, although most of the nomads who move through this area, pasturing their herds of camels and cattle on the stubble in harvested fields as well as in the grassy plains, are not actually of Digil and Rahanwiin affiliation. These are described as visiting graziers (*daaqsita*) and have merely a relationship of economic interdependence with the settled cultivators. They exchange milk and dung, and sometimes also money, for rights of access to stubble grazing and wells and water-ponds in the dry seasons.

Within Somalia as a whole, the Digil and Rahanwiin who speak a separate dialect of Somali constitute a distinct subculture, but in this chapter we shall only be concerned with particular aspects of this in so far as they relate to the structural distinctions associated with the southern practice of cultivation. Those Digil and Rahanwiin who live as nomads move similarly to their northern nomadic kinsmen in small groups of close kin with their nomadic hut, or tent, loaded on burden camels, their flocks of sheep and goats and herds of cattle, settling temporarily wherever grazing conditions and water resources are suitable. The camels on the other hand, again as in the north, form a separate herding unit in the charge of young men, although wherever possible some milch camels are attached to the other less widely moving domestic unit based on the husbandry of sheep, goats, and cattle.

No single Digil or Rahanwiin clan is wholly devoted to nomadism, however, and throughout this area where people of these groups do practise pastoralism it is ancillary to their fundamental concern with cultivation. Thus here, in contrast to the north, the primary focus of Digil and Rahanwiin social organization is the maintenance of territorial solidarity in relation to arable land, water-ponds, and wells. The basic local unit is the village/community consisting of several, and sometimes as many as a few hundred,[2] nuclear families living in round mud-and-wattle huts (sg. *mundille*) surrounded by a patchwork of fields and gardens.

Unlike the situation among those northern nomads who have recently adopted cultivation in the north-west (see Lewis 1961a: 114) each village here has a distinct local name, and some of the larger villages have a history going back several generations. Although some villages are in their male population based essentially on a small patrilineal segment of the clan to which they belong, more typically villages contain men of several different lineages and are therefore heterogeneous in agnatic composition. Their inhabitants, moreover, are well aware of this scattering of kinsmen and state explicitly that it serves to promote overall clan unity (cf. Colucci 1924: 57). Thus, although, as will presently be shown, lineages are the foci of social and political identity and of heritable rights in land and water, they seldom appear as distinct territorial divisions within a clan. Unlike the position among such peoples as the Nuer (Evans-Pritchard 1940) or the Bedouin of Cyrenaica (Peters 1960) territorial divisions within the clan do not generally mirror the clan's lineage segmentation.

Villages are based on artificially excavated water-ponds in the dry-farming areas, and on stretches of river with associated irrigation canal systems among the wet-farmers. Every village has of necessity rights of access to at least one such source of water, both for domestic use and for the watering of sheep and goats and cattle. Camels are watered along the rivers and at deep wells especially constructed for this purpose. Whatever their lineage affiliation, all the members of a village are regularly associated in the construction and maintenance of water-ponds, the actual watering of stock, and similarly in any aspect of cultivation which requires collective endeavor. There is thus a distinct sense of village unity and autonomy, although this may be cut across by the various lineage and other external ties of village members.

Notwithstanding the identity of the village, however, and unlike the position in so many other African cultivating societies, there is no office of village headman as such. Village affairs are organized by the elders of the various lineage fractions living together, and collective work in cultivation, water-management, hunting, recreation, and ceremony are assigned to parties of young men under the leadership of a youth of appropriate character dignified with the title of "head of the young men" (Aw barbar). Within the total territory claimed by the clan, constituent villages are not regularly grouped in an ever-widening series of territorial divisions. Indeed, between the clan in its role as a sovereign territorial entity and the village there is no intervening category of territorial unit. Except where contiguous villages share the same lineage segment affiliation, there is little sense of any wider territorial solidarity outside the village until the clan as a totality of villages is reached.

In keeping with this lack of any clearly defined hierarchy of territorial divisions, the clan's internal politico-administrative system is not territorially defined but is based on lineage segments. The clan has a fixed skeletal structure of segments and each lineage has an office of headman (with usually several assistants) whose importance decreases with decreasing segment size. Thus, although as with the northern nomads, at every level of grouping all adult males have a right to speak in the group's council, there is here a definite and permanent administrative organization paralleling the internal segmentation of the clan. The largest primary segments of a clan each have at least one officially recognized, and until recently, stipended headman, known traditionally as Gob,[3] but in the Italian-inspired administrative jargon now generally styled "Capo;" and a large clan with a strength of several tens of thousands of people may have half a dozen such offices vested in it. These segment leaders traditionally exercise informal judicial as well as political functions, but did not possess formal courts such as those presided over by chiefs in more centralized African societies. Overall clan policy is decided by meetings of the headmen of component segments acting as representatives for their kinsmen, and some clans have a final single titular head ("Capo qabila") representing the clan as a whole on a similar basis in its external relations.

As already indicated, segments within the clan vary in size and consequently in their political importance. Usually, however, one particular segment, often the smallest, has a special ritual status to be discussed presently. And there is regularly also a group of religious leaders who, as part of the clan structure, or external to it and then serving several clans, perform such specialist tasks as the ritual blessing of new villages and water-ponds and the protection of the crops from the unwelcome attentions of bird pests. They also officiate at marriages, deaths, and other ritual occasions: their duties thus to some extent often overlap with those of the ritual segment of the clan referred to earlier.

The Structure of Corporate Groups

We are now in a position to examine the structure of corporate groups as this is expressed throughout the Somali culture area in terms of the payment and receipt of compensation for injuries and death. Among the Digil and Rahanwiin, participation in these arrangements relates not merely to the maintenance of personal security and livestock interests, but also to land-holding and associated watering rights. For land titles are primarily vested in clans, and secondarily in their constituent segments. Each of the forty or so Digil and Rahanwiin clans, with populations varying between 5,000 and 100,000 are thus essentially land-holding corporations. They also act as units in the payment and receipt of compensation and thus participate in the nation-wide systems of indemnification.

As with the northern pastoral nomads, here also there is a general correlation between the structural proximity (or remoteness) of groups and the amounts of blood-money which they customarily offer as compensation for a killing or lesser injuries. Thus, Digil or Rahanwiin clans that are territorially and socially in close contact and consequently on friendly terms pay smaller amounts of damages than those which are more distant. For example, the Elai of Bur Hacaba, who are the largest single Rahanwiin clan (some 100,000 strong), their smaller neighbours the Helleda, and the neighbouring and formerly subject Eyle clan, all occupy adjacent lands round the three hills of Hacaba, Jejis, and Heibe. These are striking granite outcrops in an otherwise level plain and the three clans are often referred to collectively, both by themselves and others, as the "People of the Three Hills." They jointly observe a single tariff of blood-compensation according to which any killing among them requires payment of blood-money at the rate of sixty camels (or £300[4]) in the case of a man's death, and half that figure for a murdered woman. With more distant groups who stand outside this tripartite agreement rates are correspondingly higher. Similarly, among the Bay Hargan territorial cluster of six contiguous clans round the wells and religious center of Saraman, forty camels (or £200) is the normal rate of compensation for the homicide of a man (and half that figure in the case of a woman). Again, externally a higher tariff applies.

Likewise, at a higher level of grouping, all those clans which fall within the Siyeed (or "Eight") moiety of the Rahanwiin confederacy exchange smaller rates of payment than those obtaining between members of this group and the other half of the clan-family, the Sagaal (or "Nine"). And between the Rahanwiin and the related but structurally more remote Digil clan-family, higher rates still are normally applied. Within the seven-clan-strong Digil group itself, there is a pronounced sense of overall unity and the usual tariff of indemnification is 2,500 shillings for the killing of a man.

Although these gradations are more systematized among these contiguous southern cultivators than they are among their northern counterparts, there is a much more striking and important difference to note. In the north, whole clans never act as single compensation-groups except temporarily in the short-lived circumstances of protracted inter-clan war. Here, however, most Digil and Rahanwiin clans exhibit this characteristic as a permanent feature, and not as something which is only evoked fleetingly in special circumstances. Thus, the solidarity of these southern clans as land-holding units is paralleled in their unity as indemnification-groups; and their internal segments, although incipiently political and capable of splitting off, are more typically internal administrative divisions of a permanent political structure.

This is evident in the internal arrangements for paying and distributing compensation within a clan. While the clan is in almost all cases a single unit in external transactions, its internal segmentation determines the arrangements which obtain in the collection and distribution of dues in which it is involved. Among the Elai, for example, an incoming blood-wealth of 6,000 shillings is divided into two parts valued at 1,000 shillings each, and a third portion of 4,000 shillings. The first is allotted to the immediate kin of the deceased — brothers, a father, or sons — while the second is paid to agnatic cousins within the minimal lineage. The remaining sum of 4,000 shillings is divided into three equal parts and distributed among the three primary segments of the clan. In outgoing dues, the murderer and his immediate patrilineal kin are responsible for providing the expenses of the deceased's funeral, while the remainder is paid by the clan as a whole on the same principle as that applied in distributing incoming awards.

In cases of internal clan homicide, however, a much smaller rate of compensation is the rule. Where the murder occurs within one of its minimal segments only a few sheep are given, over and above the burial expenses. And between more remote segments this tariff is only slightly increased. This drastic reduction in the amounts paid and received reflects the high degree of unity which the clan exhibits as a single compensation-paying group. In the north, comparable features are only evinced at a much lower level of grouping, for among the nomads the most stable solidary units are not whole clans, but only small fragments of them.

The Adoption of Clients

Politico-legal commitment in terms of payment and receipt of damages is, as I have said, intimately bound up with the distribution of rights to arable land and water among the Digil and Rahanwiin. It is only by continuing to meet these legal responsibilities and liabilities that a person enjoys secure tenure of rights of access to these vital clan resources. If a stranger wishes to join a clan other than that of his birth he can only do so, and thus acquire rights to cultivable land and water, if he undertakes to make common cause with his hosts and to pay and receive compensation with them. This is graphically seen in the procedure for the adoption of clients, which is standard in form among all the Rahanwiin and Digil clans.

Amongst the Hareyn clan of Molimud, for example, a would-be client approaches the clan elders and headmen with a small gift of money and a camel, which is slaughtered for their benefit. In front of a formal assembly of elders, the client pledges his allegiance to the Hareyn as a whole and to the various internal segments of the clan to which he has been allocated. The formula runs as follows: "I am now Hareyn, my segment is the Garaskunle lineage of the Warasile segment of the clan: my leader is Malak Alio. My blood is with Garaskunle. Whatever the Garaskunle undertake I shall participate in. If war breaks out I shall fight beside them; if they remain at peace I shall also be at peace as they are; if prosperity and plenty are their portion, I shall share these. But if drought and disaster overtake them, I shall endure these evils with them. Thus I renounce my birth place: my clan is now Hareyn and so it will be as long as I live."

Having in this fashion undertaken to share the burdens as well as the joys of association with his patrons, the new client is allocated land for cultivation and his new holding is publicly demarcated by the elders of his segment. Such a newly installed client may not dispose of his land except to members of his patron group; nor can he immediately add to his holdings by buying further land. Should he leave his patrons, his rights automatically lapse; but if he stays on with them and dies among them, his heirs will inherit his fields. If, however, his heirs elect to leave their father's adopted group, they in turn will forfeit their inheritance, although they may claim compensation.

This institutionalized adoption of clients, which attaches strangers not to individual patrons but to groups and is extremely rare among the northern nomads (cf. chapter 4) but very common among the southern cultivators, is crucial to any understanding of the differences in structure between the two Somali groups. Unlike their northern counterparts, the Digil and Rahanwiin contain large numbers of adopted clients in various degrees of assimilation. Thus, in discussing the status of the members of their groups, both confederacies of clans draw a broad general distinction between those they call *deeh*, or adventitious accretions, and those they call *dalad*, authentic lineal descendants. More specifically, three categories of local resident are usually recognized in terms of the formula: *dalad iyo duhul iyo sheegad*, authentic descendants, long-standing and assimilated clients, and recent client recruits.[5] These last have less secure land rights than members of the other two categories, which in fact fade into each other to become virtually indistinguishable, save in a ritual context. The newest accretions are also often subject to such disabilities as not being considered fully eligible for appointment to the office of traditional battle leader or lineage headman; and, correspondingly, until their commitment with their protectors has ripened with the passage of years, they may not be treated as full members in terms of the payment and receipt of blood-compensation.

Thus, despite the formula for adoption quoted above, many new clients retain at least partial blood-compensation involvement with their own kin outside their hosts' group. Eventually, however, if a client wishes to identify himself completely with his hosts he must surrender his outside commitments. Only thus can he acquire full rights in his place of adoption and transmit these unfettered to his descendants. Most clients, consequently, go through a gradual process of assimilation which is fortified by endogamous marriage in the host clan, and which with the passage of years and ultimately of generations eventually fully absorbs new accretions in what were originally host groups. An access of further new clients, of course, intensifies this merging and enhances the assimilated status of those who preceded them.

Such processes of client adoption are not peripheral, but quite central to any proper understanding of the constitution of the Digil and Rahanwiin clans in their present form. The vast majority of the members of these clans today are, in fact, of client origin. Although in the course of collecting and investigating hundreds of genealogies in this area, I encountered a few individuals and small groups that had become clients within the present generation, the great majority of the present Digil and Rahanwiin peoples appear to be the descendants of much older foreign accretions, some certainly going back as far as ten generations. Many, indeed, are of such long standing that their present representatives have lost count of the number of generations that have elapsed since their original act of adoption and no longer retain precise knowledge of their former origins and provenance.

More than this, according to their own clan histories and other evidence, these southern Somali clans have in nearly every case developed from an original act of alliance (*balan*, promise) among disparate clusters of other clan fragments and fractions. They are thus essentially federative associations, although they have a genealogical structure, and I know of no single major Somali clan of whatever grouping or provenance that is not represented among them today and that has not in some measure participated in this federative and adoptive process.[6] Indeed, so many layers of foreign settlement have been deposited by successive waves of immigrants that in a great many clans the original founding nucleus of authentic Digil and Rahanwiin has not only been vastly outnumbered but has eventually withered away altogether. The peoples of the region themselves, although they try to conceal it from outsiders, compare this situation to that of an old tree whose life has ultimately been sapped by an over-luxuriant parasitic creeper. This image is peculiarly appropriate. Not only is it couched in the common idiom of plant growth in which all Somali describe group formation and decay, but also the word used for such a climbing plant (*saar*) is in fact applied equally to designate adopted clients.

Thus, for example, of the large Elai clan with a total population of some 100,000 persons, none of the twenty-two official salaried headmen in 1962 were apparently authentic descendants of the clan ancestor Elai. And if any genuine descendants of this ancestor survived I did not meet them. Instead those who now call themselves Elai, owning fields within the clan lands, and participating in its compensation-paying arrangements, are, in fact, drawn from every conceivable Somali clan, and a large proportion are of northern nomadic provenance. To varying extents these circumstances of heterogeneous clan composition are paralleled among all Digil and Rahanwiin clans, although the Elai probably represent the extreme limit of this process of admixture, federation, and client adoption (cf. Colucci 1924: 51).

Yet despite the fact that the present population is largely descended from alien clients and includes such ethnically diverse elements as remnant Oromo and Bantu communities in various stages of assimilation, it is the dialects and in large measure the culture of the orig-

inal Digil and Rahanwiin founding settlers that have survived. The culture of this original core community has, apparently, been accepted by
all subsequent immigrants and thus perpetuated at the expense of the
dialects and cultures of succeeding generations of northern clients. First
generation settlers who have come from the north usually speak both
dialects of Somali, but their children born and reared among the Digil
and Rahanwiin speak the dialect of the latter. These features of Digil and
Rahanwiin history support the general evidence of tribal tradition to the
effect that the process of clan formation in this area has been a gradual
one extending over several centuries.

Hence the great majority of the Digil and Rahanwiin tribesmen
live today in clans which are not those of their original ancestors, and
their contemporary functional genealogies are those of these new clans
to which they are currently affiliated. These southern clans have typically much shorter genealogies than those of the northern nomads. A
person normally counts some five or six named generations to the ancestor of his minimal segment, and another four or five supervene between
this point and that of the name representing the clan as a whole. These
latter names, significantly, correspond exactly to the internal segmentation of the clan. This is very different from the genealogical structure
of northern Somali clans, where adoption and federation on this scale
do not occur, and political mergers are not represented genealogically
save in exceptional circumstances (cf. above, chapter 4).

Where in the south longer and more detailed genealogies do occur,
as is sometimes the case, these are mainly of two types. People of authentic *dalad* founding stock, who form a minority in any clan, tend to possess longer and more diversified genealogies. Where, on the other hand,
ordinary affiliates of a clan who cannot trace such connection produce
long genealogies of northern Somali type, these reveal their original
clan identity and do not relate to their current, adoptive affiliation.
This, frequently, they only know in terms of their attachment to the
hierarchy of clan segments and associated headmen which represents
their contemporary politico-legal identity. Hence, for the majority of the
Digil and Rahanwiin, clan pedigrees are at best "genealogical charters"
(cf. Bohannan 1952) rather than true genealogies of northern Somali
type. And for many even this description exaggerates their genealogical
character, which might be better described as little more than a schema
of political divisions cast in the form of a genealogy.

Despite this high degree of clan heterogeneity and the absence of
a widely ramifying genealogical structure recording the various proliferation of ancestors and descendants over the generations in northern
Somali style, in each Digil and Rahanwiin clan there is usually one seg-

ment which is especially singled out and given the term *'urad* (first-born, in northern Somali), or more expressively *mindihay* (knife-bearer). This segment has traditionally the privilege of initiating all joint clan occasions, of, for example, entering battle first. But at the present time it is its ritual role that is most significant. Among the northern pastoralists the characteristic pattern of tribal ritual life within Islam is the annual commemoration of lineage ancestors, each order of lineage segmentation up to and including that of the clan celebrating its eponym's rites separately. Among the Digil and Rahanwiin, however, where a precise and tightly drawn genealogical structure is lacking, this is generally replaced by an annual collective rain-making ceremony (*roobdoon*) performed by the clan as a whole. On these occasions the ritual slaughtering of livestock in sacrifice to God is initiated by the "knife-bearing" segment (cf. Lewis 1966: 260).

The segment that plays this important role is considered to represent the most authentic settler stock of the clan: indeed, it is often directly referred to as *dalad*, a term that, as we have seen, ideally designates authentic lineal descent from an ancestor. The implication is thus that in every Digil and Rahanwiin clan there is normally at least one segment (often the smallest) which either in fact contains some true descendants of the original clan founder (or founders), or successfully maintains this pretension. The members of such ritually dominant segments are not typically scattered throughout the villages of a clan and do not therefore provide an articulating thread uniting the clan genealogically in the way that the members of dominant clans and segments do among the Nuer or the Lugbara. At the level of the clan, they are simply one, though a special one, of the various constituent segments. Nevertheless, in ritual contexts they represent the unity of the clan as a land-holding corporation, and thus symbolize the unity which Digil and Rahanwiin clans exhibit despite their formal internal divisions and their extreme heterogeneity.

This unity, which rests fundamentally upon the defence of common land and water interests, is, as I have already suggested, reinforced by the way in which village ties cut across those of segment membership. A further factor of importance here is the high degree of clan endogamy (indeed of classificatory patrilateral and matrilateral cousin marriage), which in direct contrast to northern Somali practice is the norm observed by both Digil and Rahanwiin.[7] When the patrilineal heterogeneity of these clans is taken into account, this form of marriage can be seen to have the effect of reinforcing weak or non-existent descent ties by a web of affinal and matrilateral links. It is also arguable that where people of the same original clan identity are scattered in different segments and villages of their adoptive clan, such ties as they continue to recognize on the basis of their true descent affiliation tend to provide further cross-cutting links making again for overall clan solidarity. For, despite the fact that all the members of these mixed clans have sworn solemnly to obliterate their former identity, in many cases this continues as an at least potential basis for social interaction. This potentiality, as the history of the Digil and Rahanwiin shows, may, however, also threaten clan unity. This is particularly the case where the members of a given clan segment largely derive from the same former clan origin, such common identity often serving indeed as the basis for further recruitment from the original clan home.

Modern Divisive Tendencies

Legislative changes in the 1960s presented new circumstances creating what is virtually an experimental situation for testing how effectively these various contrary pushes and pulls make for solidary Digil and Rahanwiin clan units capable of withstanding external fissile forces pressing upon their heterogeneous structure. These pressures emanate from the modern political scene. In its drive to replace tribal particularism by national solidarity, the Somali government in 1960 passed legislation officially abolishing the status of client and upholding the right of every Somali citizen to live and farm where he should choose, irrespective of his particular clan or lineage affiliation (Law of 2 March 1960). In similar vein and partly directly aimed at the local Digil and Rahanwiin political party, subsequent legislation forbade the use by political parties of tribal names. The Digil and Rahanwiin party adroitly met this difficulty by adopting a new title, the initials of which still corresponded to those of the former tribal organization. But there is no doubt that in the six years since independence this local party lost ground to the major national parties. At the same time, the fuller political involvement of all Somalis in the wider arena of national politics, which are dominated by fluctuating alliances between various clan power-blocs, has generally led to a quickening of lineage political awareness.

The effect of these and other factors has undoubtedly been to stimulate particularistic movements within the Digil and Rahanwiin and to encourage those former clients of proud northern clan origin particularly to assert their independent status. The consequent fluidity in imputed group affiliation among the Digil and Rahanwiin which this has undoubtedly promoted has, however, been countered by the continuing need for individuals to belong to viable compensation-groups which would effectively protect the security of their lives and property and those of their dependants.[8] Some conception of the interplay of these rival forces in a situation where the final result is difficult to predict can be seen in the following case-history.

A man of Hadama origin came and settled among the Hareyn about 1940 and was given land to cultivate and was allocated to a segment of his protecting clan. Some years later, his son was involved in a quarrel about a married woman in the course of which he was killed by the husband. The husband belonged to another segment of the Hareyn, and after the fight fled to a town where he was arrested by the police and eventually sentenced to fifteen years' imprisonment. The segment of which the dead man was a client claimed blood-wealth, and eventually received a few sheep and a camel from the lineage of the assailant. After all this trouble, the father of the deceased decided to leave the Hareyn and return home to his natal clan, the Hadama, to whom he naturally related the circumstances of the affair. The Hadama quickly sent a delegation to the Hareyn claiming 6,000 shillings as blood-money for "their deceased clansman," as they put it. The Hareyn countered this claim, saying that the man in question was one of their adopted clients and the matter had already been settled internally.

The Hadama retaliated by going to court. After much litigation, the high court ruled that the Hareyn should pay blood-money to the Hadama and that, in these circumstances, this should be valued at 8,000 shillings. The Hareyn responded to this judgement by declaring that in that case the man would have to leave their land permanently and forfeit his fields. The government, however, ruled, and this was given local effect by the District Commissioner, that the man concerned need not do so. Since the Hareyn had given him land, the status of client being no longer officially recognized, it did not matter what his tribal affiliation was. The man returned to the Hareyn, but said he was Hadama. How long he would be able to stay was doubtful, however, since it seemed that the local Hareyn were trying to send their unwelcome visitor to Coventry and to deny him normal watering facilities and help in cultivation.

I do not know the final outcome in this case. But as well as indicating the interaction of the new separatist trends among the Digil and Rahanwiin, which government action tended to support, this brief history illustrates very clearly how rights to land, access to water, and personal security (expressed in terms of indemnification) are traditionally conceived of as three inseparable aspects of group affiliation.

Conclusions

In seeking to understand southern Somali social structure, we have been driven to refer repeatedly to their economic and historical cir-

cumstances; and, in underlining the effect of these factors, I have frequently invoked the northern pastoral nomads as a control in analysis.
Northern Somali social structure here is all the more relevant, of course,
since, as we have seen, a large proportion of those who today call themselves Digil and Rahanwiin are in fact of northern nomadic provenance.
So that in examining southern Somali structure we are also tracing, to
an extent that would be difficult to measure exactly, the modification of
the pastoral nomadic way of life in new ecological circumstances.

Let me now try to clinch my argument that without invoking the
aid of these economic differences in their particular historical settings,
we could not properly understand the structural differences between
these branches of the Somali nation. I refer again to the major distin-
guishing features of southern Somali structure with which we began:
the expansion of politico-legal solidarity; the accompanying development of a more stable clan authority system; and the wholesale adoption
of clients.

Consider first the circumstances of the northern nomads. With
movable property as the focus of corporate interests, and in an environment where pasture and water, the two prime necessities of life, are
in short supply and unequally and irregularly distributed in successive
seasons, the pastoralists have developed a social system that permits the
maximum deployment of the individual herder and his stock and mili-
tates against the formation of large stable corporate groups. There are few
situations, save those of feud and war, when the security of the herder
and his stock is threatened, which require sustained and intensive cooperation on any considerable scale. Authority, likewise, is minimal and
fluid, for little is required of it.

Underlying this essentially fluid arrangement of people and
allegiences, the lineage system provides an enduring and unambiguous
framework of grouping which is mobilized and given specific definition
by contractual alliance as need arises. The security of the individual's
personal and mobile property is provided for by his membership, in every
situation, of a specified blood-compensation group. This small association of agnatic equals only unites as an effective corporate entity when
hostilities threaten or compensation has to be paid or received. Wider
alliances are evoked as occasion demands along the lines of agnatic connection with the aid of contractual agreements of the same kind as those
binding together the members of the minimal and most frequently mobilized compensation-paying group. Moreover, where disproportionate
size forces groups to find security among distant allies, contrary to the
theory of segmentary lineage opposition, such unions are not normally
thought of as permanent and do not entail the sort of genealogical assim-

ilation and manipulation which is characteristic of Digil and Rahanwiin clan structure.

In the south, on the other hand, the expansion of stable and effective, rather than merely *potential* political solidarity, is facilitated by the advantages which population strength gives to groups in advancing claims to arable land and water-points and to maintaining their holdings against enemy incursion. For traditionally, clan title to land is obtained and maintained only by effective occupancy, which in the past, if more rarely today, frequently entailed conquest and defence. Moreover, admittedly at a much lower level of association, cultivation requires a larger circle of sustained, regular cooperation — especially for water-pond excavation and maintenance — than is normally necessary in the nomadic economy. And since the units of land-holding are in principle here, fixed and permanent, and not as in the north dispersed in a temporary and essentially transient pattern of distribution over pasture land and a multitude of different water-points, the incorporation of strangers implies a much more complete kind of social assimilation. The client, after all, acquires heritable rights to a fixed piece of land; and it is through this that he is strongly identified with the group that exercises traditional sovereignty over the land of which his holding is part. In contrast, among the northern nomads, temporary association for defence or aggression with remote agnates, or with those who are not patrilineal kinsmen, carries with it no fixed heritable patrimony.

The very different southern pattern of client adoption would seem itself to have been reinforced as a permanent associative device by the great admixture of peoples which the region has witnessed over a long period of time and by the remoteness of many client fractions from their original kin. For in those rare cases where something approaching the southern pattern of client adoption occurs in the north, the assimilated group are usually so remote from their own kin that they can no longer maintain effective ties with them and thus cannot count on their support when it is needed. The resulting heterogeneity of southern Somali clan structure, especially where clients of the same origin are allocated to different clan sections, tends to foster a wider and more diversified solidarity, which is further encouraged by clan endogamy and the dispersal of clan segments in different areas of settlement within the common clan territory. These, I believe, are the factors which encourage the expansion of southern political solidarity to the level of the clan, which give the clan as a territorial and politico-legal unit a notable degree of solidarity, and which promote the development of a more hierarchical and more stable authority system within it.

Notes

1. See also Helander, 1994.
2. See also Massey, 1987, p. 57.
3. Elders or headmen are also known traditionally as *aqiyaar* (cf Massey, 1987; Helander 1994). During the regime of Mohamed Siyad, they were renamed *nabaddoon*, "peace-seekers," see below, chapter 7.
4. 1960s values.
5. Helander, 1994 records that *dalad* is also contrasted with *daqan*, "acculturated" from the word for custom or culture.
6. One of the least common elements appears to be people of Isaaq origin.
7. Out of 167 marriages which I recorded 50% were with cousins; Helander, in press, found that 37% of his marriage sample of 149 marriages were with cousins. Massey, 1987, p. 54 recorded a figure of 25%. See also Gigli, 1993.
8. The continuing solidarity of the Digil Rahanwiin under conditions of maximum insecurity was evident after the collapse of the Somali state in the formation of the Somali Democratic Movement in 1991 : see below, chapter 9.

Chapter VII

KIM IL-SUNG IN SOMALIA:
THE END OF TRIBALISM?

Introduction

Despite Kathleen Gough's[1] eloquent appeal for the analysis of development under socialist conditions in the Third World, Western Marxist social anthropology has seemed more concerned with its own parochial pursuits than with the transformation of traditional institutions in self-defined Marxist states.[2] It is thus left to others, who may not always possess the appropriate credentials, to undertake this task. This chapter attempts to explore and assess the main currents of structural change in the Somali Democratic Republic, a state which had been under military rule since 1969 and officially Marxist since 1970.[3]

Here, as in so many other parts of the world today, the immediate problem confronting the student of contemporary politics is that of successfully penetrating the official rhetoric to discover the underlying political realities. The difficulty is not simply the usual one of finding out what really happens in high places; how and by whom decisions are taken. There is the further and wider issue of ascertaining how, and according to what principles, ordinary people order their lives, since their thoughts and actions are carefully monitored and are not readily open to general inspection. That familiar object of anthropological certitude, the 'ethnographic present', here recedes into a thick mist, posing delicate interpretative problems of the kind more usually encountered in oral history. This is daunting, especially when, as in the present case, part of my subject matter did not officially exist!

The Somali Revolution and its ideology:
Scientific Socialism

After nine years of fratricidal clan party politics following independence in 1960, there was undoubtedly public support for the "bloodless" *coup d'état* with which the army seized power in Somalia on the propitious date of October, 21 1969.[4] The new military leaders naturally sought to distinguish themselves as sharply as possible from their venal civilian predecessors (many of whom were summarily imprisoned). Hence, while generally maintaining the neutralist stance of previous Somali governments, where the latter had inclined towards the West, they tilted the balance in the opposite direction, towards Russia (already the main source of military aid), China, and Korea. As the initial wave of public enthusiasm gradually subsided, the new rulers' implicit mandate to govern lost much of its force. They were, consequently, under increasing pressure to produce a coherent and explicit political ideology at once legitimizing and consolidating the "Revolution" (as the *coup* was retrospectively styled) which had brought them to power, promising to cure all of the country's ills. The natural choice was some form of Socialism and, as became clear on the first anniversary (October, 1970) of the *coup*, that particular variety known as Scientific Socialism, based on a pragmatic local application of Marxist-Leninism.

This was taken to be fully compatible with the primordial attachment of the Somali nation to the religion of Islam. As the head of state, General Mahammad Siyad Barre, declaimed in a speech marking one of the major Muslim holidays, a few months after the *coup*:

> Our Islamic faith teaches us that its inherent values are perennial and continually evolving as people progress. These basic tenets of our religion cannot be interpreted in a static sense, but rather as a dynamic source of inspiration for continuous advancement... To help our brethren and our fellows, we must go beyond the concept of charity, and reach the higher and more altruistic concept of co-operation on a national scale. We must strive with enthusiasm and patriotism to attain the highest possible state of general welfare for all.[5]

In any case, as the President declared in response to criticism from a different quarter in a speech delivered[6] in the middle of 1972: "The founders of scientific socialism were not against religion in particular but they exposed and disproved the reactionary elements of religion that dominate [the] sound reasoning of mankind and hence hinder [the] progress of society."

If socialism does not exclude religion and is actually part of Islam, there is, however, no question about the unique transcendental status of the latter. As the President explained[7] on another occasion (January 1972):

> As far as socialism is concerned, it is not a heavenly message like Islam but a mere system for regulating the relations between man and his utilization of the means of production in this world. If we decide to regulate our national wealth, it is not against the essence of Islam. God has created man and has given him the faculty of mind to choose between good and bad, between virtue and vice. We have chosen social justice instead of exploitation of man by man and this is how we can practically help the individual Muslim and direct him to [a] virtuous life. However, the reactionaries want to create a rift between socialism and Islam because socialism is not to their interest ...[8]

There is no question of the death of God here, or of the vulgar secularization of Islam. With this emphatic religious grounding, scientific socialism, Somali-style, known literally as "wealth-sharing based on wisdom" (hanti-wadaagga 'ilmi ku disan)[9] is closely linked with such key concepts as "unity" or "togetherness" (waddajir), "self-reliance" (is ku kalsoonaan), and "self-help" (iskaa wab u qabso).[10] As these associated principles suggest, scientific socialism was first and foremost an ideology for development designed to annihilate the three major enemies which General Siyad repeatedly insisted confront his people: poverty, disease, and ignorance. These scourges could only be overcome by a sustained effort of the national will in which all sections of the population set aside their selfish interests, shrugged off contaminating neo-colonial influences and joined the common struggle for national prosperity. Women had as much to contribute as men: and the young, "tomorrow's leaders," had a particularly important role to play.

Here tribalism and "multipartyism" were singled out as anachronistic barriers to progress to be discarded in favor of a new and truly mature sense of national integrity. As General Siyad incisively stated the issue in a minatory address to regional judges: "Tribalism and nationalism cannot go hand in hand.... It is unfortunate that our nation is rather too clannish; if all Somalis are to go to Hell, tribalism will be their vehicle to reach there."[11] Tribal nepotism and corruption hence became equally heinous offenses, incurring severe penalties, and the obscure nonkinship term jaalle (comrade, or friend) was pressed into circulation to replace the traditional polite term of address "cousin" (ina'adeer) which was strongly discouraged because of its kinship associations. Earlier nationalists, religious and secular, had appealed to the transcendent brotherhood of Somalis, regardless of clan or lineage. The new stress on *friendship* appealed for co-operation and unity in which ties of blood counted for nothing. The productive energy that would thus be released was to be harnessed in a carefully planned sequence of national campaigns designed to achieve success on all the fields of battle destined for victory by the "glorious" Revolution.

These major national campaigns (s. *olol*, battle-formation) were reinforced by more specific local "crash programmes" (s. *parnaamaaj*) throughout the country. Salvation lay in honest toil: each worker benefiting in direct proportion to his efforts (*hawl iyo hantiwadaag*), spurred on by the terse slogan: "Less talk and more work" (*haddalyar iyo hawlweyn*). This tight-lipped new dynamism was epitomized in the word chosen to express the Revolution itself: *Ka'aan* which meant literally "rising" or "standing" and refers originally to nomadic movement.[12]

The dynamism which the sublimation of archaic lineage loyalties should yield received direction and was brought to a final climax of enthusiasm in the personality cult that had been assiduously developed round the head of state. "The Victorious Leader" (*Guulwaadde*) General Siyad, was presented in the official hagiography and iconography as dauntlessly leading his people in the unremitting war against all their foes. Countless posters, poems, songs of praise, and speeches proclaimed his sublime role as the "father" of a nation whose "mother" was the Revolution. Inspired by Scientific Socialism, this mystical union, dissolving mundane kinship loyalties, was the source of all prosperity and the infallible guarantee that the nation's struggle would be successful. Amongst its most precious progeny were the "flowers of the revolution," those destitute children, often without parents, who had been gathered into Youth Revolutionary Centers all over Somalia where they were fed, clad, and trained to serve their country. Their gratitude to the nation and its beneficent head ("il buono condottorre")[13] was unquestioned and, unsullied by divisive lineage constraints, set a shining example. It was this transcendent dedication to the motherland and her virile consort that was to replace the old genealogies that divided the nation into so many hostile camps.

The government newspaper, the *October Star*, printed since 1973 in the new Somali (i.e. Roman) script, supplied its readers with an edifying thought for the day, often in the form of a pithy exhortation culled from the long dramatic perorations of a man[14] who, before his elevation in 1969, was better known for his blunt military epithets than for polished oratory. A selection of these thoughts and sayings, in the form of a little blue-and-white (the national colours) pocket manual, published in 1973,[15] enjoyed wide circulation. Wherever he went, the President was greeted by mass applause and adulation, feted and saluted by his loyal subjects who literally danced before him — to Korean choreography. Every public occasion, no matter how small or trivial, ended with its participants reaffirming their pledge of loyalty to the Revolution and to its beneficent architect.

This lofty image of invincible power contrasted sharply with the disarming humility and directness which the head of state reserved for his face-to-face encounters with his comrades, his much publicized eagerness to listen to and share their problems, and his humble life-style and edifying compassion for the poor and underprivileged whose plight was a recurrent theme in so many of his speeches. The refreshing absence of ostentatious luxury or pomp and ceremony, when the President received visitors for homely man-to-man exchanges, emphasized the sincerity and directness of a leader who succeeded in conveying the impression that he was genuinely a little bewildered by the populist cult surrounding his public person. And like the splendid conductor he was, in his speeches praising the proud achievements of the Revolution he regularly, self-depreciatingly reminded his audience that their success reflected their efforts as much as his and called upon them to congratulate themselves on their exemplary dedication to the cause.

The Maoist Facet

Many of these features, particularly this elaborate personality cult so foreign to the traditional egalitarian values of the Somali nomads,[16] with the associated emphasis on public pageantry, mass rallies, sports, and gymnastics, conveyed an intriguingly oriental flavour. Local parallels could of course be found in such relatively accessible sources of influence as Nasser's Egypt, and less significantly, Tanzania. More remote parallels seemed even more striking. In addition to the obvious Russian influence, there was certainly more than a trace of Maoism in the cult which had been created round 'Chairman' Siyad, and the North Korean model was equally relevant. Although Kim Il Sung had not yet set foot in Somalia, General Siyad had twice visited North Korea, where he was cordially received, and numerous senior officials have been to Korea on training courses, as others had been to Russia and China. On ministerial bookshelves in Mogadishu the works of Kim Il Sung far outnumbered those from any other communist source. There was, in addition, the shared military emphasis of the two regimes. Other significant parallels included the Korean unification issue, recalling Somalia's own struggle to extend her frontiers to embrace those nationals living under foreign rule over the border in Ethiopia, Kenya, and the French Territory of the Afars and Issas;[17] and, crucially, North Korea's remarkable success in maintaining her independence while enjoying both Russian and Chinese patronage.

Kim Il Sung's much publicized *juche* principle, of "being true to one's inherent character" which so closely resembled the paired Somali concepts of self-reliance and self-help gave a more specific ideological edge to these correspondences and further enhanced the appropriateness of the North Korean model. We shall be in a better position to judge how illuminating this diffusionist perspective is when we have looked more closely at the implementation of socialist policies in Somalia.

State Control: The Official Structure

After the *coup*, Somalia was ruled by an all military (including some police officers) Supreme Revolutionary Council (SRC), aided by a largely civilian Council of Secretaries, the latter exercising quasi-ministerial functions but not possessing ministerial power. Key departments, such as Defence, Information and National Guidance, and Internal Affairs[18], however, remained in the hands of members of the SRC. Unlike its more recently formed Ethiopian counterpart (the *Dirg*) which was said to include ordinary soldiers, the SRC consisted, from its inception, entirely of officers of the rank (then) of captain and above. Since the arrest of one of the initial Vice-Presidents, General Korshell (then police commander) in April 1970[19] and the public execution of another (General Ainanshe) with other "counter-revolutionary plotters" in July 1972[20] the composition of the SRC remained remarkably stable. As might be anticipated, there were more frequent changes and reshuffles in the personnel of the subordinate Council of Secretaries. This unequivocal pattern of military dominance at the center was replicated at all levels of administration throughout the state. Shortly after the army had seized power, all civilian district and regional governors were replaced by military officers. From the beginning of 1974, however, civilian officials began to resume these functions.

The command structure of the Somali army thus formed the backbone of the state[21] which was literally a military rather than a police state; and much symbolic play was made of the fact that the term for the armed forces, *Hoogga*, means literally "force, might and power." This martial structure was fleshed out, both at the center and in the provinces, with a formidable array of ancillary agencies, each with its own power structure leading back ultimately to the President, in some cases directly and in others via other members of the SRC. Crucially significant here were: the President's Political Office (formerly his public relations service and the provisional nucleus for a contemplated party organization);

the National Security Service; and the National Security Courts with virtually limitless power to try a wide spectrum of "political offenses" ranging from "tribalism" to treason.

The heads of all these organizations were members of the SRC, that of the NSS having, as we shall see later, a particularly significant position. The Political Office shared with the Ministry of Information and National Guidance (headed until December 1974 by an energetic Vice-President), the important task of national thought control. These agencies were, as it were, primarily concerned with the preventive medicine for the revolutionary health of the nation. Where they were unsuccessful, the NSS and National Security Courts stepped in. The young *apparatchics* of the Presidency Office, partly trained in Moscow, were specifically charged with the delicate task of expounding Marxist-Leninism in its local, Somali version. Additional intellectual support was provided here by the Somali Institute of Development Administration, the political studies nucleus of the national University.

The most prestigious center for instruction in the aims and implementation of the Revolution was the former military academy in the capital, Mogadishu, renamed Halane after a young Somali lieutenant who gave his life trying to save his country's colors in the Somali-Ethiopian conflict of 1964. Here regular in-service training for all categories of officials was organized, including courses for the highest ranks in the civil service. Thus, for instance, the many ambassadors retained from the previous civilian regime were recalled shortly after the *coup* and sent for intensive training to Halane. There, in addition to spartan paramilitary discipline (which some found a tonic), they learned the meaning of the Revolution and how its aims were to be implemented in their service abroad. Halane had great symbolic and functional importance; it was, to quote the zealous Secretary of State for Information, Vice-President Col. Jaalle Ismail Ali Abokor, "almost synonymous with the October Revolution."[22] All secondary school leavers now spent six months in compulsory military training and "socialist orientation" at Halane before proceeding to do their national service as teachers in remote parts of the country. (Vocational training generally, it should be added parenthetically, reflected the self-reliance ideal and was realistically geared to the nation's needs. So, for instance, medical and veterinary training specialized in the locally relevant areas rather than trying to comply with international standards.)

Practical orientation for the public at large was provided by the people's militia, the so-called Victory Pioneers or "revolutionary youth" (*guulwadayaal*), with their bright green unisex uniforms and sinister Orwellian-eye, symbol of vigilance.[23] Formed in 1972 and recruited largely from the urban unemployed, this organization provided revolutionary training facilities and the prospect of employment. The latter was an important consideration where, in urban centers particularly, the government sought to control the labor market and unemployment and inflation posed serious problems. These official volunteers were expected to play a leading role in local development projects and "crash programs" as well as helping to organize routine civics and social welfare. Their women's branches were prominent in community care. Since some members were popularly assumed to have had close links with the National Security Service, it was generally felt to be dangerous to ignore their appeals for "voluntary" co-operation in kind or cash to help with the latest campaign.

These organs of thought control were augmented by the carefully calculated propaganda which poured forth incessantly on the national radio and in the press — the daily *October Star* and monthly *New Era*. Although the impact of the latter had become more important since the introduction of written Somali,[24] the radio was still the principal instrument for disseminating propaganda amongst the population at large, especially amongst the nomads. Radio controllers had successfully adapted the now established pattern of broadcasting to include the new revolutionary message in such a way that the latter seemed a natural and inevitable extension both of traditional Somali values and of Islam. So, in the typical structure of the daily program, readings from the Quran were followed by a Somali commentary, then by exhortatory proverbs, and finally by passages from speeches of the head of state and his colleagues, presented in such a way that all coalesced in a seamless continuum. In this fashion, ends and beginnings were constantly juxtaposed, and Scientific Socialism was made to appear the cornerstone of Somali traditional culture, a transformation not as implausible as it may appear.

So much for the central organization of government. Outside the capital, in 1974, Somalia's former eight provinces were reconstituted (and, where necessary, renamed to exclude clan names), as fifteen new regions (from 1975, sixteen), comprising sixty-four districts (excluding the fourteen districts of Mogadishu). Each province had its regional revolutionary council, presided over by the military governor acting as "chairman" (*guudoonshiye*) and assisted by the local military and police commanders, the regional NSS chief, and the representative of the President's political office whose main task was to see that the local Orientation center (*hanuunin*) was properly organized and well attended. As I observed myself in the summer of 1974, in some major urban centers the routine evening meetings at local orientation centers were often poorly attended. In the provinces, however, I have seen impressively

large turnouts at the weekly Friday meeting in the provincial orientation center.

With the help of locally recruited vigilantes, workers' committees,
local dignitaries, and women's representatives, the official apparatus of
the central government was brought into the life of the community.
Some regions had well-trained and highly efficient local government
officials. But there appeared to be considerable variation in the effectiveness of local government institutions. A key issue here was naturally
the role of the traditional clan-heads, formerly known in southern
Somalia by the mongrel Arab-Italian term, *capo-qabila*. These tribal leaders were officially abolished, or at any rate re-christened "peace-seekers"
(s. *nabad-doon*), and became theoretically bureaucrats capable of being
posted to any part of the country. This regional pattern was replicated on
a smaller and more modest scale at the district level with again the same
combination of military and other officials and local dignitaries.

As will be evident, great stress was placed on propaganda and
thought control. Even the smallest permanent settlement in the countryside was expected to have its orientation center with, ideally, a suitable complement of Marxist-Leninist literature and portraits of the
reigning trinity: *Jaalle* Siyad, *Jaalle* Markis (Marx), and *Jaalle* Lenin.
Orientation centers with their public-spirited attendants, were intended
to provide an approved alternative basis for social and political activities,
indeed to replace the old lineage structure which the government sought
to destroy. They represented the new nationalism based on friendship and
patriotism, not kinship, and were designed to form the nerve centers of
the vibrant new revolutionary life. In some urban areas, they did appear
to have become a focus of neighbourhood social life in competition with
that based on mosque or lineage association (officially banned).

People were encouraged to arrange their weddings at these centers,
thus (theoretically at any rate) marrying in revolutionary rather than
clan style and without exchanging marriage payments, traditionally collected and disbursed on a kinship basis. Other associated measures
designed to undermine lineage loyalties and to increase the individual's
dependence on the state included: government provision of burial
expenses, the banning of collective blood-compensation payments, the
penalty of execution by firing-squad for murder and other tough sanctions to control crime. All these, clearly, were more likely to be effective in towns than among the illusive nomads who make up the major
part of the population.

This formidable apparatus extending from the President's office to
the grass roots throughout the country seemed more designed to ensure
that national policies were faithfully followed than to establish a creative

dialogue with ordinary citizens. The latter was, however, something on which the claimed to President set great store and regularly emphasized in his perorations to administrative officials. The following extract from an address to a national seminar of district and regional officials (chairmen, representatives of the PRO and NSS officers) delivered by General Siyad on April 3 1973 conveys the message in the General's own inimitable style:

> It is incumbent upon me to explain to you the aim behind the Local Government Reform Law and how serious its implementation is considered. The law is based on the just policy of socialism, which stipulates that the people shall take part in running their own affairs. The way this could be done is not to let all power be concentrated in Mogadishu, or on one man, but for the people to have their say. Secondly, we used to be a one-city state. We want to fight against this tendency and establish a country of many regions and towns that are living and thriving. This is intended to create self-sufficient districts that can erect self-sufficient councils that can erect their own factories, to create local employment and finance their own education. How can this and other revolutionary decisions be implemented? The people can attain this, and run their own affairs and not be dictated to by colonial style administrators ... The provincial people should participate in the task fully till self-sufficiency is attained ... the management of the people's affairs should be put in their own hands. The Chairman is just to oversee and not to interfere.[25]

The periodic arrests and exemplary sentences which followed murmurs of local dissent or questioning suggested a rather one-sided exchange. And when striking local developments were achieved, as in some districts they had been, these could often be attributed in large measure to the energy and ambition of a particular governor or other key official.

Development and the Management of the Economy

If the population was so extensively and minutely controlled so, in theory, was the economy. Briefly, the position here was that imports and exports were generally controlled by government agencies, a notable exception being the export of livestock on the hoof (the main trade item). Bananas, the principal cash crop, were marketed and exported solely through government agencies. Hides and skins from the pastoral sector were dealt with similarly. All grain grown privately was bought by a government agency, the Agricultural Development Corporation, and sold at controlled prices through retailers or distributed directly through orientation centers. Each farmer was allowed to keep a proportion of his crop for his own domestic consumption. This system, which also provided regional storage facilities, sought to destroy the parasitic activities of mercenary middlemen. But it was not clear whether the amount of grain the producer was allowed to keep was sufficient, under existing market conditions, to provide a sufficient incentive for maximum production.[26]

Private enterprise was not restricted to small-scale farming: there were many privately owned large-scale banana estates; and despite half-hearted occasional attempts to portray the nomads as herding their livestock in pristine communes, virtually the entire nomadic economy retained its traditional status with private ownership of livestock. The economy was thus, in practice, mixed. Nationalized industries such as the Jowhar sugar complex[27] (the seat of many scandals), and the Kismayu meat-canning factory, existed cheek-by-jowl with private companies and interests, the official emphasis on co-operatives being most ostentatiously displayed in such small urban businesses as pharmacies, many of which boasted appropriate revolutionary-style names.[28] The largest and most successful, spontaneously formed agricultural commune was ironically a traditionally based religious settlement in the north, El Birdale. According to a sympathetic, and to the best of my knowledge accurate Russian report,[29] this involved some 600 families with a population of about 4,500 people who grew their own food as well as rearing their own livestock, and produced cash crops which included grains, citrus fruits, coffee, and the narcotic plant, *Catha edulis*, chewed as a stimulant in Somalia and Ethiopia. The cooperative had its own tractors, bulldozers, trucks, and other equipment, and at least one qualified agricultural officer; it received substantial support from the Somali Development Bank.

The stress placed on agricultural development, particularly in the relatively rich riverine Juba-Shebelle basin in the south of Somalia, with the minimum aim of achieving self-sufficiency in grain production, was strongly reflected in the Five Year Plan (1974-8) in which, prior to the disastrous 1974-5 drought, almost 30 per cent of the budget (£200,000,000)[30] was earmarked for agricultural development (in comparison with 5 per cent for education). Special attention was given both to the reactivation of the previously unsuccessful state farms, and to the formation of further co-operative and crash program farm settlements designed to absorb surplus unemployed population from the town and nomadic areas (a matter of critical urgency after the 1974-5 drought).

If the show-piece of the nation's effective self-help schemes was the impressive sand-dune stabilization project near Merca to the south of Mogadishu,[31] the largest, most ambitious crash program was unquestionably the (February 1975) Rural Development Campaign. This was a logical extension of the "Cultural Revolution" achieved in 1973 in the urban areas through the quite successful mass literacy campaign using the new latin Somali script (adopted in 1972). After long and careful preparation, this ambitious rural campaign was launched with appropriate pomp and ceremony in July 1974, when virtually all the urban intermediate and secondary schools in the country were closed to provide a task force of over 30,000 students and teachers which, at an estimated cost of £10,000,000, poured into the interior in triumphant truckloads. Grouped in parties of eight, with a teacher as leader and assisted by visiting veterinary and medical personnel, these young pioneers sallied forth to teach the nomads how to write their own language in the new script, hygiene, modern techniques of animal husbandry, basic civics, and the aims of socialism. Equipped with blankets, a folding blackboard, water-bottle, and other basic kit, and drawing a daily allowance of two Somali shillings (approximately 15 English new pence) these privileged urban students were to share the fruits of the Revolution with their neglected nomadic comrades, staying as guests with nomadic family groups and repaying hospitality by teaching their hosts to read and write.

Here, as in the previous urban mass literacy drive, the President supplied the guiding motto : "If you know teach, if you don't learn." As he explained in a speech marking Women's International Day on March 8, 1974:[32] "The key... is to give everybody the opportunity to learn reading and writing.... It is imperative that we give our people modern revolutionary education... to restructure their social existence.... It will be the weapon to eradicate social balkanisation and fragmentation into tribes and sects. It will bring about an absolute unity and there will be no more room for any negative foreign cultural influences." The interrelated goals of modernization, nationalism, and independence were here all combined, a modern integrated nation comprising not merely those "who speak the same language,"[33] but also who read and write it. Nor was this simply utopian idealism, since there was some evidence that the urban literacy campaign had quickened sentiments of national identity and self-awareness.

As might have been anticipated, this unprecedented assault on the refractory nomads turned out to involve an exchange of knowledge and culture in which the young urbanized students (some of whom showed marked reluctance to venture into the unfamiliar bush) in many cases learned as much as they taught. It was certainly a rewarding, character-building experience for many of these youngsters; and while there is no doubt that the nomads showed that they could learn to write as quickly as their urban countrymen, it remained to be seen how many of the claimed 1,750,000 new recruits[34] to literacy would retain their command of writing.

An enterprise of this kind and scale was bound to encounter technical difficulties which, in practice, varied from region to region. In some cases the nomads turned out not to be where they were expected by campaign organizers. It was also often difficult to persuade them to combine regular instruction with their normal herding tasks, even when watering charges at government wells were waived to attract the herders to settlements where they would be more accessible to indoctrination. What was totally unforseen, although it might have been forecast, but in the end turned out greatly to enhance the success of the scheme was the intervention of the worst drought in recent Somali history.[35] In contrast to the earlier Ethiopian drought, once the extent of the devastation became apparent, the government, to its credit, made no attempt to hide the disaster, but mobilized all its resources to save the lives of drought-stricken nomads. A state of emergency was declared, a "holy war" proclaimed against the drought, and energetic appeals launched to secure famine relief from all possible foreign sources.

In these circumstances, the first priority of the rural development campaign became simply that of famine relief, and the majority of the young nation-builders found themselves helping to set up and staff the relief-camps which were required to accommodate almost 250,000 destitute nomads. Once the camps had been established and stocked with relief foods and medical equipment, their inmates became a conveniently captive audience which could not only be taught the aims of the revolution but also induced to practice them in local self-help schemes.

Thus if the drought transformed the rural development campaign[36] into a massive famine relief operation, the original aims of the enterprise were recovered by converting the famine relief camps into orientation centers. This, of course, was purely a temporary expedient. The long-term future of these totally impoverished nomads, who had lost virtually all their livestock, posed a more challenging problem. But this adversity could also be turned to advantage. As the government was quick to perceive, here was a golden opportunity to achieve two of its most cherished aims at the same time: sedentarization and de-tribalization. With the existing level of unemployment in the towns, the only two realistic possibilities which presented themselves were to settle as many of the nomads as possible in "crash" farming schemes in the inter-riverine region in the south, and to establish the residue in fishing communities along the coast where the rich fishing resources had scarcely been exploited. Both involved the movement of people to new locations, hundreds of miles from their traditional grazing areas, and their settle-ment amongst clans and lineages with which they were unlikely to have any immediate connection. This unprecedently vast movement of peo-ple was actually effected by a Russian airlift (and not with Arab aid as the Somalis had earlier hoped). As President Siyad's speeches at the time indicated, the government realistically feared that its nationalistic objec-tives might be jeopardized by a backlash of clan and lineage feeling on the part of those so abruptly uprooted and juxtaposed (see chapter 8).

It is too early to assess the long-term impact on traditional kinship ties of this dramatic movement of population. To set it in perspective, however, it must be appreciated that the existing population of the southern inter-riverine area was of extremely heterogeneous composi-tion and included a very substantial proportion of people of nomadic ori-gin who, over the centuries, had made their home in this region and become more and more involved in cultivation.[37] Their very mixed composition, reflected in the name of their largest tribal unit, the Rahanwiin, literally "large crowd," made these partly sedentary south-ern Somali the epitome of the new transcendent nationalism which the Revolution sought to realize. It was difficult, however, for the govern-ment to hold them up as a shining example of the ideal nationalistic community without referring to their own synthetic clan identity. There was also the additional consideration that they were traditionally dis-paraged by the arrogant nomads, precisely because they were both seden-tary and of mixed lineage composition. Of course this had not prevented northern nomads settling amongst them as clients, probably under acute environmental pressures such as the 1974 drought.

Similarly, although the proud nomads do not traditionally eat fish and use "fish-eater" as a term of abuse, fishing communities (as e.g. the somewhat despised Reer Manyo) have for centuries existed on the edges of the nomadic world in the coastal ports. The boundaries between nomadism, cultivation, and fishing are thus far from being as hard and fast as they are traditionally drawn by the nomads. Historically, there have certainly been movements back and forth between these economic categories: in their capriciously arid environment the Somalis would scarcely have survived at all without such flexibility in adaptation.[38]

The Infrastructure: Traditional Constraints

If the drought made the Rural Development Campaign much more than the mere ritual exercise it would largely otherwise have been, it did not have the revolutionary force of its Ethiopian counterpart. A few heads rolled: but not *the* head. However, it does seem to have contributed to the major change in the structure of government instituted in December 1974. This involved the replacement of a large proportion of the Secretaries of State and the formation of five new Coordinating Committees (for politics, social affairs, economics, justice and law, and security), with a membership drawn from the SRC and the Council of Secretaries augmented by additional advisers (some ex-Secretaries of State). The widely publicized intention here was to bring into the center of government and policy-formation a fresh infusion of new blood in the shape of the young, ideologically oriented intellectuals, and to clear the decks for the concerted achievement of the objectives of the Revolution.[39] It was also announced that a political party of a kind "unique in Africa" was about to be launched. This evidently took longer to realize than was originally expected, for it was not until July 1 1976, that the party, under the title Somali Socialist Revolutionary Party, was formally inaugurated.

Sufficient has now been said of the formal framework which has been created in Somalia in the name of Scientific Socialism. We must now shift our emphasis to try to establish what lay behind this imposing edifice, directing our attention towards those bastions of the traditional order: Islam, and tribalism in its particular Somali lineage form. Both these have an external as well as an internal component, so that we cannot exclude foreign policy from our examination. Here the unifying perennial issue remained that of the future status of the Somali-inhabited areas adjoining Somalia, the French Territory of the Afars and Issas,[40] the Ethiopian Ogaadeen, and the northern districts of Kenya. Like all its predecessors, the military government protested its dedication to the goal of Somali self-determination in these regions but, in contrast to the incisive vigor of its internal policies, pursued the issue with marked restraint. The constraints imposed by General Siyad's chairmanship of the Organization of African Unity during the critical period of Ethiopia's extreme vulnerability in 1974/5 may, as some commentators argue, have exerted some influence here. If so, this was reinforced by a number of other considerations. One was the fact that the new Ethiopian military regime had developed a strong socialist orientation, adopting policies remarkably similar to those in Somalia and hailed (predictably) by some Somalis as imitations of their own revolutionary efforts (as e.g. in sending all the students into the countryside to preach the Revolution).

There was also the equally complicated issue of Russia's priorities. The Russians had a considerable strategic investment in Somalia[41] which was reported to include nuclear weapon-servicing facilities near the port of Berbera and, after their massive drought aid, more reason than ever to expect (though not necessarily to receive) a grateful Somali response. At the same time, like the Chinese, they were also clearly keenly interested in current events in Ethiopia where their chances of ousting the Americans were greater than they ever were under the imperial regime. In 1976, Russia controlled Somalia's oil supplies as well, of course, as replacements, and ammunition for the sophisticated Russian equipment used by the Somali army and air force.[42] In seeking as advantageous a position as possible here, the Somali regime was acutely aware that the closer and more explicit its dependence upon Russia, the more complicated and less rewarding its links with the right-wing, oil-rich Arab states. Then there was the question of Chinese aid and interests which, again, were not limited to Somalia but also embraced Ethiopia. In these circumstances, it was not surprising that Somalis of varying political conviction looked with envy at Kim Il Sung's remarkable success in performing such a delicate balancing act on the Sino-Russian tightrope.

Somalia's chairmanship of the Organization of African Unity in 1974 brought, at considerable local expense,[43] a significant increment of diplomatic glory and increased bargaining power and freedom to manoeuvre. Here Somalia attempted with some success to usurp the role previously played to good effect by the Sudan, as mediator between Black Africa and North African Islam. On a longer term basis, Islamic identity itself suggested another option, but one entailing the recalcitrant problem of reconciling Mohammed with Marx. If this posed delicate internal issues, it also raised equally acute and less easily controlled difficulties externally, and these compounded each other as had become increasingly obvious since Somalia joined the Arab League in 1974.

The obstacles encountered in assuaging Arab doubts about Scientific Socialism were thrown into sharp relief by the extraordinarily ill-timed public execution of a number of local men of religion at the height of the famine, when the Somali Foreign Secretary was desperately pleading for emergency aid in Arabia and the Gulf States. Their crime, which in the Arab point of view made the Somali treatment of it even more heinous, was that they had allegedly preached in the mosques against the President's plan, announced on Somali Women's Day (December 1974),[44] to grant women equal rights in inheritance and in other respects, all this being, of course, contrary to the traditionalist interpretation of Islamic Law. The execution of these Somali sheikhs astonished the Somali public and outraged many of the more conservative Arab governments. When, on the same day, two Somali air force MIGs crashed in Mogadishu after colliding in the air, many saw the hand of God. Others suggested that one plane, equipped with rockets, had set out to kill the President, while the other had been sent up to intercept it. No wonder that their urgent wooing of the Arabs, including the insertion of a regular page in Arabic in the daily *October Star*, met with little success and led to the indefinite postponement of the Arab League meeting which should have taken place in the summer of 1975 in Mogadishu, when the Somalis had hoped to secure sufficient aid to resettle the destitute nomads without calling on other sources. If this enabled the Russians to seize a further opportunity of demonstrating Siyad's dependence on them, it also encouraged him to show that he was master in his own house by locking up a number of leading pro-communist figures, including, for good measure, a kinsman. Those who wished to, could draw the convenient inference that these over-zealous socialists had urged the killing of the defiant sheikhs which was now seen to be a disastrous error of judgement.

If the outcome of the tempestuous union between Somali Islam and Scientific Socialism was still in doubt, what of the fate of that other major traditional constraint, clanship? Banned shortly after the *coup*, officially buried in April, 1971, and resurrected from time to time in President Siyad's numerous ominous warnings to backsliding neo-colonialists, Somali "tribalism," as we have seen, is clearly a perversely persistent force. If it did not continue to exist, it would scarcely have been necessary to wage such a relentless battle against it. The Marxist theory of power would suggest that we should start looking for this sinister anti-revolutionary cancer at the very heart of the state. When we do this we discover at once that, in common with its predecessor civilian cabinets, the SRC contained representatives of all the major lineage blocs in the country. The statistics in Table 1 comparing its composition with that of earlier Somali governments, speak for themselves.

Although it was an indictable offence to say so publicly, it was in terms of this wide representativeness that the SRC continued to be regarded by the majority of the Somali population. Even more revealing was the fact that in 1974 (and up to 1986), the clandestine code-name for the military regime was MOD. M stands for the patrilineage (Marrehaan) of the President; O for that of his mother—and this means the Ogaadeen people who live in the critically sensitive Ogaadeen border region of Ethiopia; and D for the Dulbahante, the lineage of his son-in-law, the head of the dreaded NSS. The implications were succinctly expressed in a popular explanatory verbal formula: "The Marrehan are drunk on power; the Dulbahante are drunk on pride; the Ogaadeen are drunk on powdered milk."

An earlier generation of Somali nationalists found it convenient to acknowledge the persisting significance of lineage ties by ostensibly consigning them to the past through the expedient of qualifying them with the English affix "ex-." Now, however, there was no place for this double-think and resort had to be made to other subterfuges which, as soon as they were reported by the NSS, become dangerously circumlocutory to utter. Thus one woman, I was told, the chief witness against a man arraigned on a charge of "tribalism" before a National Security Court, was pressed by the court chairman to declare the basis on which she could testify with authority against the accused. Eventually with great reluctance, she conceded that: *before the Revolution* she and the accused *had* belonged to the same "ex-." In such a minatory climate, ingenious Somali sophists developed a new idiom for expressing the regime's code-name MOD. They spoke of October 21 (=M), of October 22 (=O), and of October 23 (=D). This is at once a more comprehensive and flexible formula, since it can be extended to express a wider range of key groups in power, and to register changes in their precedence and relative influence at different times.

TABLE 1
Composition of Somali Governments by
major lineage blocs, 1960-75*

	1960[1]	1966[2]	1967[3]	1969[4]	1975[5]
Daarood	6	6	6	6	10
Hawiye	4	3	4	5	4
Digil and Rahanwiin	2	3	3	2	0
Dir	0	1	1	0	2
Isaaq	2	3	4	5	4
	14	16	18	18	20

*Cabinet Ministers only are included here and, after 1969, members of the Supreme Revolutionary Council.
1. The first administration of Somalia formed after independence in 1960, headed by premier Abdirashid Ali Shirmarke (Daarood). The President and nonexecutive head of state was Adan Abdulle Isman (Hawiye).
2. Government formed under the leadership of Abdirazaq Haji Husseyn (Daarood), Adan Abdulle Isman remaining President of the Republic.
3. Government formed by Mohamed Haji Ibrahim Igal (Isaaq) from the northern (ex-British) regions of the Republic. Dr. Abdirashid Ali Shirmarke (Daarood) had now become President.
4. Second Government formed by Mohamed Haji Ibrahim Igal following March 1969 elections, Dr. Abdirashid Ali Shirmarke remaining President.
5. Supreme Revolutionary Council, as of 1975, following various changes in composition since the military *coup* of October 1969. The

Council was officially dissolved in July 1976 with the formation of the Somali Socialist revolutionary Party. This had a Supreme Council of 73 members and a politburo of 5 (including the 3 SRC Vice-Presidents and the head of the National Security Service) presided over by the Head of State and Party Secretary General, General Mohamed Siyad Barre.For further developments before Siyad's collapse, see Lewis, 1988, pp. 226-267 and below, chapter 9.

Leavened as it was by the wider representativeness of the SRC, MOD was a powerful recipe for rule in Somalia. If it is part of the Somali political tradition that a man should depend for his ultimate security upon the loyalty of his agnates, as we have seen his mother's brothers' people are also very important allies. His maternal ties with the Ogaadeen gave the President a lever with which to modulate the level of clan pressure for the liberation of those Ogaadeen who languished under Ethiopian rule. Despite the acute vulnerability of Ethiopia during the internal turmoil and chaos of 1974-5, General Siyad's apparent reluctance to take this desperate course suggested that he set more store by staying at home to lead the Revolution there than by engaging in uncertain adventures on Somalia's borders. Evidence of the pressure to which this tie also, however, made him subject, was indicated by reports current in late 1975 of a threatened purge of high-placed Ogaadeen clansmen in the Siyad administration.

The Dulbahante symbol in the national monogram was perhaps even more immediately important. For the Dulbahante formed the bridge linking the two ex-colonial territories which in 1960 united to form the Somali Republic.[45] They thus combined the British and Italian colonial heritages which still produced competition between Anglophone and Italophone factions and played a far from negligible role in the political structure of modern Somalia. We should note in passing that, despite all the anti-colonial rhetoric, particularly marked since the *coup*, the Italian connection retained its importance and, as well as harking back to an older totalitarian tradition, was conveniently adaptable to both communist and anticommunist trends.

Hence, when we look closely at the composition of the SRC and the connections of key figures and interest-groups in General Siyad's government we find an inner core bound together by traditional loyalties and surrounded by an outer circle drawn from opposing groups carefully balanced so that none should gain an influence that could not be counteracted by others. And if for the moment ascendancy appeared to lie with the MOD trinity, those who were outside this charmed circle philosophically observed that others had their chance in the past and found comfort in the reflection that every dog has its day.

Socialism and Siyadism

It would be easy to exaggerate the importance of this infrastructure which was so different from the external appearance. But the fact that it was entirely suppressed —forbidden knowledge that was a kind of public secret — and that the general public *believed* these ties to be crucially significant is not something we can ignore. President Siyad did not disregard them and we should take our cue from him, noting the suspiciously strident tone of many of his public condemnations. Of course, the total political reality we are attempting to disclose was more complicated than this. It is not simply a question of Marxist rhetoric at the surface level, and lineage ties underneath. The significant factions which jostled for power in the Somali hierarchy and sometimes acted independently, and in defiance of others, were not solely based on lineage. Doctrinal and ideological issues, Marxist and Islamic, entered the picture, as well as competition between the Italophone and Anglophone parties. The very fact that there were stern official warnings of the "theoretical confusion and hesitation [which occur] when demagogy takes over some of the Marxistically educated youth" indicate that ideology was, for some, a real issue, which, if pursued too enthusiastically, could have dangerous consequences. It is this audience that General Siyad addressed when he sternly announced that there was only one universal form of Scientific Socialism which was pragmatically adaptable to all conditions, including those of Islam. The General had understandably little patience with those who presumed to question his interpretation of the doctrine. As he contemptuously observed,[46] such slavish textbook ideologues miss the point when they "say that Comrade V. I. Lenin confiscated such and such property after the Great October Revolution; or in [the] 1940s Comrade Mao Tse-Tung did this and that in his country against the reactionary forces. These people are totally ignoring the historical context of the teachings of the great socialist thinkers. They recite quotations from the founders of scientific socialism out of their proper context." And woe betide them in Somalia he might have added. In a very different context, the same point was made by a young Somali Marxist intellectual who concluded a heated debate with a prominent French Marxist anthropologist with the uncompromising declaration: "I don't need Marx: Marx needs me!"

This of course requires some reformulation of the conventional Marxist dialectic of class struggle which, in its simplistic, literal form, as General Siyad forthrightly declared, had little relevance to the traditional Somali social structure. In the struggle to liberate the nation from the oppressive evils of ignorance, disease, and poverty the most intractable and pernicious enemy was not capitalism but tribalism. "Capitalism," as the President exclaimed in his 1974 May Day address, "has no power in our midst, none of its basic pillars are evident among us. The explosive arsenal is TRIBALISM, which benefits the reactionaries that care the least about the progress of their nation. I urge all Somalis to wage a war against tribalism and [to] spearhead the struggle against this social evil that is contrary to our unity and socialist belief, in order to enhance our future chances of social, economic and technical achievements."

What so far seemed to be generally accepted by the various factions — ideological and tribal — that are obliquely attacked in these and other public utterances was, paradoxically, the ultimate supremacy of General Siyad himself as the primary source of legitimate authority. In this sense his writ seemed unquestioned, although to judge from his often violent public denunciations it did not prevent nepotism and corruption amongst his senior colleagues.[47] Such charges, one might have thought, would have naturally been followed by exemplary punishments, but this does not always appear to have been the case. This, of course, would again be consistent with a fragmented power structure in which, within certain ill-defined and apparently shifting limits, factions with some degree of freedom of action pursued their own particularistic interests. Cynical interpreters might also say that the head of state found it convenient publicly to censure malpractices that he could not control or that enjoyed clandestine protection.

Particularly in such conditions of *Sturm und Drang*, there were traditional precedents for the kind of leadership General Siyad provided. Personal authority of this kind and on this scale has, however, in the past usually only been accorded to national religious heroes waging the holy war (*jihaad*) against the infidel. There are two outstanding examples of this tradition who are relevant here. The first is the great sixteenth-century Muslim leader, Ahmad Gran (1506-43) who nearly succeeded in permanently subjugating Ethiopia and whom some Somalis regarded as a direct lineal ancestor of the head of state.[48] The second is Siyad's maternal relative (who was also connected by marriage to the Dulbahante), Sayyid Mohamed 'Abdille Hassan, the famous "Mad Mullah" who led the remarkably successful guerrilla war against the British, Ethiopian, and Italian usurpers between 1900 and 1920.[49]

The charisma of these two great heroes, which General Siyad sought subtly to subsume and appropriate, drove him constantly to present himself as a perennial crusader in the endless struggle against all

Somalia's foes. In this fashion, the lay and the religious (which Somali, traditionally, strictly distinguish in their opposition between "man of God" and "warrior") merged in the reverse direction as General Siyad proclaimed himself the divinely guided leader of his people. No wonder some Somalis said, under their breath, that Somali Socialism was a religion. No wonder either that religion should have been such a sensitive issue and one directly touching the legitimacy of a leader who sought to transform his secular uniform into the glorious raiment of those who fight in the army of the Lord.

Life in Somalia was indeed a battle in which victory could only be achieved through the heroic efforts of the rightly guided savior of the nation. Not only did natural calamities such as the 1974/75 drought and the government's response to it confirm this, but so did internal acts of treachery within the state. As the head of State's speeches incessantly reiterated and as the arbitrary arrests and unpredictable rehabilitations of his subjects confirmed, the state was filled with potential adversaries, dedicated to the destruction of socialism. As the General himself proclaimed: socialism could not exist without opposition which must be overcome by a ceaseless struggle for victory. In this war it was General Siyad who defined the enemy and kept the battle score. Thus though Lenin, Mao Tse-Tung and Kim Il Sung all had their place[50] in the homespun philosophy of development and power that General Siyad and his coterie had constructed, the local political realities suggested that Scientific Siyadism might be an apt description for what was done in Somalia in the name of Scientific Socialism.[51] Certainly whether one looks at it from an economic or political point of view, socialism was a means rather than an end.

The Death of Tribalism?

Since they were elected, however fraudulently, and because they relied on public support, the previous civilian politicians were ultimately dependent upon the loyalty of their clan and lineage kinsmen whose interests and demands they could not totally ignore. Lineage ties no longer had this official franchise. As long as he could safely control the "means of destruction" (to borrow Jack Goody's pithy phrase), with loyal servants in key positions to do his bidding, General Siyad could theoretically disregard traditional lineage loyalties. However the evidence we have reviewed indicates that, despite the official campaign against "tribalism" (which may have had its roots in a serious endeavour to promote national solidarity), clan and lineage ties still carried a high political charge, not least within the SRC and in the innermost sanctum of the

President's coterie.

More generally, while the public had good reason to know that it could be extremely dangerous to be seen to press lineage claims for position or profit, it was still in these terms that the government's representativeness was ultimately assessed. How could it be otherwise when the majority of the population were pastoral nomads whose whole social structure was based on the segmentary lineage system described in earlier chapters? It would be unrealistic in the extreme to suppose that, even with the help of the drought, this traditional order could have been drastically transformed by the 1975 rural development campaign. Moreover, while many of the measures we have mentioned (the official abolition of blood-money, and bridewealth, the substitution of orientation centers for segmentary sociability, etc.) discouraged these traditional forces, other factors worked in the opposite direction. So for instance, before the 1974 drought, state rent control in the towns encouraged businessmen and civil servants to invest in livestock cared for by their kin in the interior. Tribalism in its special Somali lineage version maintained much more than a mere residual presence. Indeed, thriving, as President Siyad rightly acknowledged,[52] on insecurity in these uncertain political conditions it waited in the wings, ready for emergencies and sudden changes of political fortune which could come at any moment. As I discovered in 1962,[53] people of northern extraction settled among the southern cultivating Somali for generations and absorbed in local tribes there, had not forgotten their original lineage genealogies. This bespeaks remarkable powers of endurance.

Thus, while in comparison with feudalist Ethiopia, Somalia scarcely offered propitious conditions for a genuine socialist revolution, its traditional institutions appeared to present more refractory and challenging obstacles to radical change than those across the border. It is not too far-fetched to suggest that the direction of transformation from anarchic democracy to a monolithic militarism was actually in the reverse direction, and brought the military power structure of Somalia in some respects closer to that of the *ancien régime* in Ethiopia. There were also, perhaps, significant analogies with the pre-revolutionary Chinese form of oriental despotism, where, as Maurice Freedman elegantly puts it, "Government existed, but its political and legal abstentions promoted self-help. Lineages depended on one another,... and they might make common cause in the face of a common danger..."[54] And if we invert Wittfogel's famous "hydraulic hypothesis" connecting centralized despotism with irrigation, further confirmation of this oriental association might be found in the very understandable enthusiasm of the Siyad regime for vast irrigation schemes. Thus while General Siyad in part recalled an older African tradition, in modern Somalia, Kim Il Sung was not entirely a red herring.

Notes:

1. K. Gough, 'New Proposals for Anthropologists', *Current Anthropology*, vol. 9, no. 5 (December 1968), pp. 391 ff.
2. Serious discussion of this issue is conspicuously absent in such symposia as T. Asad (ed.), *Anthropology and the Colonial Encounter* (London: Ithaca Press, 1973); D. Hymes (ed.), *Reinventing Anthropology* (New York: Vintage Books, 1974); and M. Bloch (ed.), *Marxist Analyses and Social Anthropology* (London: Malaby, 1975).
3. This chapter which draws on the results of my earlier research in Somalia (principally in 1955-7, 1962, and 1964) relies for recent information on three short visits made since 1969, the last and longest in the summer of 1974 when, under the auspices of the British Academy, I was able to spend two months travelling widely in Somalia. I acknowledge my debt to the Academy and to the Somali Government for its generous hospitality.
4. This timing is largely fortuitous since the *coup* was precipitated by the apparently unconnected (and unexpected) murder of the previous civilian President on 15 October 1969. It should also be noted that the five points on the Somali national star represent the five Somali territories (see below) and have no relation other than coincidence to counterparts elsewhere. For a fuller account of the precipitants of the *coup*, see I. M. Lewis, 'The Politics of the 1969 Somali Coup', *Journal of Modern African Studies*, vol. 10, no. 3 (1972), pp 383-408; see also Payton 1980.
5. Somalia, Ministry of Information and National Guidance, *My Country and My People: Selected Speeches of Jaale Major General Mohammed Siyad Barre*(Mogadishu: State Printing Agency, 1974), p. 284.
6. *Ibid.*, p. 83.
7. *Ibid*, p 75
8. Although he had numerous advisers, who helped to prepare major policy speeches, the President frequently spoke without notes.
9. The term *hanti-wadaagga* was invented by announcers on the British Broadcasting Corporation Somali programme in the late 1950s to refer to communism.
10. This term was in circulation in the mid-1950s in the then British Somaliland Protectorate where the expatriate administration strongly encouraged self-help schemes for school construction, farming and other development projects. The booklet prepared on the subject by the Somali Ministry of Information for the Organization of African Unity conference in Mogadishu of June 1974 points out that self-help policies were also applied in the Soviet Republic, China, and North Korea.
11. Here the guiding slogan was: 'Tribalism divides, Socialism unites.'
12. This term replaced the Arabic loan-word *tawri* which was used initially, but subsequently discarded, partly because it can mean revolution in the sense of circular movement, and also suggests an upsurge which may later collapse.

Ka'aan has none of these negative connotations. It suggests a relentless force whose progress can neither be arrested nor deflected.

13. Literally, 'The Good Leader'. In describing the aims and objectives of the Somali revolutionary regime, I have deliberately used officially current words and phrases to give as vivid an impression as possible of the political rhetoric. This is how the leaders of the regime saw and described their aims.

14. Unlike the ex-Red Army Major, Kim Il Sung, General Siyad had no official communist background. He served as a police inspector during the British Military Administration of Somalia (1940-50) and received most of his subsequent military training (including courses in politics and administration) under the Italians. See Jama' 'Umar 'Ise, *Thawra 21 Uktuubir: Asbaaabuhaa, Adhaafuhaa, munjazaatuhaa (The Revolution of 21 October: Its Causes, Its Objectives, Its Achievements)* (Mogadishu: State Printing Agency, 1972) pp. 57-8.

15. *Khudbadihii Madaxweynaha — G SK-Ee Soomaaliya, Jaalle Siyad,* 1969-1973 (Mogadishu: State Printing Agency, 1973).

16. The nomads make up approximately three-quarters of Somalia's population of c. 5,000,000. For a detailed account of their uncentralised traditional political system and its connections with the old party system in Somalia, see I. M. Lewis *A Pastoral Democracy* (London: Oxford University Press for the International African Institute, 1961).

17. These three missing communities were symbolized in the Somali Star, the national emblem, whose two remaining points represented the former British and Italian Somalilands united in the Somali state.

18. In the reorganization of December 1974 (see p. below), however, this post was allocated to the police commandant who was not a member of the SRC. Many would interpret this as a move sideways.

19. Reportedly released in the general amnesty issued in October 1975 on the occasion of the celebration of the Sixth Anniversary of the Revolution.

20. An interesting account of the ideological disputes within the SRC, and the conflict between 'pro- and anti-Western' factions which were contributory factors in these events is offered by the Italian communist journalist Luigi Pestalozza, *Somalia, Cronaca della Rivoluzione* (Bari: Dedalo Libri, 1973), p. 141.

21. The head of state was, naturally, ultimately commander in chief of the armed forces immediate responsibility, however, lying with the secretary of state, General Mohamed Ali Samanter, who was reputed to be an undisguised atheist. It is noteworthy that there were a few older Generals of higher rank who were not members of the SRC.

22. Somalia, Ministry of Information and National Guidance, *Our Revolutionary Education* (Mogadishu: State Printing Agency, 1974), p. 40.

23. This symbol is identical to that which appeared mysteriously in 1974 in the map symbolizing national unity adopted by the Armed Forces movement in Ethiopia.

24. See below.

25. *My Country and My People,* p.270.

26. For some information on these topics in the agricultural areas of the north-

west, see A.I. Samatar, 1989.

27. Before the coup, the state held the controlling share in this enterprise.

28. Further nationalization measures were announced in October 1975, affecting the import and distribution of vehicles, machinery, textiles, and household utensils.

29. See P. Kuprijanov, 'Somalian Village: Social and Economic Transformations', *Proceedings, Third International Congress of Africanists* (Addis Ababa, 1973)

30. For comparative purposes it is interesting to note that in the ordinary budget of 1975 for approximately £30,000,000, defence expenditure was costed at £7,500,000.

31. Somalia, Ministry of Information and Guidance, *Somalia's Self-help for Self-reliance* (Mogadishu: State Printing Agency, 1974).

32. Published in *New Era* (Mogadishu), March 1974, no. 13, pp. 9-18.

33. This is the most succinct definition of nationalism usually proposed by political scientists. See e,g, K. Minogue, Nationalism (London : Batsford, 1967), p. 154. See also Gellner, 1983.

34. This item was included along with other notable achievements of the revolution in General Siyad's opening address to a seminar at the People's Hall, Mogadishu, on 20 October 1975.

35. See I. M. Lewis, *Abaar: The Somali Drought* (London: International African Institute, 1975); and Somalia, Directorate of Planning and Co-ordination, *Revised Programme of Assistance Required to the Drought Stricken Areas of Somalia* (Mogadishu: State Printing Agency, 1975).

36. The original title of 'Rural Prosperity Drive' was quickly changed in view of the drought to the more neutral 'Rural Development Campaign'.

37. See chapter 6.

38. Cf. I. M. Lewis, 'The Dynamics of Nomadism: Prospects for Sedentarization and Social Change', in T. Monod (ed.), *Pastoralism in Tropical Africa* (London: Oxford University Press for the International African Institute, 1975), pp 426-42.

39. For a detailed description of the form and responsibilities of the new Committees, see *New Era* (Mogadishu), January 1975, pp. 11-12.

40. Formerly known as French Somaliland, this tiny overseas territory has a local population of some 120,000, divided between the Issa and other Somali and the currently, politically dominant Afar. See V. Thompson and R. Adloff, *Djibouti and the Horn of Africa* (Stanford: Stanford University Press, 1968).

41. For an apparently well-informed but obviously anti-communist assessment of these see B. Crozier, *The Soviet Presence in Somalia, Conflict Studies*, no. 54, February 1975.

42. Somalia was reputed to possess the finest military force in sub-Saharan Africa, fifth in manpower after Nigeria, Ethiopia, Zaire, and Uganda, but with much superior equipment: including over 200 tanks, 300 armoured cars and personnel carriers, 200 heavy guns and SAM missiles. The air force was reported to have 60 MIG fighters and a squadron of Ilyushin light bombers.

43. This included the purchase of a fleet of Mercedes Benz limousines to ferry the visiting heads of state about in the comfort to which they were accus-

tomed. A Somali intellectual commenting on this and other extravagances, pointed out to me that there is such a thing as Gross National Pride as well as Gross National Product.

44. The speech is published in *New Era* (Mogadishu), January 1975.

45. i.e. the British Somaliland Protectorate, and the Italian administered (and former Italian colony) of Somalia, under United Nations trusteeship from 1950 to 1960. For the history of these territories and the legacy they bring to the political life of Somalia, see Lewis, 1988.

46. In a speech to the 6th Orientation Course at Halane on 9 June 1972. See *My Country and My People*, p. 83. See also, A. S. Abdi, 1981.

47. Some of whom, like their counterparts in other uncertain political conditions elsewhere, are alleged to have had numbered Swiss bank accounts. I have reason to believe that some of the allegations of this kind are well-founded.

48. Here Somalis usually confuse two historically separate individuals, the great Muslim champion, the Imam Ahmad 'the left-handed' as the chroniclers of the period and present-day Ethiopians and Somalis alike call him, and his Somali namesake and lieutenant, a valiant battle-leader of the Muslim forces. The latter is not referred to in the chronicles as *Imam*. See Lewis 1992, p. 187.

49. Sayyid Mohamed is also immortalized as the greatest poet in recent Somali history. For a brief account of his life and nationalist struggle, see Lewis, 1988, pp. 63-91

50. Basil Davidson's wistful proposal that we should also see the influence here of the MPLA freedom fighters in Angola seems rather implausible. See, e.g. B. Davidson, Somalia: Towards Socialism, *Race and Class*, Vol. 17, no. I (Summer 1975), pp. 19-38. His utopian assessment of modern trends in Somalia was also, in my opinion, optimistic, to say the least. For a better-informed assessment see A.I. Samatar, 1988.

51. *Cf.* for an interesting Marxist critique reaching similar conclusions, A. Wolczyk, 'Il "socialismo" Somalo: un industria per il potere', *Concretezza* (Rome, Jan 1972), pp. 23-6.

52. Speech of 19 April 1971 in *My Country and My People*, p.177. For the same interpretation of the role of lineage, cf. Lewis, 1961, p. 302. The widespread insecurity and lack of food resources associated with the collapse of Siyad's rule in 1991 prompted what is probably the most vicious upsurge of clan loyalties in the history of the Somali people. See Chapter 9.

53. Lewis, 1969, p. 68. See also Chapter 6.

54. M. Freedman, *Chinese Lineage and Society: Fukein and Kwangtang* (London: Athlone Press, 1966), pp 114-115

Chapter VIII

THE RISE OF THE SOMALI
NATIONAL MOVEMENT:
A CASE STUDY IN CLAN POLITICS[1]

Precipitants to dissidence in Northern Somalia

In December, 1961, barely six months after its union with ex-Italian Somalia to form the independent Somali Republic, a short-lived military coup sought unsuccessfully to restore the autonomous status of the Somaliland Protectorate (see Lewis, 1988, pp 173-178). Thus, the history of northern dissidence, partly reflecting conflict between the British (northern) anglophone colonial tradition and the Italian experience in the south, as well as clan differences, can be traced back virtually to the original act of union between the two component states. This dissident strain was increasingly muted as northerners in general, and Isaaqis in particular, gained more and more economic and political power in the south culminating in securing the position of the premiership in 1967 and holding it until the military seized power in 1969. However, the tendency throughout this period to concentrate aid and trade in the south at the expense of the north gathered new momentum under the Daarood tyranny of Mohamed Siyad Barre and his regime of scientific socialism (as we have seen in Chapter 7). Isaaqis were not excluded from token positions in the Siyad power machine. This included an Isaaqi Vice-President and Foreign Minister, both of whom soon acquired a reputation for their fulsome contributions to the Siyad personality cult which became such a marked feature of Marrehaan rule and which northern Somalis in general found particularly distasteful.

The 1974/75 drought and famine (mainly concentrated in the north) contributed to unrest in that region, particularly since the government's relief measures (despite advice to the contrary) included the movement of drought-stricken northerners (amongst them Isaaq clansmen) and their relocation in cultivating and fishing settlements in the south. Northerners had already begun seeking work as immigrants in the Gulf States in the late 1960s and early 70's, but the volume of this "muscle-drain" swelled greatly after the drought as new immigrants joined kin already established there (see Chapter 5, page 122). The North thus became further drawn into the wider market economy to a greater extent than the south, and its expanded involvement in exports (livestock) and imports made it correspondingly vulnerable to government interference through control of trading licenses.

Further, more powerful political forces, leading eventually to armed insurrection, were unleashed by the 1977/78 war between Somalia and Ethiopia over the issue of self-determination for the Ogaadeen (Daarood) Somalis in eastern Ethiopia. In the initial stages when the Somalis were scoring dramatic victories against their traditional enemies, the Ogaadeen war engendered a high level of national solidarity in Somalia and General Siyad's regime was never more popular (see Lewis, 1988, pp 233-242). The ignominious defeat in 1978 and the consequent vast refugee influx of hundreds of thousands of Oromos as well as Daarood Somalis from the Ogaadeen (see Lewis, 1986,) prompted bitter recriminations, conducted characteristically along clan lines.

The first public reaction was an unsuccessful coup launched in April 1978 by a group of military officers predominantly of the Majeerteen clan (Daarood) which had tended to dominate Somalia's civilian governments (see Lewis, 1988, pp 166-204) and whose leading politicians had been nursing a grievance since Siyad assumed control. After this coup against Siyad failed, those of its leaders who had escaped arrest regrouped and combined with several other small leftist movements to form a guerilla group which eventually (October, 1981) took the name, Somali Salvation Democratic Front. This organization made its operational headquarters in Ethiopia (cf Compagnon, 1990, pp 30-31, Galaydh, 1990, p.20), whence, with Ethiopian support, it launched initially successful attacks on Somali installations across the international frontier. Although the SSDF at first included Isaaq and Hawiye members on its executive council, the movement increasingly acquired a Majeerteen character and by 1992 had become synonymous with the political structure of the Majeerteen autonomous region.

Dissension within the ruling Daarood clan-family in Siyad's Somalia spawned the SSDF. Hard on the heels of this rebellious current, the Isaaq clansmen of the former British Protectorate began to seek an appropriate means to express their opposition to Siyad's regime. Initially, immediately after the Majeerteen coup, Siyad seems (characteristically) to have briefly tried to court the Isaaq, encouraging discussions between the representatives of his clan and theirs. However, this did not last long, as the Isaaq became victims of oppressive military rule and clan discrimination in the north to the benefit of the Ogaadeeni (Daarood) and Oromo refugees who had been imposed on their country in such huge numbers. Relations between these refugees and the local (mainly Isaaq) residents were understandably complicated, particularly in view of the long history of confrontation and conflict over grazing and water in the Northern Ogaadeen between pastoralists of these rival clans. Housed initially in huge camps containing up to 60,000 people, the refugees were totally dependent on international relief delivered through the United Nations High Commission for Refugees whose operations became an important economic resource for the Somali regime and another strand in the multi-sector national economy.

At the same time, the Ogaadeen factor in Somali politics acquired new impetus now inside Somalia. The army started illegally recruiting Ogaadeenis and Oromos from the refugee camps as well as employing the (Ogaadeen) Western Somali Liberation Front (cf Lewis, 1980) as a subsidiary militia to maintain control of northern Somalia. Isaaq civilians were regularly harassed by the WSLF, especially in the border area. In September 1979 an Isaaq delegation went to see President Siyad, complaining of these and other abuses. Isaaq officers started deserting from the army and in 1980 established a militia called *Afraad* ("fourth unit") which was formally part of the WSLF but which was also intended by its founders to counter WSLF pressure on the Isaaq population - fighting between the Isaaq *Afraad* and WSLF proper soon broke out. In 1980 Siyad appointed one of his clansmen, General Mohamed Hashi Gani, military commander of the northern regions. Gani quickly deprived the Isaaq *Afraad* of weapons and transferred the unit from the border area where it was in conflict with the WSLF. The process of Daarood colonization of the north including seizure of property and economic favoritism at Isaaq expense, greatly intensified under Gani's brutal rule, with the systematic application of all the apparatuses of state repression which increased in number and scope after the formation of the Isaaq-based Somali National Movement in April 1981. The regime also created armed militias among the neighbouring non-Isaaq clans (chiefly the Daarood: Dulbahante; and Dir: Gadabuursi) which were encouraged to attack Isaaq nomads.

The creation of the Somali National Movement belatedly responded to the growing sense of Isaaqi alienation; alienation reflecting the forces stirred up by the disastrous Ogaadeen war, the friction between government-backed Daarood refugees and Isaaqi citizens, economic and political discrimination, and the almost complete absence of serious development activity in the north. As we shall see, once the SNM had been formed, its engagement in military and other activities provoked correspondingly savage reprisals by Siyad's forces on the Isaaqi civilians in Northern Somalia who were treated as hostages. This, in turn, further contributed to the movement's wide popularity and ultimate success. It also brought more and more Isaaqis to seek political asylum abroad - not least in Britain. The SNM was thus, from the beginning, a typical reactive Somali clan-based organization responding to hostile external pressures and seeking to protect and forward clan interests. It owed its origins primarily to the strength of clan ties in the migrant Somali communities in Saudi Arabia and in Britain. Inter-clan behavior in these migrant communities was closely linked with the clan political situation in Somalia and, of course, could also have repercussions there (cf El-Solh, 1991, p 545). Thus, according to the wider political situation, the SNM, at times sought to widen its membership to appeal to other clans.

Before we consider how the two major expatriate Isaaq communities contributed to the establishment of the movement we should not forget that, despite their oppression and the impossibility of open political activity, the home-based Isaaq community also played a role from the beginning. This included some of those Isaaq army and police officers who had been transferred by the regime to Mogadishu, as well as a few intellectuals, ministers, assistant ministers, and high ranking government officials. These people were not happy with the regime but could not leave the country, being effectively prisoners. Some Isaaq elders and educated people who had been forgotten by the government in the towns of Hargeisa, Berbera and Burao, also made a significant contribution. All the other educated Isaaq had been transferred to the south.

Despite the distances between the home and overseas Isaaq communities, and the oppressive censorship and communications control exercised (not particularly efficiently) by Siyad's functionaries, people were able to keep in touch with each other, directly or indirectly, and news of developments within and outside Somalia was regularly broadcast on the Somali service of the BBC and by other foreign radio stations which were widely listened to. The importance attached to these services, particularly during the Siyad dictatorship, was forcefully underlined in 1981, when the British government was considering abolishing the BBC Somali program, by a delegation which went to protest to the British embassy. The delegates told the ambassador that they understood the need for economies, but if Britain was to seek savings in this area they would prefer that the embassy were closed and the BBC Somali service saved. News as well as messages and political commentary in the form of innocent-seeming love poems recorded on cassettes which greatly extended the scope of Somali oral culture (cf Lewis, 1986), also helped people in the different communities to share information notwithstanding surveillance. The clan-based remittance system (see Chapter 5) also encouraged the maintenance of effective contact between the migrants and their kinsmen at home, and expanding air-services to the Gulf facilitated mobility despite the constraints imposed by the Government through passport control. Last, but not least, and again despite government surveillance, abundant use of the telephone was made by overseas clansmen to maintain contact and guardedly exchange news with their kin in Somalia.

The Saudi Arabian Group 1977-1981

As early as 1977 the Somalis who were in Jedda in Saudi Arabia started collecting money in order to print a newspaper. The man behind this effort was Mohamed Hashi Ilmi, a former engineer and businessman from the Habar Awal Isaaq clan. Mohamed Hashi Ilmi later became one of the founders of the SNM. The group held their meetings in the house of another prominent figure, Omar Meygag Samatar. It was believed that among the people attending the meetings were some who reported to the Somali embassy in Saudi Arabia. Osman Ahmed Hassan of the Habar Tol Ja'lo Isaaq clan, who was a senior member, became chairman.[2]

Under Osman Ahmed Hassan's chairmanship, the Saudi Arabia group took its first steps towards something more concrete and political. In the beginning, the members could not agree on whether to create a formal political party or a looser political organization. There was also some discussion about creating a base in Ethiopia (like the SSDF) but many people were against that.

In 1979 most of the members left the group. Only six remained and held their discussions in a Yemeni coffee-shop in Jedda. In 1980, how-ever, the group was revived when those in Jedda discovered that there were other groups working along similar lines in Riyad, Dahran and Khobar.[3] Every three months the groups from Jedda, Riyad, Dahran and Hober held common meetings. Little by little the number of members increased and a new chairman and secretary were elected.

Mohamed 'Ali Farah, a Habar Tol Ja'lo, and a well known per-sonality, was elected as the first chairman of the united group. He was a former member of the northern Legislative Council, (belonging to the Somaliland National League), and, after independence, of the Somali

National Assembly. In the Saudi group, following him the position of chairman was held by Ahmed Mohamed Farah and then by a man of the Habar Yuunis clan. The meetings of the group were held in the house of Ismail Mahamud Hurre Buba, Idegale, a Somali businessman, when his family was not there.[4]

The majority of members[5] were Isaaq and it would be difficult to describe the group as other than an Isaaq organization. This is also apparent from the way funds were collected for various purposes. When, for example, the group decided to collect 100,000 rials (approximately $30,000) for the printing of a newspaper the whole amount was collected on a "tribal basis." That meant that each Isaaq clan in the Gulf contributed a set amount of money. (According to Mohamed Ali Farah, the sum was $50,000 and was collected by clansmen resident in all the Arab countries).

The group subsequently decided to widen its membership and tried to recruit from the Dulbahante clan (Daarood) and the Gadabuursi clan (Dir). Prominent Dulbahante men who were approached included Ahmed Mohamed 'Abdille Sakhran and the clan leader Garad 'Ali Jamaa. In the end, through no fault of their own, it transpired that they could not carry their clansmen with them. The same applied to the Gadabuursi.

Initially, money was collected from noted individuals who could afford a contribution of 1,000 rials each. Most of the money was needed for paying people to become full-time representatives of the group to travel abroad in order to organize a political party. They wanted also to give their families at home an allowance which would enable them to live comfortably. Additionally, from June, 1980 the Saudi group sent money to England to support the SNM occasional newspaper "Somalia Uncensored" (first issue June, 1981). More than once, apparently, they sent 10,000 rials. As we have seen, the group had members in Riyad, Hober and other places. However, in reality it was mainly the people from Jedda who were most involved in the group's activities.

According to its first Chairman Mohamed Ali Farah, the Saudi group possessed a semi-official name from its early days (probably 1979): it was known as the "Somali Islamic Democratic Movement". In 1980, however, they held a small congress and decided to change the name. The word "democratic" worried those who had communist or socialist leanings and raised difficulties in its combination with the word "Islamic". As one source suggested, since all the members of the group were Muslims there was no reason for the word Islamic to be included in the name.

This suggests two things: First, in Saudi Arabia among the Isaaq

people there must have been a number of people of socialist or communist orientation who appeared to have had a say in the way things were
organized. Others, however, were evidently more or less solidly Islamic.
There was thus, virtually from the beginning, a tension between secular and Islamic ideals, and as will be seen, some members of the SNM
wanted it to have a strongly and explicitly Islamic character.

The second point to note here is the existence of the name
"Somali (National) Movement" in Saudi Arabia since 1979-80, a year
before the official launching of the movement in London. This implies
that, on this version of events, the SNM was conceived in Saudi Arabia
by Isaaq ex-patriates, was born there as a result of a congress, but for practical and logistical reasons was launched in London the following year.
Indeed, this is what Mohamed Ali Farah argued.

He maintained specifically that at the 1980 congress it was decided
that a number of people should abandon their jobs and dedicate their
energy and time to the SNM. These people were to travel to London to
organize the movement there. England was suggested as the place where
the movement could come out publicly because it was a democratic
country in which political activists could work unimpeded.[6] In Saudi
Arabia the launching of any political movement or association was
against the law. A second reason was that the migrant Somali community in Saudi Arabia could not openly declare that they wanted to overthrow the government of a member state of the Arab League which was
substantially supported by Saudi Arabia - despite differences from time
to time between the Saudis and Siyad, particularly over "Somali
Scientific Socialism" (see Chapter 7).

The group wanted Osman Ahmed Hassan (Habar Tol Ja'lo) to go
to England and become the chairman of the party. At that time, as we
will see shortly, the first discussions in London between the Saudi group
and the London group had borne fruit. Osman Ahmed Hassan refused
to become chairman. He argued that there are two types of people: the
ruthless and the democratic. A party should have a ruthless leader and
Osman Ahmed Hassan did not want to become known among his
friends as the man who started purging people and party enemies.[7]

The other candidate whom the group thought of was Hassan Adan
Wadadid (Habar Yuunis), but according to the information the group
received from London, he refused. In any case, things went ahead as
planned and in the early months of 1981 a number of Saudi group delegates went to London for discussions with their compatriots there who
were working along similar lines. The names of the delegates were 'Abd
al-Salaan Yassin, Ahmed Ismail 'Abdi Duksi, Hassan Adan Wadadid
and Mohamed Hashi Ilmi.

The London Group 1979-1981

Omar Ilmi Dihoud of the Arab clan had studied in the Medical Military Academy of Leningrad and was a colonel in the national army. His relationship with the Somali government was not very cordial: he was eventually accused of being anti-socialist and anti-Marxist after showing a lack of enthusiasm for the Soviet presence in Somalia. In 1979 when Omar Ilmi Dihoud went to England for medical treatment, he was soon drawn into politics and encouraged the few Somali intellectuals who were at that time in London to form a political organization. Among these were Hassan 'Isa Jamaa (Arab clan) who was working for the Somali Section of the BBC, Ismail Mahmud Samatar (Habar Tol Ja'lo) who was doing a course in engineering and 'Ali Jamaa Timir, a man who very quickly disappeared, Omar Ilmi Dihoud, Ismail Mahmud Samatar (Habar Tol Ja'lo), Ahmed Mohamed Sufi (Habar Yuunis) and 'Abd al-Rahman 'Abd al-Qadir Farah (Habar Yuunis) held regular meetings every Wednesday in the Marlborough Pub beside London University. Their aim was to establish a form of political grouping.

Before that, the Somalis in London who opposed the regime did not adopt radical measures. For example, in 1978-9, through its embassy in London, the government was collecting money supposedly to assist the Somali refugees from Ethiopia. As the people were in general against the government, however, they were reluctant to contribute to this effort which, of course, was bringing Daarood immigrants into Isaaq territory. The embassy called for meetings with the students in order to discuss the problem. The ambassador argued that he was asking for support for the refugees, not the government. The matter was left there.

In 1979-80 the only sizeable, formally organized body of Somalis in London was the Somali Student Union of the United Kingdom whose general secretary was Ismail Mahmud Warsama. In line with the sweeping political changes of the period that were shaking the Islamic world (the Iranian revolution, etc.), the Somali students wanted to address their own local problems and the problems of their country. The Union held several meetings in the University of London Union, the YMCA, the Africa Center and other places. These meetings were not very productive however.

One reason was that some of the students were pro-government, so that any kind of collective political action that was conceived and put into practice was bound to be of a vague and indecisive character. As Ahmed Mohamed Sufi, a member of the Union and, later on, an SNM activist in England argued, the Somali Student Union of the United Kingdom was not the political cradle of what later came to be the Somali

National Movement.

Contrary to the view that the Student Union was the only organized body of Somalis in London in the period 1979-80, Omar Ilmi Dihoud records that in March 1979 the few intellectuals of the Marlborough Pub formed the Somali National Democratic Party which soon changed its name to Somali National Party (SNUP). The members agreed to pay a weekly contribution of one pound. SNUP was particularly interested in the seamen who formed the backbone of the Somali community in the United Kingdom. The seamen were regarded as elders, hence the importance of their consent and support. Omar Ilmi Dihoud was appointed as co-ordinator of the party's activities with the special task of contacting all the Somalis who were living in the United Kingdom. For that reason he visited Sheffield, Cardiff, Manchester and Liverpool where he tried to persuade his Somali compatriots to share his condemnation of the abuse of power by the Daarood clan family.

At this time, a new Somali ambassador was appointed in London. This was Mohamed Jamaa who belonged to the Dulbahante clan of the Daarood clan family. (He replaced Mohamed Adan Ghaibi, another Dulbahante, who was appointed ambassador to the United Nations). Mohamed Jamaa had a good reputation and while serving in Iraq was supposed to have been very helpful to the Somalis there. However, Omar Ilmi Dihoud was suspicious of the new ambassador and pointed out that he had worked as a diplomat for eight years without formal qualifications. It was then decided that SNUP would not have any meetings with the embassy. The party sent Ali Hire and Mohamed Huri to the seamen to persuade them not to attend any meetings. Indeed, when the embassy called for a meeting in the East End of London, where the Somali community was concentrated, only ten people turned up. The party stepped up its efforts. A second meeting called by the embassy was attended by a mere fifteen people. At that point, the SNUP leaders felt that they had gained the support of the people.

At a public meeting that the party organized at Toynbee Hall after these incidents, a member of the seamen's community showed the assembled people a letter he had received from the embassy informing him of the cost of renewing Somali passports which had risen to £71. Passports were very important to the Somali seamen who were living in England: without passports they could neither work, nor return to Somalia. Seventy-one pounds was an amount the seamen could not easily afford. This passport problem provided an issue for the students in general and the few Somali intellectuals to take up and develop into a more generalized campaign against the government.

The SNUP hastened to exploit the situation in the best possible way. Some of the members, however, were afraid of coming out and talking openly against the regime. Omar Ilmi Dihoud decided to push ahead. The SNUP thus called for a meeting on May 15, 1980, with the elders of the Somali community of London. On that occasion Omar Ilmi Dihoud openly accused Siyad Barre's government of promoting the interests of one clan family only, the Daarood. He declared that the people had reached the limits of their patience and that an opposition political organization should be formed. What Omar Ilmi Dihoud had in mind was an organization of a more political character than the SNUP. At first sight, this might appear strange since, after all, the SNUP, was a party formed by people who opposed the regime. As we will see shortly, later events and information from a number of sources will explain this paradox and provide a deeper understanding of the dynamics of the period that led to the formation and launching of the SNM.

The SNUP proposal to form a political organization was adopted by the elders, and the Somali-London Association was formed on May 15, 1980. (According to some informants the Somali-London Association was called the Somali Community Association). Before proceeding, we should consider here the view of another person who was involved in the formation of the Somali-London Association, Ismail Mahmud Warsama. He maintains that at that time, besides the Somali Student Union, there was no other organization that included a sizeable part of the London Somali community. This assertion seems to suggest that SNUP was not a real party with an internal structure and a following. Indeed SNUP was presented by Omar Ilmi Dihoud, its founding father, as a four or five member organization. It might thus be more accurate to regard the SNUP not, as a political party, but as a small group of intellectuals who became the spearhead of every new organization or formation that led to the emergence of the SNM.

One could thus maintain that the only mass Somali organization that existed at that time (1979) in London was indeed the Somali Student Union. Under the organizing skills and ideological eagerness of the SNUP members, it became apparent that an organization of broader structure than the Somali Student Union was needed in order to respond to the problems of the Somalis in a more concrete and, ultimately, more political fashion. An organization that would include not only the students but the seamen and the elders of the community as a whole was needed. It is in this light that one should see Omar Ilmi Dihoud's plea for an organization of a more political character. The crux of the matter was the organic relation between the student-intellectuals on the one hand, and the seamen-elders on the other. Only if the latter were also involved could there be a political corpus in the Somali sense of the word.

For that reason the Somali-London Association (or Somali Community Association) was formed. The Association was organized as a political opposition group by those members of the Somali Student Union who were against the government, the community of seamen, and the members of SNUP. The central committee that was elected included five people from the seamen's community and four from the SNUP.[8]

The committee of the Association asked for an interview with the ambassador. At the meeting, the Association complained to the ambassador that the new price for passports was far too high and that another solution should be found. The ambassador replied that having a passport was a privilege, a gift from the government that cost only £71. He also expressed his disagreement with the formation of the Association which, he claimed, was against the government's laws and regulations. Concluding the meeting, the ambassador suggested that the Association should be disbanded and a joint committee of seamen and embassy staff formed in order to discuss any difficulties. When the Association delegates refused to accept his suggestions, the ambassador started threatening them and the meeting ended in dead-lock.

The interesting point about this meeting is that the Daarood members of the committee of the Somali-London Association did not turn up and so the ambassador was able to accuse the rest of being "tribalist" since they were all from the Isaaq clan-family. According to 'Abd al-Rahman 'Abd al-Qadir Farah, the embassy interview had been carefully prepared. In fact, after the meeting of the Somali-London Association at which it was decided to request an interview with the ambassador, the Daarood delegates had informed the Somali embassy about what the Association was planning. The ambassador then advised them not to turn up.

A week later, the non-Isaaq members of the central committee denounced the Somali-London Association because, according to Omar Ilmi Dihoud, the embassy refused to recognize it: it was openly against the government; and the majority of its members were Isaaq. Nevertheless, the Association decided: (i) to celebrate June 26, when the Isaaq-dominated Somaliland Protectorate achieved its independence from the British in 1960; (something that the government of Somalia always ignored) (ii) to form a political organization; (iii) to protest against the raising of the passport fees. Again, here we see as one of the objectives of political organization the formation of a political organization!

As a representative of the Somali-London Association, Omar Ilmi Dihoud went to Scotland Yard to ask for permission to protest against the Somali government. He did not raise the passport issue; he said that the Association wanted to protest against the Somali government because it was a Marxist government which permitted no freedom of choice and expression, no free elections, and blocked all the roads of trade. The Somali-London Association demanded a government owned by the people, not a government that owned the people. The Association also expressed its wish to have good relations with both East and West.

Scotland Yard asked for the passports of some of the Committee members of the Association, and after some time contacted them and gave them permission to demonstrate. The first to be contacted was Ismail Dube from the Habar Yuunis clan who informed Omar Ilmi Dihoud. A demonstration was planned for August 10 1980. The Association needed time to campaign for this and Omar Ilmi Dihoud spent much time and money travelling to Sheffield and other places to publicize the demonstration. Nur Ilmi, an ex-seaman, supported the Somali-London Association with a donation of £500. It should be pointed out here that the seamen in general were suspicious of the Somali-London Association activists. Because of the nature of their job, the seamen were associated with the Somali embassy or, rather, depended on the embassy which did its utmost to subvert the Association. At some point, the seamen thought that what the activists really wanted was to obtain permission to stay in England as political refugees. Nur Ilmi's role, then, was of the utmost importance as he had to explain to the seamen, that is, to the Somali expatriate community at large, that this was not the situation and win them over.

At the organizational level, the formation of the Somali-London Association did not end the experiments of the activists in creating something broader and "more political". As we have seen earlier, this was explicitly acknowledged as one of their aims. That meant the formation of an organization that could appeal to all the Somali communities in the United Kingdom: and could be presented as a political movement or party. This broadening of the framework would lead to a qualitative change to a more general, purposeful opposition movement directed against the regime in Somalia.

Even before the demonstration on August 10, 1980, some people wanted to elect a UK committee before taking any action. In effect, that meant postponing the demonstration. The former SNUP members who were members of the committee of the Association rejected that proposal arguing that joining the demonstration would reveal who was against the government so that people could later know whom to trust. Otherwise, they warned, spies from the embassy could attach themselves to the Association and destroy it from within. For its part, the embassy itself was trying very hard to persuade the various Somali communities to postpone the demonstration and elect a committee that could negotiate on all the existing problems with the ambassador. According to our informants, the embassy even offered money to the communities.

The situation in London must have caused some concern to President Siyad Barre's government in Somalia which decided to involve itself in a discreet but quite direct way. Mohamed Ahmed Silanyo from the Burao branch of the Habar Tol Ja'lo clan, (as were the majority of the sea-faring community), at that time minister of commerce, was given direct orders by Siyad Barre to dismantle the whole Somali-London Association. Consequently, when he came to London for medical treatment three weeks before it, he met with Somali ex-patriates and tried to persuade them not to participate in the demonstration.

Although he was a minister in Siyad Barre's government for many years, Mohamed Ahmed Silanyo had the reputation of opposing the regime from within the cabinet. He was believed not to be directly involved in any acts of violence or embezzlement, and in a curious way was able to satisfy both the government and the opposition. This ambiguity in his role enabled him to become chairman of the SNM in 1984. At the meeting with the seamen, Mohamed Ahmed Silanyo suggested that there were currents in Mogadishu against Siyad Barre and that a militant act like a demonstration could backfire. He thus urged them to change their minds. He failed and the demonstration took place as planned. Although it was quite small it was nevertheless an important event since it was the first bold, direct action by an organized body of Somali ex-patriates against their government. The organizers of the demonstration gave a number of interviews but not to the Somali section of the BBC because some of the Somalis who were working there were pro-government.

Then the embassy released a statement which our informants characterized as "stupid". The embassy claimed that the demonstration consisted of a few troublemakers and women and children, as if the women and children were not Somalis. In the end, even the Somali section of the BBC was obliged to ask the Association for an interview. In its own right, that development was very important, but at the same time it encouraged a premature sense of euphoria and prompted wishful thinking that the collapse of the regime was imminent. When the dust settled, the members of the Association realized that this was not the case. They understood that they were a small immigrant community far away from Somalia. Continuous demonstrations were not the solution. What kept them going, however, was their optimism and their hatred for the regime. At a practical level, something more was needed.

After the demonstration, the Somali-London Association held a congress in Liverpool on August 17, 1980 for all the United Kingdom Somali communities. There were about twenty delegates from the various communities. Under the auspices of the Somali-London Association, the London community, which was more militant than the others, was supposed to be the leader of the opposition. As was expected, the Somali embassy sent its own delegation from London who tried to insist that they were the true representatives of the Somali community in London and that the others were a bunch of irresponsible troublemakers. 'Abd al-Rahman 'Abd al-Qadir Farah gave a speech arguing that the Somali expatriates had nothing against the ambassador who, as a matter of fact, was a very good man. They were against the regime in Somalia, not against its functionaries in London. Responding, the ambassador (who was Dulbahante) accused them of being "tribalist" since the majority were Isaaq and maintained that they should forget about the problems of Somalia and concentrate on their problems in England.

The congress participants sided with the Somali-London Association delegates and expelled the embassy delegation. After that, they proceeded to form a new organization that was called the UK Somali Welfare Association.[9] In contrast to the Somali-London Association, the UK Somali Welfare Association was the first organization that brought together people from all the different Somali communities of the United Kingdom.

The chairman of the executive committee of the UK Somali Welfare Association was Said Farah of the Dulbahante, the same clan as the ambassador; Ahmed Mohamed Sufi (Isaaq - Habar Yuunis) was the general secretary. The fact that the chairman was not Isaaq suggests that until that time the London group, that is, the activists who were behind all the movements and organized the meetings and the demonstration, did not act in the name of the Isaaq clan-family only, although there may have been some scepticism and apprehension as to the probable success of a non-clan organization. In any case, as we were told, "nobody saw anything wrong with Said Farah's clan, but unfortunately he was not particularly sympathetic towards what we were doing and was trying to manipulate us".

Indeed, when the group decided to organize a second demonstration Said Farah refused to attend it.[10] In order to deal with the situation in a firm but non-confrontational way, Omar Ilmi Dihoud proposed that every member of the executive committee who refused to attend meetings or demonstrations twice, should be expelled from the committee.

Said Farah was not expelled but was officially ignored. Eventually he was replaced by Farah Jihad, an Isaaq from Birmingham. In any event, the chairman was a figure-head. Everything was organized by the general secretary, Ahmed Mohamed Sufi, and the core of the former SNUP activists.[11] Behind both the Somali-London Association and the UK Somali Welfare Association was the same group of people, the few ex-SNUP activists. Their role was critical. As 'Abd al-Rahman 'Abd al-Qadir Farah pointed out, the passports issue had been used by the London group, that is, the ex-SNUP activists, to shake up the Association and move it in a more militant direction. It was Omar Ilmi Dihoud who went to Scotland Yard and booked a day for the demonstration.

The UK Somali Welfare Association lasted for sometime although some of its members supported the government. On October 19, 1980 a second demonstration was organized. This time it was bigger than the previous one. Some of the Association's opponents wrote letters to Local Government Bodies in the UK asking them to ban the activities of the Association. Facing problems of internal cohesion that could lead to disaster some of the Association's members decided to launch a political party. As Ismail Mahmud Warsama put it, they did that in order to save the UK Somali Welfare Association from total collapse.

The launching of the Somali National Party took place in November, 1980. The idea was opposed by several members of the Association. Ahmed Mohamed Sufi, at the time one of the opponents of the idea of a political party, contends that what they were afraid of was that they did not have experience, financial resources or enough man-power to move in that direction. So the first time that the idea was discussed it was dismissed. But in the end the desire for it became very strong. The Association members voted at a hall in east London. The chairman was probably 'Abd al-Rahman 'Abd al-Qadir Farah. On that day everybody supported the idea of forming the party. According to Ismail Mahmud Warsama, the chairman of the new party was Nur Ilmi (an elder of the seamen's group), the secretary was himself, and Ahmed Mohamed Sufi was himself the treasurer. Other members of the committee were Omar Ilmi Dihoud, 'Abd al-Rahman 'Abd al-Qadir Farah, Shire 'Ali, etc. The party had around 150 members.

One of the staunch proponents of the idea of a political party was Omar Ilmi Dihoud. Another enthusiast was 'Abdullahi Gulaid but because he was working he could not devote himself completely to the party. For Ahmed Mohamed Sufi, 'Abd al-Rahman 'Abd al-Qadir Farah and others the party was their full-time occupation. Ahmed Mohamed Sufi was not sure whether the party had its own constitution at that period or even if they had agreed upon a definite name. They had heard, nevertheless, that there were some people coming from Saudi Arabia to meet them. So they did not formally inaugurate the party, as SNM, before these colleagues arrived in London. The name "Somali National Party," was probably used even after the arrival of the Saudi Arabian group in the first months of 1981.[12]

Structural Tendencies and Practical Limitations

Before proceeding to the period when the Saudi Arabian and London groups met together to form the Somali National Movement, it will be useful to examine some of the reasons behind the appearance and disappearance of the various groups, parties, and organizations of the period 1977-80 in London, and to see how and why the situation in Saudi Arabia differed. This will also throw light on the internal politics of the SNM in the period 1981-84.

The problem that was inherent in the organizations that preceded the SNM (the Somali National Democratic Party, the Somali-London Association, the UK Somali Welfare Association and the Somali National Party) was that they were, at the same time, too exclusive and too inclusive. The Somali National Democratic Party was not a party in the true sense of the word. It was a small group of dissidents who could voice in a coherent and eloquent way the dissatisfaction of the community with the government and the political situation in general, but who were not affected on a serious day to day basis by the same restrictions as, for example, the seamen. For the latter, the passport problem was central to their lives in a very direct way. Thus, the move from SNUP to the formation of the Somali-London Association was a step that for the first time brought together the activists and the community generally united against an external foe.

Further, the Somali-London Association was more viable than the Somali Student Union not simply because it brought together the students with other members of the expatriate Somali communities, but also because it provided a conceptually appropriate forum for the community as a whole. As a group, the students or intellectuals alone had no special status in the community, in the sense that their position was undefined, vis a vis, the formal structure of the community which was tribal and led by its elders (often retired seamen). This point was explained in more than one way by our informants who argued that the SNM proved to be successful because it was a grassroots movement which sprang from the tribal structure of Somali society and not a movement based on the theoretical discourse of a few intellectuals or the blind determination of a few hotheads.

The move from the Somali Student Union and the SNDP to the Somali-London Association should thus be seen as a development to something that is closer to the clan texture of Somali society, which also involved recognition of the importance of the elders. But it was still far removed from what was ultimately desired since it only included the Somalis who lived in London. As many informants argued, something "more political" was needed. That meant, consciously or unconsciously, a form of organization that was closer to the way politics were articulated in Somali society generally, namely, through the employment, in one way or another, of the clan structure to reach a wider area and a larger number of people.

The new Welfare Association now covered the entire canvas of the Somali communities in the United Kingdom, thus implying at least in theory the blessing of the seamen, the "elders" of the Somali community. That is what was meant when we argued that the organizations that preceded the Somali National Movement were too exclusive. The UK Somali Welfare Association was less exclusive than the Somali London Association which, in turn, was less exclusive than the SNUP. The SNUP was an organization consisting of Isaaq intellectuals who had no direct relationship with the Somali expatriate community in general. In 1979 it became the bedrock of the Somali-London Association. As the name implied and the composition of its committee suggested, the clan background of its members was mixed. The same can be said for the U.K. Somali Welfare Association. However, in their organizational hierarchies at least, both movements became purely Isaaq. It is of interest to recall here that the Somali ambassador (himself, of course, a "tribalist") accused the Somali-London Association of being "tribal." Even if this was not technically the case, the impression was there.

What is evident in the trend towards more explicitly "political" organizations is that each new form was more strictly purged of non-Isaaq elements than its predecessors -at least in the leadership. This does not mean necessarily that there was a deliberate policy of exclusion of non-Isaaq members, although there were some moves in that direction. For instance, when 'Abd al-Rahman 'Abd al-Qadir Farah was interviewed by the BBC Somali program, he had been advised not to express support for the SSDF which was primarily a Daarood organization.[13] This issue was discussed with many members of the London group. All denied that there was any notion of "Isaaqism." Ahmed Mohamed Sufi maintains that the SNM did not start out as an exclusive Isaaq movement; he admits it became one, but not intentionally. 'Abd al-Rahman 'Abd al-Qadir argues that the London group wanted a movement that was both national and heterogeneous in clan composition. However, he recognized that the seamen thought differently and, in a way that was closer to Somali realities, and that was the direction in which events moved. The final form, the Somali National Party, was a more or less frankly Isaaq body built around the team of Isaaq ex-SNP activists.

It is difficult now to judge whether the SNP leadership as a whole was in favor of such a policy, but in the light of subsequent events a number of people appear to have been opposed to clanism as an organizing principle. The rank and file members were more conservative: for them there was nothing else. The formation of the SNM in 1981 and its meteoric success suggest that they were right. The few individuals who did not espouse clanship and left the movement accomplished nothing important in politics.

The Saudi group, significantly, did not go through a similar process of organizational evolution. Our information suggests that, from the beginning, it was formed by Isaaq clansmen and did not encounter major organizational or structural problems in the period 1977-81. The solidity of its form and the stability of its internal structure can be attributed partly to the fact that it was run, from the beginning, by people of high standing and authority within the community. The founders and members of the Saudi Arabian group knew and accepted that the only possible way to organize a viable political movement was along clan lines. Unlike the London group, they were also, of course, operating in a relatively traditional, kin-based society. The way money was raised for the organization was a good example of how the community worked along clan lines.

The group did not consist of young activists on the one hand and elders on the other, so there was no problem of reconciling the structure of the organization with that of the wider community. The movement was conceived as the vehicle for the community's interests. Although it is probable that the majority of migrants were Isaaq, we lack information on the clan affiliation of the other members of the Somali community and their relative strengths. When our sources spoke of the "community" it was the Isaaq to whom they were referring. Whenever other clans or clan-families were mentioned, this was in the context that the Isaaq approached them to enquire about their feelings regarding joining the struggle; but in the end, as was probably expected, found that they were not interested in what the Isaaqis were doing.

The Saudi and London groups converge

In September 1979, Omar Ilmi Dihoud had a meeting with another intellectual, Mohamed Omar Hashi of the Habar Awal clan, a businessman who was at that time in London. It was agreed that Omar would stay in London and try to form a movement while Mohamed returned to Somalia to work there. He undertook to organize something there as soon as he heard from the London group. Nothing in fact seems to have happened in Somalia until 1981,[14] and in the meantime, the London activists concentrated their attention on developments in Saudi Arabia. After the second demonstration in front of the Somali embassy in London, Omar Ilmi Dihoud sent a message to the Saudi group in the form of a tape which recounted the activities of his London group and informed his Saudi compatriots that there were many eager supporters in England but a shortage of experienced activists. The tape was well received by the Somalis in Arabia who decided to spend some of the funds they had collected on sending three delegates to London in January, 1981.

Meanwhile, in November, 1980, while the London group was preparing to publicly launch the Somali National Party, three Somali businessmen from Saudi Arabia contacted Omar Ilmi Dihoud. They reported that the Somalis of Saudi Arabia and Qatar wanted to join their clansmen in England but were not yet quite ready. They argued that the launch of the new party should be delayed until January when their representatives could be in London.

In the same period, about November 1980, 'Abd al-Rahman 'Abd al-Qadir Farah went to Egypt, Saudi Arabia and Dubai for personal reasons and had a chance to meet representatives of the local Somali groups. Ismail Mahmud Warsama suggests that 'Abd al-Rahman went to the Middle East as a representative of the Somali National Party which, at the time, felt the need for a broader basis. Ahmed Mohamed Sufi maintains that the Saudi group heard about the London group on the radio and decided to make contact with it. Clearly we have here a number of versions differing slightly. Which group first approached the other? In the eyes of our sources, the answer to this question will establish which group took the initiative in the foundation of the SNM.

In any event, 'Abd al-Rahman's trip to the Middle East was productive and his meetings with the Saudi group's representatives fruitful. The Somali migrants in the Middle East were comparatively well-off, which for the less well-endowed London group and for the movement in general, was very important. In Cairo in January 1981 'Abd al-Rahman met 'Abd al-Salaan Yassin (Habar Yuunis) and Mohamed Hashi 'Ilmi (Habar Awal) both of whom were to play important roles subsequently. 'Abd al-Rahman believes that the Saudi Somalis wanted to contact their London counterparts at the same time as the latter wanted or needed their brothers from the Middle East. One consideration, he argues, was to recruit people of the Habar Tol Ja'lo and Arab clans in order to achieve a balance of power in the movement's leadership. At that time, apparently, the Saudi group did not have representatives of these clans who were prepared to devote themselves to the cause: 'Abd al-Rahman was able to introduce them to members of these clans who were already active in London.

The two Saudi-based Somalis were convinced and accompanied 'Abd al-Rahman to London and went to stay in his apartment in West Kensington which, according to him, became the center of the SNM. Hassan 'Isa (Isaaq, Arab) and Ismail Mahmud Warsamme (Habar Tol Ja'lo) were also in London, so the four major Isaaq clans were equally represented. All that was now necessary was to find a name for the party and launch it officially.

'Abd al-Rahman's version of these events seems a little selective. It seems clear that the Saudi group wanted to move their operations to London for at least three reasons: there would be no government constraints in London on launching the party; from London news of their policies and activities could be readily disseminated to Somalia; there was a sizeable and growing Somali community in London which was moving in the same direction politically as they were. 'Abd al-Rahman's statement that the Saudi group was interested in clan balance is obviously significant - as the following pages will show. But it is questionable whether this was the primary reason encouraging the Saudi Somalis to wish to collaborate with their kinsmen in England. However this may be, it seems certain that the Saudi Somalis assumed that, whatever its name, their organization would be Isaaq-based. As we have seen, the situation in England was not so clear cut: some of the activists believed that their dissident movement should be national in spirit and mixed in clan composition. The seamen, however, were more realistic (as well as conservative), and considered that it was impossible to run an effective national organization drawing support from the different clan groups. Some of the younger activists assumed that the movement would be Isaaq-dominated, but hoped that it could include others as well.[15] As one of the sources put it, "the students [the London group] had to come to terms with Isaaq nationalism."

From November 1980 until 'Abd al-Rahman's return from the Middle East in January 1981, the London group was pre-occupied with fierce debates and a certain amount of confusion. The Somali National Party was in place but, following the Saudi proposal that it should not be launched publicly until January 1981, it had not been announced to the media and people were becoming impatient. In the meantime, the existing UK Somali Welfare Association split into two factions. One maintained that the whole idea of a political party was wrong and that the British government would never consent: they proposed acting under the mantle (and name) of the Somali community. The other group led by Omar Ilmi Dihoud held the opposite view, urging that they wanted to be registered as political activists. In the ensuing ballot held to decide the issues, Omar and his supporters gained thirty-five votes while their opponents secured thirty votes. The issue was hotly debated and some of those present became so angry that they started insulting and hitting each other. The three Saudi Somalis became very concerned and implored the London group to keep these developments to themselves and not to publicize anything until the official Saudi group joined them in January or February. This was agreed.

The first of the Saudi activists arrived in late January to be followed by the others in March. The group consisted of Dr 'Abd al-Salaan Yassin, Hassan Adan Wadadid, Ahmed Ismail 'Abdi Duksi, and Mohamed Hashi Ilmi.[16] 'Abd al-Salaan Yassin had been teaching at Riyad University and was appointed to prepare the movement's political program, implying that the Saudi Somalis played a major role in the formation of policy. Of all the Saudi Arabian delegates, 'Abd al-Salaan and Mohamed Yusuf Artan (Habar Tol Ja'lo) were those working most closely with the London group. According to Omar Ilmi Dihoud, the London group had reservations about the Saudi group because of their "ideology." They also appeared somewhat reserved and did not seem to want to have close contact with the ordinary members of the Somali immigrant community. Ahmed Mohamed Sufi recalls that the Saudi delegates were generally older than the London activists and usually had considerable political experience or had held high positions in the Somali civil service as well as often substantial careers in business. This, with their financial resources, made their support valuable. On the other hand, their different background led to a number of disagreements which soon came to the fore.

Discussions about the constitution and name of the movement took place in 'Abd al-Rahman's apartment in West Kensington. It was immediately evident that power had to be transferred from the UK Welfare Association to the new organization. Sensing the background tensions and differences between themselves and their Saudi colleagues, the London group thought that it would be appropriate to call the new organization a "party." The activists included leftists, Marxists, as well as religious people and others without any strong ideological commitment; to contain these tendencies, they proposed calling the new organization a movement rather than a party. The Saudi group favored a strongly Islamic orientation to which the London activists were generally opposed. Sticking to their position that, ideologically, the movement had to be widely based, they declared that religious issues could be taken up once they had successfully defeated the Somali dictator. 'Abd al-Rahman 'Abd al-Qadir Farah, Omar Ilmi Dihoud and others warned of the consequences that such a development could have in light of the Islamic revolution in Iran and the negative position of the West towards that. In the end, the Saudi group gave way. As 'Abd al-Rahman put it, that was a minor victory: the London group won the battle but lost the war since the SNM later became an Islamic brotherhood fighting a holy war (*jihad*) against the Somali dictator. As we shall see, however, this judgement is an exaggeration and requires some modification.

When the title "Somali National Movement" was approved, discussion continued on the movement's constitution. A draft was developed in March, 1981. Delegates from Saudi Arabia and the United Arab Emirates then arrived and they decided to hold a public meeting in Connaught Hall, in London, on April 6, to launch the movement. A few days before that date, a secret delegate from Somalia[17] arrived, who reported that Isaaq notables in Mogadishu had held a clandestine meeting and concluded that the cause might not succeed if the movement was dominated by the Isaaq. Hawiye leaders were reported to be ready to join in but wanted more time.

This news caused considerable difficulty because the prospect of joining forces with the Hawiye (to whom the Isaaq were distantly related in clan terms), was important. The Saudi Arabian representatives were sceptical however, saying that they had frequently been told this without anything coming of it. In the light of this possibility of Hawiye support, they nevertheless decided to adopt a new tactic: they informed the messenger that the conference would take place but, that instead of appointing a central committee to run the organization, they would elect for the time-being, a steering committee. Their intention was to hold a larger conference in October 1981 when "everybody" would be invited.

Most of those elected to the steering committee were from the Saudi group who saw themselves as the movement's founders: they included 'Abd al-Salaan Yassin, Ahmed Ismail 'Abdi Duksi, Ahmed Yusuf 'Abdi, Ahmed Zeila, and Mohamed Hashi Ilmi. Ismail Mahmud Warsama and Hassan 'Ise were elected from the London group. A four-page press release bitterly criticized the nepotism, corruption and chaos into which Somalia had sunk under the Siyad dictatorship and outlined the case for overthrowing it to reestablish a just and democratic system. This declaration of war against the Siyad regime was couched in general terms and referred to the Somali state as a whole rather than concentrating on the situation in the north. On the day after the party's launch, the BBC Somali program interviewed two spokesmen as well as the Somali ambassador and the leader of the Somali community in Cardiff. The SNM representatives were cautious in their treatment of the Greater Somalia issue, expressing support for the idea of Ogaadeeni self-determination but also stressing the importance of maintaining good relations amongst the peoples of the Horn of Africa. They firmly dismissed charges that they had links with Ethiopia or Libya. In response, the ambassador claimed that the SNM only represented a small minority of expatriate dissidents and criticized their position on the Ogaadeen, solemnly pronouncing that "the Somali people are not for sale."

In the months following the conference, the SNM leaders met a delegation from the Somali Salvation Front[18], the guerilla organization which had developed out of the unsuccessful coup launched by (mainly), Majeerteen army officers in the wake of the 1977-78 Ogaadeen war. The delegation which included figures from two non-Isaaq northern clans as well as from the Majeerteen was led by a prominent Gadabuursi dissident whose brother was a minister in Siyad's government. The main point of the mission was to discuss the possibility of the two movements joining forces. The SNM temporized, referring to their forthcoming October conference at which they would expand their activities. In the meantime the two organizations would work together closely, but separately.

As many people had predicted, the Hawiye were not represented at the conference which was held on 18th October 1981 in the International Student Union, London University. There were fourteen delegates drawn from England, Saudi Arabia, and the Gulf States as well as the London-based steering committee. On 27th October the conference issued a press release along similar lines to the April one but accompanied by a detailed "position paper" entitled "A Better Alternative" which proclaimed inter alia that "Any Somali who believes in the objectives and principles of the SNM... is eligible for membership."

The official statement on Somalia's prospective political structure, issued immediately after the conference (October, 1981) referred very realistically to the fundamental clan fabric of the Somali "traditional" political system: "The challenge at present confronting aspiring Somali political leaders is to find a lasting solution to the question of clanism without, in the process, destroying Somali society as we know it." The SNM sought to combine "the advantages of Somali democracy and egalitarianism with the benefits of modern national government." The system proposed would be one which elevates the concept of *heer*, or inter-family social contract, (see Chapter 2), to the national level.

More concretely, the decentralization envisaged would be within a "unitary" rather than "federal" state. The country would be divided into four or five administrative regions each with a regional government consisting of an "elected governor, a regional assembly and regional administration... responsible for policing, health service and public sanitation, education up to college level... magistrate and high courts, veterinary pastoral and agricultural development, water services, electricity, regional roads and transport, forestry...." This would represent a genuine devolution and decentralization of power in contrast to the existing system where the regional structures were created and controlled by General Siyad at the center (cf. Chapter 7). With responsibilities clearly defined in the constitution, central government would be left to control defence, foreign and financial policy and national development. The "division of power between the executive, legislature and judiciary...[would be]... clearly defined."

The frank acknowledgment of the continuing political realities of clanism and the undertow of Isaaqi nationalism which they detected and even found further evidence of in the proposals for new regional divisions of the state fuelled the suspicions of those London activists who rejected "tribalism" in favour of "nationalism." Self-declared "liberals" like 'Abd al-Rahman 'Abd al-Qadir Farah, Ahmed Mohamed Sufi, and Ibrahim Sheikh of the Habar Yuunis and those the liberals labelled Isaaq "chauvinists," like 'Abd al-Salaan Yassin and Ahmed Jimaali, had heated discussions about clanism. To some liberals the Isaaqi nationalists appeared "to assume that all the Isaaq were good whereas the Daarood were congenitally bad." For the "liberals" the strategic problem lay in their assessment that the support the SNM could count on from the Isaaq was not enough to topple the Siyad regime. They proposed that "Isaaqism" should be left to the ordinary members of the movement, while the leadership should aspire to wider nationalist ideals. This was not accepted by their opponents which, as we shall see, had important consequences for the internal unity of the SNM.

The election of the members of the executive committee distributed the available posts among the main Isaaq clans. The Habar Awal gained the lion's share: chairman, secretary for internal affairs and "secretary at large." The Habar Yuunis won two seats: secretary for foreign affairs, and party secretary; and the Habar Tol Ja'lo was treated similarly with the posts of secretary general and treasurer. The position of political secretary was filled by a member of the Arab clan. The Saudi group did particularly well, gaining five of the eight offices with the remaining three going to the London group.

In addition to clan rivalries among the candidates and contradictory ideas about the role of Islam, another line of division amongst the

most experienced leaders was between former members of the
Somaliland Protectorate's rival political parties. Thus, Ahmed Jimaale
(Ahmed Mohamed Gulaid), the businessman from Jedda who was
appointed chairman, was a veteran politician of the old National United
Front and editor of their Arabic journal (see Lewis, 1988, p. 151), while
the secretary-general, Ahmed Ismail Duksi, had been a member of the
rival Somaliland National League (see Lewis, 1958, p. 255) but belonged
to the Habar Tol Ja'lo clan which was generally associated with the
NUF. Since leaving Somalia for Saudi Arabia after the military coup of
1969, Ahmed Jimaale had worked for the Saudi government with which
some people suspected he had a particularly close association. He was
certainly not strongly fundamentalist, however, indeed he had something of a reputation as a drinker and was rather unpopular in some
quarters. But partly on account of his seniority and the appropriateness
of his clan (which had supplied the first northern Somali premier), as
well as the fact that no other candidate put his name forward, he secured
the chairmanship.

Here we see the operation of the principle, so marked in Somali
politics, of "my clansmen, right or wrong" since, whatever their misgivings, in the context of inter-clan rivalry, Ahmed secured the votes of his
clansmen who, apparently, made up about half of the delegates who
voted at the meeting. Obviously, at the highest level of grouping, clan-
family solidarity could be effective as a basis for action, but at a lower
level within the movement, clan loyalties were inevitably divisive.
Genealogically, the descendants of the eponymous founder, Sheikh
Isaaq (see Chapter 4) are grouped in three matrilaterally defined divisions: Habar Awal, Habar Garhajis, and Habar Tol Ja'lo. The Habar
Awal consist of two very large lineages ("clans" or "sub-clans")
descended from two brothers: Sa'ad Muuse and 'Ise Muuse, and a smaller
lineage grouping, the Ayuub. Habar Garhajis includes what are structurally (in my terminology, see p. 19) three "clans:" the Habar Yuunis,
'Iidegalle, and Arab. The Habar Yuunis are the largest and most widely
distributed of the three and tend to play a dominant, though not uncon-
tested role in Isaaq politics, being well-represented in all the main towns
of central Somaliland. Finally, the Habar Tol Ja'lo comprise the descendants of four brothers, by the same mother, who form what are structurally four "clans'" of which, however, one - the Habar Ja'lo
-outnumbers the collateral groups.

As political co-operation (amply laced with internecine rivalry)
has extended amongst the Isaaq within the SNM, the convention has
developed of treating the Isaaq as consisting of eight groups: Habar Awal
(historically dominant in trade and modern politics),; Habar Yuunis;

'Idegalle and Arab; and the four Habar Ja'lo 'clans.' As the SNM gathered momentum in the years following its foundation, in the absence of population statistics, the Habar Tol Ja'lo sought to sustain the claim that they are entitled to half the seats in the movement's leadership while the Habar Yuunis and 'Idegalle, collectively Garhajis, were entitled only to one. This was validated, or legitimated, in genealogical terms: four of Sheikh Isaaq's sons form the Habar Tol Ja'lo, while the Habar Yuunis and 'Idegalle are descended from Garhajis - one of Sheikh Isaaq's sons. Clearly different claims to representation can be based on genealogical position, alleged relative size, geographical distribution, etc. There is ample scope for rival interpretations and justifications and for abundant political manipulation and manoeuvre. The concept of clan balance which tended to guide, or at least influence, the distribution of offices and leadership in the movement and later (from June 1991) Somaliland government, was always subject to a certain ambiguity and different interpretations. This was reflected in the fairly rapid circulation amongst the clans of the most senior positions in the movement's formative years from 1981-1984.

As an organizing force, clanship was not only applied in the manner in which the leadership was chosen, it was also the leading concept guiding and defining membership in the organization. As the financial arrangements of the Saudi group imply, membership was not primarily on an individual basis: money was collected by lineage in the same way as blood compensation (*mag*). Whole communities were regarded as corporate members. This meant that almost by definition, the communities of other clan-families were excluded. These assumptions also informed the approaches the Saudi group made to Daarood and Gadabuursi notables in 1979. These personalities "failed to carry their clans with them" and, consequently they themselves were excluded. Corporate membership was useful not only in keeping large numbers of people together within the SNM framework, but also in excluding others. Non-Isaaq groups were reluctant to join the SNM. This was used by the leadership to justify disregarding non-Isaaq potential recruits. Their stock response to criticism here was: "Where are all these non-Isaaq people who want to join the SNM?" For 'Abd al-Rahman 'Abd al-Qadir Farah the situation was hopeless. As he put it, "If you try to persuade a Somali that you are not tribalistic, he will become suspicious and think that you are crazy, or that you have something else in mind." So the nationalist approach that sought to include all the clan-families under the same umbrella was regarded by most people with suspicion.

Still, some of those in the London group did not want the matter to rest there. 'Abd al-Rahman 'Abd al-Qadir Farah, Ibrahim 'Ali

Weyrah, Ibrahim Sheikh and Ahmed Mohamed Sufi (all of the same clan - Habar Yuunis) got together and decided that they should try to change the internal structure of the SNM. A meeting was held with members of the executive committee: Ahmed Jimaali, Ahmed Ismail 'Abdi Duksi, 'Abd al-Salaan Yassin and a few others. They asked first that the organization of the party should be changed: they proposed to replace the practise of collective membership by individual membership. The committee, however, did not approve and dismissed their allegations of clan politics.[19] As it happened, there were other more pressing problems which, as we shall see, were to lead to the removal of the committee chairman himself.

Ahmed Jimaali was not with the delegation that originally went to London from Saudi Arabia. According to Dr Omar Ilmi Dihoud, the rest of that group were hostile to him and within two months of the October, 1981 conference, they managed to unseat him. From the beginning, the Saudi group had misgivings about Ahmed Jimaali as a clever man who might overshadow them. According to some sources, they had tried to stop him from becoming chairman but he had gained the support of the London group. As we have seen, the latter had reservations about the Saudi group whom they suspected of wanting to "go back to the traditional way of living and to share power on a clan basis. They did not like drinking and were far too religious for politicians." They wanted to form an Islamic movement, but the London group rejected this idea. In comparison with his Saudi colleagues, Ahmed Jimaali was more liberal and more secular.

In their efforts to overthrow Ahmed Jimaali, the Saudi activists got in touch with Omar Ilmi Dihoud, secretary for information in the United Kingdom, telling him that the only reason Ahmed had been elected was that many people from his clan were present at the conference. They requested the holding of another conference, an idea which Omar rejected. The Saudi group decided to move secretly against Ahmed Jimaali. They were reinforced by the return to London of Ahmed Ismail 'Abdi Duksi who had missed the October conference. Ahmed Jimaali himself gave them plenty of ammunition: he was rather casual in performing the chairman's duties. Following his election, he was reported to have spent a month and a half in Cardiff with very little contact with the SNM London office; thereafter he took his family back to Egypt where he spent another month before informing his colleagues that he would return to London in March. In the event, Ahmed was removed while he was in Jedda: he was accused of working for an Arab intelligence service: Saudi Arabia was never directly mentioned. For public consumption the ex-chairman was simply labelled a "spy" and his place was taken by Yusuf Sheikh Maddar (also Habar Awal), son of the famous sheikh of the religious settlement at Hargeisa (see Lewis, 1988, p. 65). This change actually took place when the leadership of the SNM had moved to Ethiopia (see below). For a short period before the SNM left England for Ethiopia, power was in the hands of the secretary-general, Ahmed Ismail Duksi.

From such information as we were able to gather, it seems that Ahmed Jimaali did not react particularly strongly to his removal. Mohamed 'Ali Farah, chairman of the Jidda chapter at the time, advised Ahmed to accept the situation for the sake of unity. He assured him that he had sent a letter to the executive committee in London, objecting to the chairman's replacement, but they took no notice. He urged Ahmed to remain faithful to the cause and to bring his case forward at a future congress. His clansmen were asked to provide a replacement, which as we have seen, they did. Meanwhile the movement was becoming more active in its public relations. In the summer of 1981, the SNM magazine *Somalia Uncensored* was launched to spread the message amongst the expatriate communities in England and elsewhere. Printed in London, this was edited by Hassan 'Ise a former BBC Somali programs broadcaster who had been forced to relinquish his job because of his SNM activities; 'Abd al-Rahman 'Abd al-Qadir was the assistant editor. Largely financed by the Saudi Somali community,[20] this journal appeared as a monthly between June and December 1981: its last issue announced the forthcoming transfer of the leadership to Ethiopia.

This controversial move had long been debated within the movement. It was opposed particularly by the ideologically oriented nationalists who viewed this as an act of betrayal of the Somali nationalist cause, especially after the crushing defeat in the 1977-78 Ogaadeen war. The danger of losing popular support by seeking help from Somalia's traditional enemy had already been illustrated by the SSDF's decision to make its headquarters in Ethiopia - despite the practical advantages of a location just over the Somali border. Opponents of an Ethiopian base for their operations tended to envisage an internal coup with popular uprisings in all the main cities and towns. This approach relied heavily on the known demoralization and poor discipline of Siyad's forces, especially in the north where the revolt was supposed to start with the capture of the northern commander. Isaaq officers in Somalia, however, thought this unrealistically optimistic and emphasized the difficulties the SNM would face in operating inside Somalia.

Convinced that the time for armed struggle had come and that nothing was to be gained by remaining in London, the Saudi faction which was now dominant was increasingly attracted by the idea of moving to Ethiopia where they expected to receive a warm welcome. They calculated that the Ethiopian leader, Mengistu, would be only too glad to add their support to that of the SSDF in his proxy war with the Siyad regime and the Ogaadeeni WSLF. Besides, it was argued, scriptural justification for seeking Ethiopian aid could be found in the famous tradition according to which, when the Prophet Mohamed's followers were being persecuted in Mecca by the Quraysh, he advised them to seek refuge in Abyssinia. Although, according to Hassan 'Ise, the leadership had already decided to transfer their headquarters to Ethiopia and had already applied for visas, this controversial plan received a further boost with the defection to Ethiopia in September 1981 of four Isaaq colonels from Siyad's forces[21]. It became obvious that despite ancient enmities, Ethiopia was the natural base for cross-border operations taking advantage of the grazing movements of Isaaq nomads deep into Ethiopian territory and the proximity of the northern capital, Hargeisa, lying within fifty miles of the frontier.

The SNM in Ethiopia

Meanwhile, a series of events reinforcing the SNM's role and aims had occurred in northern Somalia itself. As the SNM was assuming its official form in the latter part of 1981, a group of young Isaaqi professionals in Hargeisa, appalled at the government's failure to maintain effective social services, determined to improve matters by concerted voluntary action. The action group, which followed the regime's much-publicized self-help formula and included doctors, teachers, and other qualified people from in and outside Hargeisa, adopted as their slogan the word *ufo*, "hurricane."[22] These public-spirited initiatives, underlining the regime's failures in the north, coincided with the mysterious appearance of SNM hand-sheets and copies of the journal, *Somalia Uncensored*. Siyad's local officials, naturally, responded by branding those involved "subversives" and arrested the supposed ring-leaders.

After being brutally interrogated, the thirty-eight detainees were prepared for trial and sentencing by the national security court, a judicial court in name only, guaranteed to travesty justice by delivering whatever verdict President Siyad ordered. The trial was due to open in Hargeisa on 20th February 1982, but rioting broke out in the town when rumours spread that three of the accused were to be sentenced to death. The riots lasted for three days and led to the military shooting indiscriminately into crowds, killing several people and wounding many more. When the court finally met and delivered its verdicts about a week later, there were long prison sentences but no executions.

Meanwhile, according to SNM press releases from the London office, a number of military units in the north had mutinied and more officers had defected to the movement.

This marked the opening on their home ground of the war between the Isaaq clansmen and Siyad's Daarood regime (pejoratively designated the *Faqash*, from the noise made by young pigs scattering) which was to last until the surrender of Siyad's forces to the SNM in January 1991. In the aftermath of the February disorders, General Gaani, Siyad's tough Marrehaan governor of the north, turned the screw of oppression, imposing emergency regulations and curfews as well as the notorious *tabeleh* system,[23] according to which a "leader," a member of the official Somali Revolutionary Socialist Party in close touch with the national security service, was made responsible for the good conduct of twenty households. Visitors had to be reported, and when a member left home to travel, the NSS had to be informed. This Orwellian system of social control was, of course, particularly aimed at discouraging SNM contacts and spreading divisiveness and fear amongst the public.

Reacting to these oppressive measures and economic discrimination against Isaaq merchants and traders in favor of Daarood officials and refugees, a group of over twenty prominent Isaaq elders on March 30, 1982, sent a long memorandum summarizing their grievances to the Head of State.[24] Typically, Siyad seems to have responded by tightening control on potential Isaaqi dissidents and SNM sympathisers. Thus in June the President ordered the arrest of two senior Isaaq figures in his government (Vice-President Ismail 'Ali Abokor, and Foreign Minister Omar Arteh), including them in a new package of political detainees (two his own clansmen), flung into jail on unsubstantiated charges of plotting against him (cf. Lewis, 1988, pp 249-250). This further alienated Isaaq public feeling and helped to mobilize support for the SNM which, transported to Ethiopia, had now to develop its military organization there and establish a viable relationship with the Ethiopian regime and its protege the Majeerteen (Daarood) -based SSDF.

Following contact with the Ethiopian embassy in London, the SNM arrived in Ethiopia led by the secretary-general, Ahmed Ismail 'Abdi, accompanied by two other members of the executive council (Hassan 'Ise Jama and Mohamed Hashi 'Ilmi). There they were joined by other personalities from the Gulf States, the treasurer Mohamed Ahmed "Zaidi," who had been appointed to the executive council *in absentia*: the post of chairman, made vacant by Ahmed Jimaali's removal, was still unfilled. Consequently an extraordinary general meeting was called and held at the small spa town of Nazareth outside Addis Ababa in March to elect a new chairman and deal with other pressing issues.

In the interests of continuity, the Habar Awal delegates (Ahmed Jimaali's clan), were encouraged to present a candidate which they did in the person of Yusuf Sheikh Maddar (from the famous family of Hargeisa sheikhs) who was duly elected. The chairman's period in office was extended to two years and the new post of vice-chairman was created. Hassan Adan Wadadid (Habar Yuunis), who had stood as a rival candidate to Yusuf Sheikh Maddar, was elected to this position, while Ahmed Ismail Duksi (Habar Tol Ja'lo), continued as secretary-general. So the three leading Isaaq clans were equally represented in the leadership. No other changes were made, and the position of the religiously oriented Saudi group was thus consolidated at this crucial time (the so-called *Wadaaddo*; literally, "men of religion").

Apart from establishing guerilla units, the two most pressing problems, not easier to resolve because they were inter-related, facing the new leadership were, naturally, how to obtain effective Ethiopian military support and how, and to what extent, to coordinate activities with the SSDF, already well-ensconced with the Ethiopian authorities and also benefitting from Libyan aid. Both these involved clan issues and could not be tackled without considering their clan implications.

Thus the Ethiopians wanted to know where the SNM stood on the question of Ogaadeen self-determination. According to Hassan 'Ise, in an early meeting with the Ethiopian leader, Mengistu, the latter asked the three SNM delegates (Duksi, Hassan 'Ise, 'Abd al-Salaan), what their position was on the Ogaadeen. Duksi, apparently gave a diplomatically non-committal reply, inviting Colonel Mengistu to let the SNM know his views on this question. Hassan 'Ise did not remember the Ethiopians raising the matter again. More specifically, in an interview on the BBC Somali programme on May 22, 1982, Dr 'Abd al-Salaan explained that in the SNM view, the Ogaadeen was an internal issue between the people of the Ogaadeen region and the Ethiopian government. At a later meeting with their Ethiopian counterparts[25] in July, 1983 at Harar, Hassan 'Ise recalled than the SNM used the presence of a wide range of Isaaqi elders from the northern Ogaadeen to demonstrate that the Ogaadeen clan itself only occupied part of the region named after it and that their "natural" capital was Gode in the south.

The other delicate matter, concerning SNM relations with the SSDF, already well established in Ethiopia and enjoying Libyan financial and military support, had to be approached cautiously, not least since, understandably, the Ethiopians expected the two organizations to work together or even merge. The latter proposition was also put forward by the SSDF leader, Colonel 'Abdullahi Yusuf (Majeerteen) who had become president of the newly constituted movement, (amalgamating

several smaller groups) in 1981 when the eleven-man executive committee included two Isaaq, one Dulbahante, and one Hawiye. Later on,
the tendency was for the SSDF to become more and more exclusively
Majeerteen and thus to consolidate its Daarood character as it was perceived by the SNM. 'Abdullahi wanted the SNM to join him and presented the Isaaq leaders with an outline political programme which,
according to Omar Ilmi Dihoud, was largely Marxist propaganda and
panegyrics, praising the Soviet Union and Ethiopia (as well as Cuba and
Libya) for their support.

The SNM, for their part, proposed that in the event of a formal
merger, the SSDF would have to elect a new leadership -a proposal that
was not at all to the taste of the authoritarian colonel. Knowing that the
SSDF was short of manpower for its abundant equipment, the SNM
later suggested, as Hassan 'Ise recalls, that they should exchange man-
power for arms, petrol, and petro-dollars. This was rejected, and the best
that the two movements could agree on was general cooperation in pursuit of their shared aim - the downfall of Siyad - and, more particularly,
to operate a common radio station in Ethiopia. Consequently in
October, the SSDF radio station changed its name from *Kulmis* (unity)
to *Halgan* (struggle): this was a timely development since the Siyad
regime regularly punningly derided the dissident radio station as *Qudmis*,
literally "those who spread rottenness."

This limited degree of cooperation was in keeping with the two
movements' more fundamental interests. From an Isaaqi perspective,
the SSDF was essentially a Majeerteen (Daarood) organization dedicated to the restoration of Majeerteen (and Daarood) hegemony in the
existing Somali Republic. As Isaaqis, the SNM on the other hand, was
primarily concerned to liberate the north - the former Somaliland
Protectorate - from domination by Siyad and only secondarily interested in the south. Within the north, their first responsibility was of
course their Isaaqi clansmen whose relations with the neighbouring Dir
and Daarood clans of Somaliland remained problematic. As Osman
Ahmed Hassan and Mohamed 'Ali Farah emphasized to us, from the
beginning the SNM wanted to retain its independence and have its
own fighting force.

Eventually the Ethiopians were persuaded that the SNM could
usefully control the border zone inhabited by their clansmen in the areas
of Jigjiga, Borama, and Hargeisa, thus parrying raids launched by the
Siyad-backed WSLF (Ogaadeenis). The WSLF launched its attacks from
Hargeisa, laying mines in the border area, making it very difficult for the
Ethiopian army to operate there. In the course of 1982-83 there were a
number of skirmishes between the Isaaq irregulars and Ogaadeen clans-

men and the Ethiopians allowed the SNM to open a base at the regional capital, Dirredawa. From the outset, SNM forces were organized on clan lines: indeed, once the war was fully underway, as Gerard Prunier (1992) who observed the guerillas in action in 1990, vividly recorded: "In a way the SNM does not exist: it is simply the Isaaq people up in arms." At the start, from their new Ethiopian bases, the SNM leaders went on recruiting missions amongst their own clansmen along the border - each appealing to his clansmen or lineage members for support. While the Ethiopians were said by Hassan 'Ise to have initially only supplied ammunition, Isaaqi nomads came with their own arms (the pervasive kalashnikov carried by virtually all herdsmen in the Horn of Africa in the 1980's) as well as weapons, equipment and transport obtained in one way or another from the Somali national army.

Isaaqi members of the army's northern units also readily deserted to join the SNM. The Somali migrant workers in the Gulf states provided funds on a generous scale for military allowances which, according to Osman Ahmed Hassan, made service in the SNM forces additionally attractive to unemployed young men. More generally, the SNM fighters lived off the land supported by their own clansmen. At the same time, some important Isaaqi military officers remained behind, ostensibly loyal to Siyad while attempting to mastermind subversion and encourage mutiny. Thus the SNM's most striking initial military success, the storming of the Mandera prison and the release of its prisoners in January 1983, was daringly directed by Colonel Mohamed Hashi 'Lihleh' who moved across the border a few months later to join his SNM colleagues there. (He had sent the original party of four Isaaq officers to Ethiopia the year before).

These SNM attacks provoked severe reprisals against the local civilian population, and the military governor declared a state of emergency, preventing the free movement of people and goods. In 1983 also, the northern economy and its Isaaq traders suffered a sudden set-back when the Saudi government insisted that Somali livestock imports should be certified as free from rinderpest. A more equivocal blow to the northern Somali economy at this time was the government's decision to prohibit the cultivation and sale of the stimulant narcotic plant qat (Catha edulis) which had become a flourishing cash-crop in the northwest and which was also imported from Ethiopia and marketed locally mainly by Isaaq merchants (see Samatar, 1985, pp. 41-56). Presented by the regime as a progressive step forward in the international campaign against drugs, the ban was interpreted in Isaaq and SNM quarters as a further attack on their economic activities and on their communication lines between Ethiopia and Somaliland, since qat traders regularly plied their trade across the battle-lines with their fast land-rovers, seeking and delivering intelligence as well as bringing supplies of the stimulant plant. As was to be expected, all this stiffened Isaaqi resistance and further benefitted the SNM struggle.

Over the border, the SNM held its second congress at Harar in July 1983 when a new clause was introduced into the constitution which, according to Hassan 'Ise, empowered the central committee to change the leadership through motions which secured a two-thirds majority. In November, at an emergency meeting of the central committee in Jigjiga, the Saudi group chairman Yusuf Sheikh Maddar and most of his *wadaaddo* colleagues were replaced by professional army officers a considerable number of whom had now deserted from Somalia. Colonel 'Abd al-Qadir Kosar (Habar Yuunis), became chairman, Adan Shinneh Mohamed (Habar Awal), vice-chairman, and Mohamed Kahin Ahmed (Habar Tol Ja'lo), secretary (later first minister of defence in the 1991 SNM government). The executive committee was reduced from eleven members to five with Hassan 'Ise, from the secularly oriented London group, surviving this purge as the sole civilian. The new vice-chairman and secretary had both been in the original group of four regular army officers who sought refuge in Ethiopia early in 1982.

The chairman, also a former officer in the national army, had fled the country and sought asylum with his family in Qatar. There he joined the SNM and, after moving to Ethiopia, became the main organizer of guerilla raids against the government. In Ethiopia, he collaborated in the planning of the Mandera prison raid: his brother-in-law who had been head of intelligence in the official Somali Revolutionary Socialist Party was arrested on Siyad's orders in June 1982. Under his leadership, the central committee of the SNM reiterated the movement's commitment to the Shariah but was obviously more secular in orientation than its predecessors. More generally, Hassan 'Ise recalled that the religious term "holy warrior" (*mujahid*) which had been introduced by the Saudi group at the Nazareth conference had been generally applied facetiously and derogatively by the Isaaq public but, as the war progressed and the toll of human suffering mounted, a religious spirit became more pervasive among the SNM freedom fighters who were rediscovering the old truth that "there are no atheists in the trenches."

Reviewing the clan composition of successive executive committees, it is interesting to note that the order in which the three main Isaaq clans were represented in the leadership changed cyclically over time. The Habar Awal who had held the top position in the second committee were now in the third post (having moved from holding the chairmancy to the secretaryship). The Habar Yuunis who had held the second position moved to the top (from vice-chairman to chairman), and the Habar Tol Ja'lo moved from third to second in rank (from secretary to vice-chairman). The new military administration remained in power from July, 1983 until August 9, 1984, a period that witnessed a marked increase in military activity. Our main sources here are the various SNM press releases and BBC World Service reports which offer a fragmented but informative picture of the situation. A typical report in early May 1984 details clashes along the border south of Jigjiga; later accounts indicate that June and July were months of heavy guerilla activity with bomb incidents in Hargeisa and SNM probes towards that town.

At the same time, there was considerable upheaval within the SNM leadership. At the fourth SNM congress in August 1984, 'Abd al-Qadir Kosar was challenged by another Habar Yuunis clansman but of a different lineage. In this situation of Habar Yuunis conflict, the Habar Tol Ja'lo seized the initiative and secured the post for their candidate, Ahmed Mohamed Silanyo. It was agreed that henceforth the chairman should remain in office for a period of three years. No secretary was appointed, but a new vice-chairman was elected from outside the Isaaq in the person of the well-known Hawiye lawyer 'Ali Mohamed Ossoble.

Ahmed Mohamed Silanyo, a controversial personality, was minister of planning in Siyad's government for thirteen years up until 1982. As we have noted, his first involvement with the SNM occurred in 1981 when Siyad sent him to London to discourage the Isaaqi dissidents there. His next contact was in 1982, when he was planning to seek political asylum in England. On June 16, 1982, he was interviewed on the BBC Somali program about his plans and took the opportunity to castigate the brutality and corruption of Siyad Barre's regime. He claimed that he had originally supported the "revolution," but that when he realized that Siyad's government was working against the public interest, he decided to leave. He also reported that he was in contact with others who believed that the "mistakes of the revolution could be rectified" from within Somalia. Although some members of the SNM were mistrustful of him, with his wide political experience and contacts he managed to become the representative of the movement in London and, from this launching pad, moved to Ethiopia and the chairmanship.

Assessing Silanyo's rapid ascent for our benefit, Mahmud Sheikh Ahmed Sheikh Muse linked the question with the clan nature of the SNM. He considered that, unless a candidate for office had done something particularly heinous and had alienated his clansmen, he could count on their support which was all important. Although Silanyo had served in Siyad's government for many years, he was not directly implicated in any grave crimes and enjoyed a considerable reputation as a political heavy-weight. As soon as Silanyo was endorsed by his own people as an acceptable leader (who had presumably supported his clansmen loyally when he was a minister), his standing and position were unlikely to be seriously questioned by other clans except at the risk of alienating his clan as a whole. There was also an urgent need at the time for unity: if people of one clan started questioning the position of the leaders of other clans there would be serious trouble. Thus the election of Ahmed Mohamed Silanyo as chairman was in line with the SNM's well-established, pragmatic (and realistic), approach to politics: the turn of the Habar Tol Ja'lo had come, especially when their candidate had, as Said 'Abdi recalled, support from the powerful 'Ise Muuse division of the Habar Awal (to which Silanyo is related by marriage) and also of the Arab clan.

Having become chairman, Silanyo managed to get the constitution amended, abolishing a clause requiring anyone who, in the past, had dealings with Siyad Barre to be examined closely before assuming any senior SNM position. This restriction, in the view of Mahmud Sheikh Ahmed Sheikh Muse, was now considered too radical to remain in the constitution: besides, it would discourage other leading Isaaq personalities from deserting Siyad. With this exculpatory change, Silanyo's election opened a new chapter, encouraging other senior ex-government ministers and officials to seek high office within the movement[26]. It was not only politicians and military officers, with their vested interests, who favoured and accepted this new situation: it was also endorsed by the elders. Following Silanyo's example, a number of other high ranking officials who had recently deserted Siyad Barre were absorbed into the SNM leadership. These included 'Abdarahman Ahmed 'Ali 'Tur' (Habar Yuunis, a very experienced diplomat and future President of Somaliland) and Ibrahim Meygag Samatar (a former minister and ambassador).[27]

Another more radical development was the election as vice-chairman of the Hawiye lawyer, 'Ali Mohamed Ossobleh, along with seven other figures from the same clan-family appointed to the central committee. This represented a major SNM policy initiative in seeking to secure support from the Hawiye whose traditional territory included the Somali capital, Mogadishu, and whose active collaboration would significantly expand the ranks of dissident forces ranged against Siyad. There were also two Daarood figures (from the Majeerteen and Dulbahante clans), one Dir (Gadabuursi), and one Rahanwiin. If these latter elections smacked of clan tokenism, the substantial Hawiye presence signalled a serious attempt to extend the clan base, and political and military effectiveness of the SNM. This move also capitalized on

extended clan sentiments since, at the highest level of kinship grouping in the national genealogy, the Isaaq and Hawiye both descend from
Irir (whose descendants also include the 'Ise and Gadabuursi Dir).
Cohesion at this level, however tenuous and provisional, was encouraged, oppositionally, by the perceived Darood character of Siyad's MOD
regime (see above, p 166) and by the latter's open appeal to Darood clans
to rally to his side against the Isaaq, an appeal which risked evoking these
wider Irir loyalties as a reactive response.

The establishment of this bridgehead, (highlighting the lack of
progress in collaborating with the faction-ridden SSDF[28] whose
Ethiopian support was declining), was naturally, a source of concern to
Siyad who had hitherto enjoyed the acquiescent cooperation of many
prominent Hawiye figures. To disrupt this menacing alliance, one of
Siyad's most pugnacious generals, according to Dr Omar Dihoud, eventually succeeded in arranging the assassination of Colonel 'Abd al-Qadir
Kosar by Hawiye gunmen.[29] There had been in any case differences for
some time between Silanyo and his Hawiye vice-president over a range
of matters which included 'Ali Mohamed Ossobleh's criticism that the
SNM was concentrating its military operations[30] in the north, which
suggested that it had secessionist aspirations. Silanyo is reported to have
resented Ossobleh's popularity and his handling of financial contributions to the movement - as Dr Omar Dihoud recalls.

At the fifth SNM conference , held eventually in March 1987, the
position of vice-president was abolished and the chairman's powers
increased by giving him the right to nominate ten of the fifty-five members of the central committee. With most of the other Habar Gidir
Hawiye members, Ossobleh had already left to become leader of the
Hawiye-based United Somali Congress and was to play a prominent
role in the formation of the 'Manifesto Group' which mobilized support
in Mogadishu in the weeks leading to the downfall of Siyad in January
1991 (see Compagnon, 1991, and below Chapter 9). Silanyo himself was
re-elected, serving until April, 1990 when his designated successor,
'Abdarahman Tur (Habar Yuunis) was elected chairman and hence
became first president of the re-instated "Somaliland Republic" in June,
1991. But this is to anticipate.

According to Hassan 'Ise, 1985-1986 was the most effective period
of SNM guerilla operations which now included forays into the south
from bases on the Ethiopian side of the frontier by what was later to call
itself the southern SNM which included Dir clansmen from southern
Somalia. While the Ethiopian and Somali heads of state where holding
preliminary discussions towards normalizing their relations, the SNM
pressed home their probes in the north, sometimes apparently with

Ethiopian help, their most daring operation being the assassination of the National Security Service regional chief at the end of 1986. Under the new northern military governor, General '"Morgan," the Siyad regime responded in 1987 by unleashing a new reign of terror on the civilian population to crush the Isaaq once and for all (cf, Lewis, 1988, p.253). The SNM reacted by intensifying the guerilla struggle, but it was only after Siyad had signed a formal peace-treaty in April 1988, (in which each side agreed to cease harbouring the other's dissident gueril-las), that the SNM campaign widened into the all out war which was eventually to lead to victory.

All out war and victory: the pervasive clan factor

It is not our purpose here to seek to chronicle the sequence of extremely brutal engagements which ensued between Siyad's forces and the SNM,[31] and which led at the end of January, 1991 to Siyad's flight from Mogadishu pursued by the United Somali Congress (Hawiye) forces which had finally brought his downfall. Our interest is, rather, to explore how the clan factor operated in this final phase of the SNM's ten year struggle. As the scope of military operations widened and inten-sified the clan basis of units became, if anything, more sharply delin-eated. In the period of all-out war (1988-1990), the SNM had five major "regular" regiments, composed, form east to west, of Habar Tol Ja'lo, Habar Yuunis, 'Ise Muuse and Sa'ad Muuse - each Habar Awal sub-clan (or primary lineage) preferring to operate separately on account of its sense of distinctiveness (a factor strongly reflected in subsequent SNM politics).[32] Inter-clan rivalries were marked and, despite their common cause, often reduced the effectiveness of military operations. This rivalry was reflected in the facetious (and often derogatory) nick-names applied to each clan: thus, according to Hassan 'Ise, his own Arab clan was known as "Flint-jaw," while the Habar Awal were labelled "Voice of America" - not as widely listened to as the "BBC," sobriquet of the Habar Yuunis; and the Habar Tol Ja'lo were know as "Fox's teeth."

Despite loose links with the Habar Giddir USC militia, the SNM maintained its exclusive Isaaq character throughout this period, urging other clans to rise up against Siyad but to organize their own fighting forces. After being earlier mobilized against the Isaaq by their clans-man, who was commander of Siyad's National Security Service, in the later stages of the conflict the Dulbahante turned against Siyad, and thus prepared the way for the re-emergence of a northern Somali state based on the old Somaliland Protectorate with its distinct clans united (Gadabuursi + Isaaq + Dulbahante + Warsangeli).

Throughout their struggle, the SNM maintained that their immediate aims were the overthrow of the Siyad tyranny and the reestab-
lishment of democratic government with much greater regional
autonomy. Here, as outlined in its first constitution (see above, p. 200),
clan units should be respected and cooperation between clans based on
traditional contractual treaties (heer). This gave the traditional elders an
important role as grass-roots decision-makers as the SNM had found
throughout their struggle. In the course of the conflict, the SNM had
indeed become more, rather than less, populist in a democratic sense.
The central committee had expanded to the magic number of 99 (the
number of the names of God in Islam) by 1990, which allowed for wide
representation across the constituent clans, Isaaq and non-Isaaq.
Following the surrender of Siyad's residual forces in the north, delegations representing all the clans of Somaliland met in February, 1991
and agreed to review the country's future place within the Somali
Republic.

The central committee meeting which followed in May, with delegates from all the northern clans, debated the issue of local sovereignty
and system of government. True to its original principles, the SNM
leadership did not favor the complete local autonomy which would
result from a unilateral declaration of independence.[33] However, there
were important external pressures from southern Somalia which had a
powerful impact on the unfolding political process in the north. The pre-
cipitate establishment, without due SNM consultation, of a "national"
government by the USC in Mogadishu and radio reports of proposed
negotiations with the SNM, inflamed public opinion. Consequently,
the caution and hesitation of the leadership, sensitive to the problems
of an internationally unrecognized state, were overwhelmed by a strong
surge of public feeling demanding immediate independence. The south
and the residual Somali Republic, based in Mogadishu, had become synonymous with the oppression and tyranny of Siyad's regime and forced
the SNM leaders to proclaim the rebirth of the Somaliland Republic on
May 18, 1991. 'Abdarahman Ahmed Tur's (Habar Yuunis) presidential
government formed on 4 June 1991 was widely based and generally representative of the constituent northern clans. Of the 23 ministerial
posts, 17 were allocated to the Isaaq clans and the remainder divided
among the non-Isaaq. The distribution within the Isaaq gave the Habar
Awal and Habar Tol Ja'lo four ministries each, the Habar Yuunis had to
be content with three, the same number as the Arab clan who, in the
person of Hassan 'Ise, a founding executive council member of the SNM,
assumed the position of vice-president.

United in victory, and at uneasy peace with their non-Isaaq neighbors, divisive clan ructions soon developed within the new government as the Habar Tol Ja'lo and leading segments of the Habra Awal flexed their political muscles. In fact this SNM government proved to be insufficiently broadly based and with its lack of material resources, compounded by the absence of international recognition, failed to consolidate its authority sufficiently to control the various lineage-based and "freelance" militias which undermined security. In this situation of the virtual absence of central authority, power passed to the local clan and lineage elders. Tired of war, and anxious to extend grazing movements and trade, and to distance the north from the chaos in southern Somalia, these traditional figures embarked on a remarkable series of inter-clan negotiations and reconciliation conferences which, over a period of two years, spread like a web of tenuous peace throughout Somaliland and in the spring of 1993 elected a new central government. In comparison with the heavy-handed and largely unsuccessful UN and other international efforts to impose peace from the top in southern Somalia, this was an impressive testimony to the effectiveness of traditional grass-roots Somali diplomacy.

Notes

1. This chapter is largely an exercise in oral history, depending primarily on accounts of the formation and rise of the SNM by some of its founders and their close associates now resident in London. Our sources were interviewed in London by either Drs Seid Abdi and G.P. Makris or Dr Seid Abdi and myself between the summers of 1991 and 1992. We gratefully acknowledge the contributions of: Hassan 'Ise Jama, 'Abd al-Rahman 'Abd al-Qadir Farah, Ismail Mahmud Warsama, Ahmed Mohamed Sufi, Osman Ahmed Hassan, Omar Ilmi Dihoud, Mohamed 'Ali Farah and Mahmud Sheikh Ahmed Sheikh Muse. For archival data we are grateful to the Research Department of the Foreign Office and the BBC Somali programme. We also gratefully acknowledge our debt to the Nuffield Foundation and the London School of Economics Staff Research Fund for the grants which enabled us to carry out this work.

2. Osman Ahmed Hassan was an important personality. An administrative officer, trained in Britain, he had been briefly Governor of the north at independence in 1960. In 1962, he was appointed for three years as Somali ambassador to France. He then became ambassador to the Soviet Union for another three years before being recalled to Somalia as Director-General of the ministry of Health. After the Revolution, in 1975, Osman Ahmed Hassan, together with other prominent civil servants, was accused of being incapable of "marching along with the revolution" and was sacked. In 1976 he migrated to Saudi Arabia and remained there until 1985 when he came to England.

3. Among the prominent members of the Riyad group were Mohamed Yusuf Artan, an Isaaq of the Habar Tol Ja'lo clan, Dr Abd al-Salaan Yassin from the Habar Yuunis clan who was a lecturer at 'Abd al-Aziz University and Ahmed Gulaid of the Habar Yuunis clan.

4. Some of the most active members were 'Ali Mohamed Warsame 'Ali Tur of the Habar Yuunis clan, Mohamed 'Abdullahi Ismail Bergel from the Habar Awal clan, Ibrahim Hajji Dualleh Dundume of the Habar Tol Ja'lo clan, Qalib Mussa of the Habar Yuunis clan. Later on came Ahmed Mohamed Abshi Mohamed of the Habar Awal clan, Ahmed 'Abdi Farah and 'Ali Bakul.

5. Ahmed Ismail Abdi Duksi, a businessman from the Habar Tol Ja'lo clan, and a former figure in the Somaliland National League, came from Uganda and joined the group. Around the same period Hassan Adan Wadadid of the Habar Yuunis clan also joined when he came out of prison in Somalia - he had been a political detainee. His recruitment was important since until that time the group did not include any Habar Yuunis heavy weights. This was crucial because the group wanted to have a balance between the clans. Until then it was dominated by several senior Habar Tol Ja'lo men. There was also a teacher from the Arab clan who later stayed with the SNM for eight years in the field.

6. Among the people who volunteered to leave their jobs and work full-time for the group and the party that was going to be launched in London were Saad Sheikh Osman Nur (Habar Awal) who in the end did not work for the party, Ahmed Gulad Sayla'i (Habar Yuunis) Yusuf Ali Sheikh Madar (Habar Awal), Mohamed Hashi Ilmi (Habar Awal), Ahmed Ismail Abdi Duksi (Habar Tol Ja'lo) , 'Abd al-Salaan Yassin (Habar Yuunis) and, later on Ahmed Jimaali (Habar Awal) who in 1981 became the inaugural chairman of the SNM. However, he is not regarded as one of the founders of the movement because he came late on the scene, and for some time did not want to come out in active support of the Saudi Arabian group.

7. This was a reference to Abdullahi Yusuf, the leader of the SSDF, who had a reputation for being violent and killing people.

8. The former were Mutsi Mutse (Dulbahante), Mohamed Ali (Majeerteen), Ismail Dube from the Habar Yuunis clan of the Isaaq and Abe Schoon, a non-Isaaq. (Our sources did not remember the name of his clan). The four SNUP members who were also elected were Omar Ilmi Dihoud, Ismail Mahmud Samatar, 'Abd al-Rahman, 'Abd al-Qadir Farah and Ahmed Mohamed Sufi. Other persons who were involved in the Association were Haji Musa, 'Abdi Warsama Awdan, Bur Ilmi (Habar Yuunis clan) and Shamis Ibrahim (the only woman).

9. Ahmed Mohamed Sufi considers that the Welfare Association might not have taken its name at that particular time but sometime later.

10. 'Abd al-Rahman 'Abd al-Qadir Farah maintains that Said Farah had become an informant of the embassy.

11. According to Ismail Mahmud Warsama, he himself became the chairman of the Welfare Association and Ahmed Mohamed Sufi was the treasurer. Other members of the committee were Hajj Omar from Liverpool, Omar

Kibar from Cardiff, Ibrahim Hashi 'Abdi and Farah Jihad. Perhaps Ismail Mahmud Warsama has confused the UK Somali Welfare Association and the Somali-London Association of which he was indeed the chairman. The second contradiction is that according to 'Abd al-Rahman 'Abd al-Qadir Farah, the congress in Liverpool and the formation of the association took place before the first demonstration in 17th August 1980.

12. Ahmed Mohamed Sufi was not sure if the name Somali National Party was brought by the Saudi Arabia Group or was "invented" by the London group.

13. Later on he came to the conclusion that the London group and indeed the SNM in general distrusted the Majeerteen as much as the Marrehaan.

14. See below, p. 205.

15. When this hope proved unfounded, a number of disenfranchized intellectu- als left the movement and founded a wider-based forum under the slogan "Somalia First" : see below, p. 203.

16. Ahmed Mohamed Sufi maintained that the first representatives of the Saudi group also included Mohamed Yusuf Artan.

17. This man was met by Ahmed Ismail 'Abdi Duksi and Hussein Abokor who did not, however, reveal his name.

18. This was the backbone organization of what, in October, 1981, became the Somali Salvation Democratic Front (SSDF) and included various leftist groups with an initial executive committee of eleven members including two Isaaq, one Dulbahante and one Hawiye (see Compagnon, 1990, p. 31). Later, the SSDF became increasingly dominated by the Majeerteen clan.

19. Later in 1982, the four dissidents left the SNM and joined other nationalists in Britain and America to found 'Somalia First' - a new inter-clan group (see *Horn of Africa Journal*, September, 1982)

20. By this time, according to Osman Ahmed Hassan, fundraising among the expatriate Somali community had become more effective. Originally rich merchants were the main source, but from 1980 the activists began collect- ing money from the workers generally, going from house to house. A quota was then established for each of the clans represented in the Gulf according to their estimated numbers.

21. The four officers were: Mohamed Kahin Ahmed (Habar Tol Ja'lo), destined to become minister of defence in the first (1991) Somaliland government, Adan Shinne (Habar Awal), Ahmed Ragge and Adan Suleyman (Habar Tol Ja'lo).

22. See: "Letter from Hargeisa," *Horn of Africa Journal* 4 No. 4 1981/2, pp. 43ff; Africa Watch, *Somalia, a government at war with its own people*, 1990 pp. 37- 41; *Somalia Uncensored*, no. 6, December 1981.

23. See Africa Watch, *cit.*, 1990, p. 69.

24. Africa Watch, *cit.*, 1990, p. 32.

25. Hassan 'Ise recalls that in his dealings with the SNM and SSDF, Colonel Mengistu was advised by Atto Demise, a Somali-speaker (Habar Tol Ja'lo) from the Ogaadeen region who had been governor of Harar and Minister of the Interior under the Emperor. Another important Ethiopian figure in these negotiations was Colonel Tsfei of the security services.

26. In this spirit of reconciliation, figures from Siyad's forces were welcomed

back as with the officer who had commanded the army when it destroyed Burao: at the 1991 SNM congress he was in charge of the delegates' bodyguard.

27. In fact, after the end of the war, prominent Isaaqis who could find their way back to the north readily found positions in the SNM.
28. See Compagnon, cit.,p. 35
29. This attack, allegedly, was master-minded by General Bille Ruffle (Ogaadeen).
30. From 1985, however, Dr Omar Dihoud recalls, southern Dir guerillas, allied with the SNM and who later took the name 'Southern Somali national movement', were active against Siyad's own clansmen in the upper Juba region.
31. For an account of these from an SNM viewpoint, see *Africa Watch*, 1990, pp. 127-169.
32. Gerard Prunier's (1992) sympathetic and perceptive study of the SNM at war, based on first-hand observation, estimated that the regular troups numbered less that 4,000 men.
33. See Drysdale, 1991.
34. See Farah, 1993.

Chapter IX

SEGMENTARY NATIONALISM AND THE COLLAPSE OF THE SOMALI STATE

In the majority of the post-colonial African states with their "Ethiopian-style" multi-ethnic composition created by colonialism, the main problem since their foundation has been the formation of a viable transcendent nationalism uniting the component ethnic groups. Hence their preoccupation with "nation-building" and the associated "frontier-fetishism" (as I have called it).[1] The Somali case seemed at independence (1960) very different. Nationalism was already part of their heritage and their problem was not that of nation-building, but of extending national *statehood* outside the frontiers of the Somali Republic (formed by the Union of British and Italian Somaliland), to embrace the remaining portions of the nation in Djibouti, Ethiopia and Kenya. Thus, at home they seemed to possess an exemplary mono-cultural nationhood and so to enjoy political circumstances which, from the perspective of the nineteenth century Scottish political philosopher, John Stuart Mill, were peculiarly conducive to democracy. Politics in the first nine years of Somalia's life seemed to confirm this interpretation.[2] But the picture changed dramatically following General Mohamad Siyad Barre's military *coup* in October, 1969, and further significant changes have occurred since then.

Hindsight highlights the fact that although the Somalis had, prior to their colonial partition, a strong sense of cultural nationalism, they did not constitute a single, united political unit. Political unity, based on kinship pervasively traced in the male line, stopped short of the culturally defined nation which was internally divided into a myriad of competing lineages. The Somalis spoke the same language, shared the

same predominantly nomadic herding culture, and were all adherents of
Sunni Islam with a strong attachment to the Sufi brotherhoods. Thus,
in a word, they formed an ethnic group or nation but not, traditionally,
a single polity. Before and after independence, nationalist politicians
naturally sought to politicize this cultural legacy and transform it into
effective, national, political cohesion.

Somali nationalism in revolutionary mode

As we have seen (Chapter 7), shortly after seizing power, General
Mohamad Siyad Barre, had adopted "Scientific Socialism"[3] (in Somali,
literally "wealth-sharing based on wisdom") with the stated aim of uniting the nation and eradicating its ancient clan divisions. "Tribalism,"
which was associated with nepotism and corruption, was officially
banned and ritually buried (1971), and "tribalistic" (ie clan-based)
behavior became a serious criminal offence. The collective payment of
blood money (mag; Arabic diya) was correspondingly outlawed and the
personal rather than kinship aspects of marriage emphasized. The universal term of address "cousin" - implying clansman - was officially
replaced by the term jaalle - comrade. Lineage genealogies, the traditional basis of socio-political identity, and their use to identify people
were banned: even the old nationalistic circumlocution "ex-clan" was
forbidden. In their place, the Head of State was presented in the revolutionary rhetoric as the "Father" of a nation whose "Mother" was his
Revolution. This stirring ideology - legitimated by reference to the holy
trinity of Marx, Lenin and Siyad - was thrust upon the masses through
intense radio propaganda and through the local Orientation Centers
which were set up throughout the state, which had itself been divided
into new provinces cutting across traditional clan boundaries. Radiating
out from the presidency, the locally organized people's vigilantes (or
"Victory Pioneers" - led by the "Victorious Leader" Siyad), and the sinister National Security Service shared the task of ensuring that this elaborate propaganda rhetoric fell on receptive ears. The repeatedly
proclaimed objective was to replace archaic, divisive lineage loyalty, by
productive revolutionary allegiance to the nation.

In the view of Ernest Gellner and other theorists of nationalism,
the decisive ingredient in national self-consciousness is literacy.[4] Where
previous civilian Somali governments had faltered, here, as we have
seen, the military had acted decisively, adopting a Roman script for the
national language and launching intensive nationwide urban and rural
literacy campaigns in 1973 and 1974 (when I happened to be in
Somalia). The much-publicised intention was, as President Siyad put it

(apparently without having read Gellner), "to give everybody the opportunity to learn reading and writing...to eradicate social balkanisation and fragmentation into tribes (i.e. lineages and clans) and sects...to bring about an absolute unity" (c.f. Chapter 7).

Clandestine clan power

While these measures overtly directed at eliminating clan and lineage divisions[5] and establishing enduring bonds of national solidarity were ostentatiously promoted at all levels in the state, the head of state himself was, as we have seen (above, p. 166), covertly relying on older, time-honored ties of loyalty. His inner power circle consisted of members of three related clans - each critically significant in its own way. His most trusted ministers were naturally from his own patrilineal clan (the Marrehaan). Next came members of the clan (Dulbahante), of his son-in-law, head of the National Security Service. The third clan, in this sacred triangle was that of the President's mother's brother, the Ogaadeen. This connection, as was argued in Chapter 7, gave the President a privileged (but ambivalent), relationship with the turbulent Ogaadeeni nationalists who had been chaffing against Ethiopian rule since its effective imposition in the late 40s.[6]

It is important to emphasize here that these three clans - the President's (M), his mother's brother's (O), and his son-in-law's (D), all belong, at a higher level of segmentary grouping, to the Daarood clan family. Although the regime at all times included representatives of other non-Daarood clans, the magic letters MOD thus represented the inner circle of Daarood power.

The chaos which spread in Ethiopia in the initial years of the Ethiopian revolution following Haile Selassie's deposition in October 1974, encouraged the Ogaadeeni Somalis to prepare to seize their opportunity. Following successful risings against Ethiopian rule in neighboring provinces by allies of the Somalis (Muslim Oromo and others), the forces of the Western Somali Liberation Front,[7] aided by troops from Somalia, began in the summer of 1977 to push the Ethiopians out of the Ogaadeen. The Somali victory was, however, shortlived. The conflict triggered a seismic shift in super-power alignments in the Horn of Africa with the Russians turning to support the Ethiopians and enabling them to regain control of the Ogaadeen.

The Refugee Factor

This defeat was followed by the huge refugee influx of the best part of a million Ogaadeenis (ethnic Somalis and Oromo neighbours and allies) into Somalia in 1978 and 1979, creating immense problems for the Somali state which became increasingly dependent on humanitarian aid from the Western bloc bilaterally and via the UNHCR.[8] Perhaps as many as half the (Daarood) refugees were placed in refugee camps in the centre of the Northern Regions of the Republic, where their main local "hosts" were people of the Isaaq clan family, whom they traditionally confronted in their herding movements. Of course, the majority of the refugees remained initially in the huge camps - up to 60,000 strong - in which they were gathered. These were often poorly supplied with sources of water let alone endowed with other natural resources which might have enabled them to achieve some degree of self-sufficiency.

The refugees were consequently completely dependent on international relief supplies and treated by the Somali authorities as temporary residents of the Republic who would eventually return to their Ogaadeen homeland in Ethiopia. This assumption, as well as their sense of clan identity, was also fostered by naming sections of refugee camps after their places of origin in the Ogaadeen. Of course, this did not prevent refugees trading surplus rations with the local northern and largely Isaaqi population. Some refugees also found local work outside the camps, and a few, who managed to gain passports, even joined the migrant Somali "muscle-drain" to Saudi Arabia and the Gulf States. Thus the refugee economy became another strand in the multi-sector Somali economy and the Ogaadeen factor in Somali politics -this time inside Somalia - acquired new force.

Post-war dissent

At its height, the Ogaadeen war had been immensely popular in Somalia and President Siyad's public standing never higher. The terrible defeat and refugee invasion (which seriously upset Somalia's existing clan demography), quickly led to widespread public demoralization and to an upsurge of "tribalism" (ie clan loyalties), as different groups sought scapegoats to explain the debacle. Hard on the heels of the Somali retreat, this led to the unsuccessful Majeerteen attempted coup, mounted against the regime in April, 1978. As we have seen in Chapter 8, after this abortive action, those who had escaped arrest regrouped, forming the Somali Salvation Democratic Front (SSDF) which made its operational headquarters across the border in Ethiopia. That the Maajerteen sought support in Ethiopia, Somalia's traditional enemy, was both a sign of their desperation and a measure of the degree of disintegration of Somali national solidarity. All the measures of Siyad's Scientific Socialism had clearly not succeeded in their task of transforming Somali national solidarity from the ancient "mechanical" to the modern "organic" mode (to follow Durkheim's terminology).

In 1989-90, the spotlight switched to the main northern protagonist in the recent civil war in Somalia, the Somali National Movement (SNM) which, as we have seen, despite its name, drew most of its support from the Isaaqi clans of central northern Somalia and articulated their profound disaffection. By this time, armed opposition to Siyad was spreading throughout the country. But, at the same time, despite their common objective - the overthrow of Siyad's Daarood regime - the predominantly Daarood and Isaaq foundations, respectively, of the SSDF and SNM added to their other logistical and leadership difficulties, preventing them from making common cause and thus weakening the overall impact of their rebellion.

Since the Ogaadeen war defeat, Siyad had still continued to support, albeit somewhat nominally, the Ogaadeeni Western Somali Liberation Front which remained an irksome thorn in Ethiopia's side. However, the destabilizing pressures exerted by the SSDF and SNM had the effect of driving President Siyad to seek an accommodation with Ethiopia, a move which was also encouraged by Somalia's Western allies (Italy, the EEC, and the USA). The Somali regime's anxiety to secure a deal with Ethiopia had been increased by the insecurity that his clansmen felt when the President was involved in a nearly fatal car crash in May 1986. Siyad, nevertheless, proved remarkably resilient. Following his re-election, unopposed (since no opposition was permitted), as head of state for a further seven year term in office at the end of that year, a new government was formed in February 1987. For the first time since the *coup*, however, the cabinet now included a "Prime Minister" in the unconvincing shape of the faithful General Samatar (Siyad's long-serving and politically unthreatening military commander).

In reality President Siyad had consolidated the position of his own clan and family within which rivalry over who should eventually succeed him was beginning to become marked. The Marrehaan now unquestionably and openly dominated the military, with Siyad's son, General Maslah, in charge of a special northern command unit. The old MOD alliance had begun to crumble, at least at the highest levels, as the Marrehaan closed ranks in the face of mounting uncertainty. The time had come to secure Ethiopian co-operation in cauterizing the SNM and SSDF.

The Price of Peace with Ethiopia

Further signalling the demise of pan-Somali solidarity, in April, 1988, Presidents Siyad and Mengistu finally signed a peace accord, normalizing their relations, and undertaking to cease supporting each other's dissidents. Thus Siyad withdrew support from the WSLF which was now opposed by an anti-Siyad organization (the Ogaden National Liberation Front), and Mengistu formally withdrew support from the SSDF and SNM. As we have seen, this detente and its potential consequences triggered the audacious SNM onslaught on military installations in Northern Somalia that quickly led to the 1988-91 all out civil war between the regime and the Isaaq clansmen.

The human cost was terrible. Thousands of civilians were killed and wounded, and at least half a million fled their homes seeking asylum across the border in Ethiopia and in the Republic of Djibouti. Thousands of refugees eventually found refuge in Canada, Britain, Scandinavia, Italy and the USA. Meanwhile, male Ogaadeeni refugees in northern Somalia, who had long been subject to illegal recruitment into Siyad's armed forces, were conscripted as a paramilitary militia to fight the SNM and to man checkpoints on the roads. Ogaadeeni refugees were at the same time encouraged to take over the remains of Isaaq shops and houses in what, after their bombardment by Siyad's forces, were effectively ghost towns. Thus, those who had been earlier received as refugee guests in northern Somalia had supplanted their Isaaqi hosts; and many of the latter, in this bitterly ironic turn of fate, had become refugees in the Ogadeen.

If the Ogaadeenis were once the tail that wagged the dog, drawing Somalia into their fight for liberation from Ethiopian rule, the situation in 1989-90 was very different. Those still in the Ogaadeen were to all intents and purposes deserted by Siyad while those outside in Somalia were co-opted into fighting to maintain the regime. Here the appeal, also addressed to the disunited Majeerteen, was for Daarood solidarity against the Isaaq. Thus other northern Daarood clans were armed by the regime and urged to joint the fight. Other northern groups (such as the 'Iise and Gadabuursi), who are neither Isaaq or Daarood, were also armed and exhorted to turn against the Isaaq. The regime's appeal for Daarood solidarity evoked a corresponding attempt by the Isaaq to invoke a wider-based, higher level "Irrir" solidarity to include the important Hawiye clans in whose territory Mogadishu, the capital of the Republic, is located. While seeking Daarood support where appropriate, the regime also endeavored to secure the loyalty of all non-Isaaq clans and, of course, to penetrate the ranks of the Isaaq.

Thus, in its desperate fight for survival, Siyad's family and clansmen sought to exploit to the full segmentary lineage rivalry within the Somali nation. They also made abundant use of coercion and rewards of all kinds, as corruption flourished. By the end of January, 1991, the

SNM had effectively overcome Siyad's forces in the north and was consolidating its position throughout the region. Many Ogaadeeni refugees had returned to their kinsmen in Ethiopia, who were now incorporated in three new "autonomous" regions within the Ethiopian state. Other mutinous Ogaadeeni soldiery in southern Somalia had established the Somali Patriotic Movement in 1989 which joined the loose coalition of movements fighting Siyad, particularly the recently formed United Somali Congress.[9]

Partly derived from its earlier association with the SNM (above, p. 212), the USC had become primarily a Hawiye organization with two main factions. One was based on the Abgaal clan, whose home town is the Somali capital, Mogadishu, and the other based on the Habar Gidir, the clan of the USC militia commander, General Aideed, (a former general in Siyad's army and ex-ambassador to India), whose territory stretches to the north as far as Galkayu. Siyad, of course, sought to exploit these divisions as well as exhorting all the Daarood in Mogadishu to kill its Hawiye citizens whether they were Abgaal or Habar Gidir. The ensuing inter-clan violence, however, threatened Siyad's position further, and, in desperation, he finally turned his heavy artillery on the Hawiye quarters of the city. This provoked the extremely bloody general uprising which led to Siyad's flight from the town on January 26, 1991, pursued by General Aideed who had recently entered Mogadishu with his forces. While Aideed was thus engaged chasing Siyad, the USC Abgaal group in Mogadishu hastily set up an "interim government" under Ali Mahdi, (a prominent Abgaal businessman), as provisional president and with ministers drawn from the members of other (non-Hawiye) clans - not all of whom had actually been consulted, far less accepted office! When this, largely self-appointed administration began to try to control the numerous armed groups at large in Mogadishu, the Habar Gidir became suspicious of Abgaal intentions and fighting erupted between the two Hawiye clans. With the calling of a USC party congress in July, at which Aideed was elected USC Chairman, with Ali Mahdi continuing as "interim president," an uneasy peace was restored.

Meanwhile, Siyad and his remaining henchmen had fled to his clan territory in Gedo where he proceeded to attempt to mobilise and manipulate pan-Daarood solidarity, forming the Marrehaan-based "Somali National Front." Appeals to Daarood unity were encouraged by the indiscriminate revenge killings of people of this clan-family, (especially those of the Dulbahante clan associated with the NSS), perpetrated by Hawiye groups in the aftermath of Siyad's escape from Mogadishu. Thus a motley group of Daarood-based forces (including, for a time, some SPM [Ogaadeen] and SSDF [Majeerteen] as well as

Marrehaan), became engaged in a series of skirmishes with USC forces in the area between Mogadishu and the port of Kismayu to the south. In April 1991, after heavy fighting and at the cost of a renewed exodus to Ethiopia and Kenya of thousands of Daarood refugees, the USC gained control of Kismayu - losing it again later in the year, but recovering it for the time being in the spring of 1992. All the Daarood, of course, were not engaged in this conflict and far from decisively defeated: the position of the important Majeerteen clan and its SSDF remained at this time still equivocal - partly because some of the Majeerteen lived in the Kismayu hinterland, far from their headquarters in the north-east. By the summer of 1991, and along similar lines to developments in the north-west, the whole region occupied by the Majeerteen in the northeast (Bari, Nugaal and Mudug provinces) had become effectively self-governing under SSDF administration.

Returning to the situation in Mogadishu, by September the USC conflict had flared up again. Mogadishu was now effectively divided into two principal military zones - one controlled by the Abgaal and the other by the Habar Gidir invaders. Other smaller Hawiye groups maintained their own zones of influence, with their militia, sometimes acting as neutrals, sometimes as partisan allies in the ensuing blood-bath which between November, 1991, and April, 1992, had almost completely devastated what remained of Mogadishu after Siyad's ravages, causing death and injury to civilians on a catastrophic scale and plunging the whole area into chaos and famine. The most effective ceasefire between the two sides, in April 1992, coincided significantly with Siyad's abortive attempt to recapture Mogadishu for the Marrehaan. How long this brief peace between the two Hawiye clans would survive General Aideed's Habar Gidir victory over Siyad's Daarood forces -forcing the latter into Kenya - was anyone's guess.

The Rebirth of Somaliland

During this long period of confused clan manoeuvring and turmoil in the south, the USC "interim government" in Mogadishu sent its Isaaq prime minister and other ministers on largely fruitless missions abroad to seek international aid and recognition[10].

Appreciating that external recognition would require widespread internal support, Ali Mahdi's government tried at the same time to persuade the SNM and other movements to join in talks aimed at the formation of an acceptable national government. (Most publicly, this was pursued at the abortive Djibouti conferences of July 1991). That the USC "prime minister" was a well-known Isaaq figure might have been expected to facilitate these complex negotiations. Actually, this had the reverse effect. He had been appointed without consultation with the SNM who, in any case, chose to regard him as tainted by a too close association with Siyad as well as possessing other negative features. Hence the SNM, whose links with the USC were in any case through Aideed and the Habar Gidir rather than Ali Mahdi, responded coolly to these overtures. This cautious response seemed to the SNM leadership amply justified as the extent of internal USC divisions became plain in the developing conflict and chaos in and around Mogadishu.

So, the SNM concentrated on its own local problems in the north. A surprising degree of peace between the Isaaq and non-Isaaq clans of the region (the former British Somaliland Protectorate) had been secured, largely through the efforts of the traditional clan elders, by the time of the SNM national congress in May 1991. There was widespread hatred and distrust of the south, (identified with Siyad's misrule), and a strong tide of public feeling favoring separatism. As we have seen above, bowing to this pressure, the SNM leadership had proclaimed on 18th May 1991 that their region would resume its independence from the south, taking the title "Somaliland Republic." This pragmatic decision also reflected the desire of the people of Somaliland to concentrate on rebuilding their country and ruined towns after their wholesale devastation by Siyad's forces which had left hundreds of thousands of landmines to remind northerners of their barbaric regime.

The Somali Republic had thus now reverted to its two former constituent colonial units - the ex-British and Italian Somalilands - a development that was bitterly, but ineffectually, opposed by Ali Mahdi's administration in Mogadishu. There were now two interim governments - neither of which recognized the other - and each of which desperately sought international emergency aid and diplomatic recognition. While the SNM government had, initially, virtually country-wide support, Ali Mahdi's government was effectively restricted to the Mogadishu area and after September, 1991, to only a dwindling part of the town itself. Outside Mogadishu, various locally-based clan forces reigned and struggled for control of wider areas.

Djibouti and the limits of Somali segmentary nationalism

The re-emergence of the Somaliland Republic (based on the former British Somaliland Protectorate), dealt a further blow to the once powerful aim of Pan-Somali unity. I say "further" because, of course, the attainment of independence by the ex-French territory of Djibouti under a Somali President (the Somali doyen of French politics), in 1977, sharply punctured Somali aspirations for wider national unity based on an extension of the existing Somali Republic (the so-called Somali Democratic Republic). From 1977 until May, 1991, there were thus two Somali states, and after May, 1991, effectively three, as the colonially defined territories assumed (or reassumed), local sovereignty. Of course, Djibouti is a special case, being a state comprising the two related eth- nic groups, the currently dominant Somali (mainly of the 'Iise clan), and the 'Afar, in uneasy combination. As President Hassan Guled's reign drew to a close in the 1990s, the inevitable jockeying for future power amongst his close lineage associates - and others - had wider repercus- sions on the delicate relations between the 'Afar and 'Iise (and other Somali), of Djibouti. Aligning themselves with pressure from the French Government to introduce a multi-party system, the "Afar formed the "Front for the Restoration of Unity and Democracy" (FRUD) which in 1991 mounted a series of guerilla operations seeking to secure control of a number of 'Afar centres outside the town of Djibouti. As tension mounted with the Djiboutian authorities, some dissident Somali polit- ical figures identified themselves with FRUD which remained, however, an essentially 'Afar organization with links to the 'Afar Liberation Front, presided over by the conservative 'Afar land-owner, Sultan 'Ali Mirreh in Ethiopia.

The 'Afar, of course, live in eastern Ethiopia as well as Djibouti; the 'Iise Somali pastoral nomads are also represented in Ethiopia and in the north-western districts of what is now the Somaliland Republic. In opposition to the Isaaqi SNM, some 'Iise formed the United Somali Front (USF) to protect and further their clan interests. They tended to look to their kinsmen in Djibouti for support and in early 1991 unsuc- cessfully attempted to detach themselves from Somaliland in order to join Djibouti. Relations between the Djibouti government and the Somaliland SNM have thus, inevitably been strained from time to time but by the spring of 1992, were informally cordial with Djibouti acting as the main point of entry for development assistance to Somaliland. By this time, as I saw myself in March, 1992, the pressure exerted by FRUD on the Somali authorities in Djibouti was replicated - not necessarily directly - by 'Iise clansmen aggressively pushing their 'Afar neighbours in the Ethiopian Awash Valley closer and closer to the river as, follow- ing a series of bloody engagements, they expanded into traditionally 'Afar pastures and trading centres along the Awash-Assab road. Somali- 'Afar relations in Ethiopia, mediated on the 'Afar side by the ALF, inevitably also had repercussions on those between these ethnic groups in Djibouti where the radical 'Afar representatives were FRUD. Another factor affecting 'Iise solidarity and relations with these 'Afar were, of course, the changing pattern of interaction between the 'Iise and other Somali clans in Somaliland, particularly, but not only, the Isaaq.

The same tendencies of reversion to clan relativist loyalties, with the alliance and disassociation of segmentary kin-groups according to the political context, characterised the general scene throughout the Somali region in 1992,[11] Siyad's much publicised official campaigns against clan allegiance had manifestly had absolutely no lasting effect, which was perhaps not surprising since they were essentially rhetorical. In my opinion, Siyad's own power politics always included a powerful clan element and served to reinforce and exacerbate ancient antagonisms in the segmentary lineage system - which, of course, he did not invent. He well knew, however, how to adapt the ancient divide and rule formula to these particular clan conditions. He befriended groups which enabled him to attack his clan enemies. In this pattern of what Daniel Compagnon aptly calls (clan) clientelism, Siyad distributed arms and money to his friends, encouraging them to attack their common clan enemies who, of course, were accused of divisive "tribalism" by the master tribalist.

The legacy of his rule, including the making of peace with Ethiopia (thus removing this factor of external threat), contributed materially to the present situation in which the Somali nation is more deeply divided along its traditional kinship lines than perhaps at any other time this century. Here we might say that if the segmentary system had not already existed, Siyad would have invented it to cling to power at the vortex of clan chaos. By destroying his country's economy, Siyad also directly promoted those conditions of general lack of resources and insecurity on which clan loyalty thrives, since clan solidarity offers the only hope of survival. Also by providing arms - directly and indirectly - Siyad's legacy of Marrehaan misrule ensured a wide and persistent prevalence of extremely bloody clan conflict.

The state collapses

The Pan-Somali ideal, founded in cultural identity rather than political unity, evoked in opposition to the colonial situation, which was so strong in the 1950s and 1960s had taken a severe battering. In 1991/92, reactively influenced by the example of the SSDF, the SNM, USC and SPM, the general tendency was for every major Somali clan to form its own militia movement. Thus clans were becoming effectively self-governing entities throughout the Somali region as they carved out spheres of influence in a process which, with the abundance of modern weapons, frequently entailed savage battles with a high toll of civilian casualties. The political geography of the Somali hinterland in 1992, consequently, closely resembled that reported by European explorers in the 19th century, with spears replaced by Kalashnikovs and bazookas. These clan areas could only be entered or traversed by outsiders (people of other clans, foreigners), with the consent of the locals and, usually the payment of appropriate fees for "protection."

This was the situation confronting those adventurous non-governmental agencies which still operated in Somalia. It was vividly and poignantly experienced by a well-respected former Somali Minister of the Interior and his friends who, on January 7, 1992, set off from Mogadishu, leading a road convoy of over seventy vehicles bound for the north (Somaliland Republic), where they arrived at Burao exactly a month later! (This journey along the Chinese road used to take some twenty-four hours to accomplish). The convoy had its own (paid), armed escorts and, in addition, was forced to hire local guides and protectors while traversing the different clan areas. Four vehicles were looted en route - one by the convoy's armed escort when it had completed its mission: other vehicles had to be abandoned and only fifty-one reached their final destination - with the help of donations of fuel from the Red Cross and Save the Children Fund. Accidents in the course of this remarkable journey accounted for eighteen deaths and about thirty injured people. On the other hand, nine babies were born en route.

As in the past, political unity was now not absolutely limited to the clan level. Related clans could, according to circumstances, ally in wider formations. So, as we have seen, the USC "warlords" in Mogadishu, however divided amongst themselves internally were perceived externally as Hawiye which tended to trigger a reactive alliance of some at least of the various Daarood clan movements at a higher level of Daarood unity and, had a similar effect on the Isaaq clans of the north. The tensions and conflicts which, in turn, broke out among the Isaaq in the Somaliland Republic's first year of existence were linked to the fact that once the Isaaq had made peace with their non-Isaaq neighbours (the Gadabuusi, Dulbahante and Warsangeli), they were themselves more likely to fall apart, along segmentary lines into their constituent clans (eg the Habar Awal, Habar Yuunis, Habar Tolja'alo, etc.). Everything that has happened in recent Somali political history is, thus, an eloquent testimony to the accuracy of anthropological analysis - but at appalling cost in humanitarian terms.

As we have seen, the segmentary Somali system provides an ideal basis for the exercise of divide and rule tyranny by unscrupulous despots such as Mohamad Siyad Barre. However, it is also the fundamental system with which all Somali politicians who aspire to roles on the national stage have to wrestle. So, paradoxically, the well-intentioned, sincere

Somali nationalist who genuinely seeks to advance the cause of the nation as a whole has, nevertheless, to operate with and through the segmentary clan system. Of course, he will be assisted, or hindered in his nationalist efforts, by external factors (such as the presence or absence of foreign pressures), and by the general security situation of the Somali people. Thus, however unlikely it may look at the time of the 1990s crisis, it cannot be assumed that the future will never see a swing of the segmentary pendulum, with a renewed upsurge (however transient), of Pan-Somali nationalism. But any realistic assessment of possible future trends has to acknowledge that Somali nationalism - despite literacy[12] -retains its segmentary character and has *not* been transformed into a "modern" organic mode.

It has, finally, to be noted that nationalism has not to be confused with statehood. Unlike the peoples of the central Ethiopian highlands (and for that matter the 'Afar), the Somali people have no traditional commitment to state government: they are profoundly uncentralized and egalitarian, and historically their encounters with state structures have tended to be fleeting and predatory. Against this background, some Somali intellectuals contemplating Somalia's disintegration in 1992, realistically concluded that the best hope for the future probably lay in a loosely organized federal state, built up gradually from clan-based local councils.

At a more abstract level, the collapse of the colonially created state represents technically a triumph for the segmentary lineage system and the political power of kinship. For better or worse, clanship has certainly prevailed, and the assertions of some Somali[13] and non-Somali[14] ideologues that clanship was an atavistic force doomed to oblivion in the modern world seem rather dated. Given then, that like nationalism, clanship is a human invention, is it in the 1990s basically the same phenomenon that it was in the 1890s? Linguistically the answer must be "yes," since the same terminology has been employed throughout the recorded history of the Somalis. Sociologically, the evidence also supports this view. Indeed, the argument of this book is that clanship is and was essentially a multipurpose, culturally constructed resource of compelling power because of its ostensibly inherent character "bred in the bone" and running "in the blood," as Somalis conceptualize it.

Clanship is, of course, an elastic principle, differentially manipulated by ambitious, power-hungry individuals. In the modern setting, with their privileged access to external sources of economic and political power, to sophisticated weapons and Swiss bank accounts, successful "big men" - like Siyad and his successors the so-called "war-lords" - can in this egalitarian society pluck the strings of kinship to their own advantage to an extent and on a scale beyond anything realised before. They are able to exploit, and partially control, the interface between their own society and the world outside. At the same time, the pervasive if uneven distribution of modern weapons has greatly aggravated the bitterness and ferocity of group conflict, with casualties too numerous to record or easily repair in terms of traditional bloodwealth payments. This seems to exacerbate the difficulties of inter-clan peace-making and dispute settlement.

However, although the scale, and perhaps intensity of operations has changed dramatically, in the past also there were always political entrepreneurs and military adventurers (*abbaanduule*) who sought to benefit from connections with external forces in the surrounding states (Muslim and non-Muslim). Historically, the widest scale of opportunistic political solidarity was that mobilized under the banner of Islam by religious figures inveighing against "infidel" infiltration.[15] Ultimately, however, all these centralizing initiatives, like that of the dictator Siyad, fell victim to the immense centrifugal pressures of the Somali segmentary system and the persuasive force of the call of kinship in this egalitarian culture.

Main Somali Clans and Movements 1992/1993

Arabian ancestry

Irrir

Digil	Rahanwiin	Hawiye Dir	Isaaq	Daarood

SDM	USC	SNM

'Ise	Gadabuursi	Marrehaan	Ogadeen

USF	SDA	SNF	SPM

Majeerteen	Dulbahante	Warsangeli

SSDF	USP

Somali Movements 1992/1993

Daarood	Marrehaan - Somali National Front
	Ogadeen - Somali Patriotic Movement
	(two main branches: Muhamad Zubayr
	lineages led by General Aden Abdallahi Nur
	(Gabio); and their rival lineages led by
	Colonel Ahmed Umar Jess).
Majeerteen -	Somali Salvation Democratic Front
	Dulbahante - United Somali Party
	Warsangeli - United Somali Party
Dir	'Ise - United Somali Front
	Gadabuursi - Somali Democratic Alliance
	(Southern Dir Clans) - Southern Somali
	National Movement
Isaaq	all Isaaq clans - Somali National Movement
Hawiye	Abgal - United Somali Congress
	led by Ali Mahdi
	Habar Gidir - United Somali Congress rival
	faction led by General Aidiid.

Digil and Rahanwiin Somali Democratic Movement

Notes

1. See Lewis, 1983, pp 67-76.
2. See Lewis, 1988, p.166-204.
3. See also Ahmed I Samatar, 1988; D. Laitin and S. Samatar, 1987.
4. Ernest Gellner, 1983.
5. The recent Africawatch report, *Somalia a fight to the Death?*, February 1992, though valuable in many other ways, quite mistakenly refers to the 1990-1992 conflict in Mogadishu between Hawiye clans as 'newly manufactured ethnic tension'. It is *not* ethnic and it is not recently manufactured - it is, on the contrary, endemic to the Somali lineage system.
6. See Lewis, 1983, pp 29 *ff*; John Markakis, 1987, pp 269 *ff*.
7. See Lewis, 1980.
8. Lewis, 1986 (b).
9. For further information on the formation of these movements see the very useful accounts by D. Compagnon, 1990, pp 29-54; and 1991; and Marchal, 1992; 1993.
10. The prime minister (Umar Arteh), who is well-known in Arab countries, seemed to have been successful in securing support from some Gulf states.

Ali Mahdi also benefited from his close relations with Italy which were reinforced by Italian distaste for General Aideed. The latter went to considerable lengths to expose the Italian Somali aid scandals which formed part of the wider pattern of political corruption under investigation in Italy in 1993.

11. Parallel developments in the decline of Somali ethnic identity and the revival of clan allegiance amongst the Somali population of northern Kenya prior to the post-1990 refugee influx are documented and analyzed in M. I. Farah, 1993.

12. See also Lewis 1986 (a).

13. This view is forcefully expounded by the Marxist Somali geographer, Abdi I Samatar, 1989.

14. In this vein, quite unconvincingly, Kapteijns (1991) seeks to distinguish 'pre-capitalist' Somali pastoralism based on 'corporate kinship' from 'capitalist' modern Somali society dominated by 'clannism.' The latter, she argues, is a new ideology invented by the new entrepreneurial 'middle class' to dominate their poorer kinsmen. No serious socio-cultural evidence is offered for this claim. For an excellent, carefully documented economic analysis of the opportunistic use of clanship by merchants and militias, see Djama, 1992.

15. The outstanding case is the Somali nationalist hero, Sayyid Mohamad 'Abdille Hassan, see Lewis, 1988, pp. 63-91; S. S. Samatar, 1982; SheikAbdi, 1993.

References

ABOKOR, A.A. (trans, A.A. Xange)
1987   *The Camel in Somali Oral Traditions*, Uppsala: Scandinavian Institute of African Studies.

ABDALLA, R.H.D.
1982   *Sisters in Affliction*, London: Zed Books.

ABDULLAHI, A.M.
1990   *Pastoral Production Systems in Africa: A study of nomadic household economy and livestock marketing in central Somalia*, Kiel: Wissenschaft Verlag Vank Kiel.

ACKERMAN, A.
1963   "Affiliations: structural determinants of differential divorce rates," *American Journal of Sociology*, Vol 69, pp 13-20.

AFRAX, MAHAMAD DAHIR
1981   *Maana faay*. Mogadishu.

AFRICA WATCH
1990   *Somalia : a government at war with its own people*. New York.
1992   *No Mercy in Mogadishu: the Human Cost of the Conflict and the Struggle for Relief*. March, Washington D.C.
1992   *Somalia a fight to the Death?*. February, Washington D.C.

ALBOSPEYRE, M.
1959   "Les Danakil du Cercle de Tadjoura" in *Cahiers de l'Afrique et l'Asie v: Mer Rouge - Afrique Orientale*, Paris: Peyronnet, pp. 102-163.

ANDERSON, J. N. D.
1954   *Islamic Law in Africa*, London: H.M.S.O.

ANDRZEJEWSKI, B.W. and I. M. LEWIS
1964   *Somali poetry : an introduction*, Oxford: Clarendon Press.

APTHORPE, R. J.
1960   "Problems of African History: the Nsenga of Northern Rhodesia," *Rhodes-Livingstone Institute Journal*, XXVIII, pp. 47-68.

ARVANITES, L.
1983   "Notes on Soomaali vocatives and polite imperatives," paper presented to Second International Congress of Somali Studies, Hamburg.

ASAD, T.
1973   *Anthropology and The Colonial Encounter.* Edited by T. Asad. London: Ithaca Press.

AYOUB, M. R.
1964   "Bipolarity of Arabic kinship terms" in H.G. Lunt (ed.) *Proceedings of the Ninth International Congress of Linguists*, pp. 1100-1106.

BARNES, J
1949   "Measures of Divorce Frequency in Simple Societies," *Journal of the Royal Anthropologcial Institute* LXXIV, pp. 27-62
1951   *Marriage in a Changing Society*, Rhodes-Livingstone Institute paper no. 20, Cape Town: Oxford University Press.

BLOCH, M.
1971   "The Moral and Tactical Meaning of Kinship Terms," *Man*, Vol. 6, pp.79-86.

1975   *Marxist Analyses and Social Anthropology.* Edited by M. Bloch. London: Malaby.

BOHANNAN, L.
1949   "Dahomean Marriage: A revaluation," *Africa* XIX, pp. 273-287.
1952   "A Genealogical Charter." *Africa*, 22: 301-15.

BOHANNAN, L. and P.
1953   *The Tiv of Central Nigeria*, London: International African Institute.

BROWN, J. A.
1956   *Adoption of Islamic Law in the Somaliland Protectorate* (cyclostyled), Hargeisa.

BURTON, R.
1943   *First Footsteps in East Africa*, London: Everyman edition.

CARO BAROJA, J.
1955   Estudios Saharianos, Madrid.

CASTAGNO, A.
1964   "Somali Republic." In Political Parties and National Integration in
        Tropical Africa, J. S. Coleman and C. G. Rosberg eds., Berkeley:
        University of California Press, pp. 512-559.

CASTAGNO, M.
1975   Historical Dictionary of Somalia. Metuchen, New Jersey: Scarecrow Press.

CASTANEDA, C.
1974   Journey to Ixtlan. Harmondsworth: Penguin.

CERULLI, E.
1918/1919 "Il diritto consuetudinario della Somalia Italiana settentrionale,"
        Bolletino della Societa Africana d'Italia, xxxviii, Naples.
1957   Somalia: scritti vari editi ed inediti, I. Rome: Istituto Poligrafico dello Stato.
1959   Somalia: scritti vari editi ed inediti, II. Rome: Istituto Poligrafico dello Stato.

CHITTICK, N.
1976   "An Archaeological Reconnaissance in the Horn: The British Somali
        Expedition, Azania pp. 117-33.

COLSON, E.
1978   "Max Gluckman and the Study of Divorce" in P.H. Gulliver (ed.) Cross
        Examinations: Essays in Memory of Max Gluckman. Leiden: E.J. Brill.

COLUCCI, M.
1924   Principi di diritto Consuetudinario della Somalia Italiana meridionale.
        Florence: "La Voce."

COMPAGNON, D.
1990   "The Somali Opposition Fronts," Horn of Africa, vol xiii, Nos 1 & 2.
1991   "Somalie: de l'état en formation à l'état en pointillé," in J. F. Medard
        (ed) Etats d'Afrique Noire. Paris: Karthala, pp 205-240.

CROZIER, B.,
1975   The Soviet Presence in Somalia. Conflict Studies, No. 54 February.

CUNNISON, I. G.
1951   History on the Luapula, Rhodes Livingstone Paper no. 21 Oxford.
1959   The Luapula Peoples of Northern Rhodesia, Manchester: Manchester
        University Press.

CURLE, A. T.
1937   "The ruined towns of Somaliland," Antiquity vol. xi, pp. 315-327.

DALLEO, P.T.
1979   "The Somali role in organised poaching in Northeastern Kenya, c.
1909-1939." *International Journal of African Historical Studies*, 3, No. 12.

DAVIDSON, B.,
1975   "Somalia: Towards Socialism." *Race and Class*, Vol. 17, No. I (Summer)
pp. 19-38.

DE VILLENEUVE, A.
1937   "Les femmes cousues: étude sure une coutume Somali," *Journal de la
Société des Africanistes*, Paris, pp. 15-32.

DICKSON, H. R. P.
1951   *The Arab of the Desert*. London: Allen & Unwin.

DJAMA, M.
"Sur la violence en Somalie: genése et dynamique des formations
armés," Politique Africaine, No 47, 1992, pp. 147–152.

DRAKE-BROCKMAN, R. E.
1912   *British Somaliland*. London: Hurst and Blackett.

DRYSDALE, J.
1991   *Somaliland 1991 : report and references*. Hove: Global Stats.

ELMI, A.A.
1991   "Livestock Production in Somalia with special emphasis on camels"
Nomadic Peoples, 29, pp.87-103.

EVANS-PRITCHARD, E. E.
1940   *The Nuer*. Oxford: Clarendon Press.
1945   *Some Aspects of Marriage and the Family Among the Nuer*, Rhodes-
Livinstone Institute, paper no. 11. Cape Town: Oxford University
Press.
1951   *Kinship and Marriage among the Nuer*. Oxford: Clarendon Press.

FALLERS, L. A.
1957   "Some Determinants of Marriage Stability in Busoga," *Africa*, XXVII,
pp. 106-124.

FARAH, A. Y.
in press   *The Milk of the Boswellia Forests*, Uppsala.
1993   Somalia: *The Roots of Reconciliation*, London: Actionaid.

FARAH, M. I.
From Ethnic Response to Clan Identity, Upsala, Acta Universitatis

FERRANDI, U.
1903   *Lugh. Emporio commerciale aul Giuba*, Rome.

FIRTH, R.
1970   "Sibling Terms in Polynesia," *Journal of the Polynesian Society*, 79, pp. 272-287.
FORD, C. D. and G. I. JONES
1950   *The Ibo and Ibibio-speaking peoples of South-Eastern Nigeria*. London: International African Institute.

FORTES, M.
1949   *The Web of Kinship among the Tallensi*. London: Oxford University Press.
1953   "The Structure of Unilineal Descent Groups," *American Anthropologist*, LV, pp. 17-41.
1959   "Descent, Filiation and Affinity, a Rejoinder to Dr. Leach: Part II," *Man*, LIX, pp. 206-212.
1969   *Kinship and the Social Order*. Chicago: Aldine.

FREEDMAN, M.,
1966   *Chinese Lineage and Society: Fukein and Kwangtang*. London: Athlone Press.

GALAYDH, Ali K.
1990   "Notes on the State of the Somali State." *Horn of Africa Journal*, New Jersey, pp. 1-28.

GELLNER, E.
1962   Concepts and Society, *Transactions of the Third World Congress of Sociology*. [reprinted in *Rationality*, B. R. Wilson, ed., Oxford: Blackwell.
1983   *Nations and Nationalism*. Oxford: Blackwell.

GESHEKTER, C.L.
1985   "Anti-Colonialism and class formation: the eastern Horn of Africa before 1950," *International Journal of African Historical Studies*, Vol 18, No.1.

GIGLI, M.
          "Exogamie et Endogamie dans un village de la Somalie Méridionale" in Mohammed Abdi, M. ed., *Anthropologie Somalienne*, Annales Literaire do l'Université do Besançon, 495, Paris, 1993 pp. 65–86.

GLUCKMAN, M.
1950   In Radcliffe-Brown and Forde (eds.) *African Systems of Kinship and Marriage*. London: Oxford University Press, pp. 166-206.
1959   *Custom and Conflict in Africa*. Oxford: Basil Blackwell.

GOODY, E.
1972   "Greeting, begging and the presentation of respect" in J. S. Le
        Fontaine, *The Interpretation of Ritual*. London: Tavistock.

GOLDSMITH, K. L. G. and I. M. LEWIS
1958   "A preliminary investigation of the Blood Groups of the "sab"
        Bondsmen of Northern Somaliland," *Man*, vol LVIII, pp. 188-190.

GOUGH, K.,
1968   "New Proposals for Anthropologists." *Current Anthropology*, Vol. 9, No.
        5 (December), pp. 403-7.

GUNN, H. D.
1953   *Peoples of the Plateau Area of Northern Nigeria*. London: International
        African Institute.

HELANDER, B.
1994   *The Slaughtered Camel: Coping with fictitious descent among the Hubeer of
        Southern Somalia*. Stockholm: Almqvist and Luiksell.

HENIGE, D.P.
1974   *The Chronology of Oral Tradition*. Oxford: Clarendon Press.

HERSI, A.A.
1977   "The Arab factor in Somali history: the origins and the development of
        Arab enterprise and cultural influences in the Somali Peninsula." PhD
        Dissertation, UCLA.

HOLLEMAN, J. F.
1952   *Shona Customary Law*. Cape Town: Oxford University Press.

HOPEN, C. E.
1958   *The Pastoral Fulbe Family in Gwandu*. London: Oxford University Press.

HOWELL, P. P.
1954   *A Manual of Nuer Law*. London: Oxford University Press.

HYMES, D .,
1974   *Reinventing Anthropology*. Edited by D . Hymes. New York: Vintage
        Books.

IRVINE, J. T.
1974   "Strategies of status, manipulation in the Wolof greeting" in
        Explorations in the Ethnography of Speaking, R. Bauman & J. Sherzer
        (eds.). Cambridge: Cambridge University Press.

'ISE, J. U.

1972   Thawira 21 Uktuubir: Asbaaabuhaa, Adhaafuha, Munjazaatuhaa (The
Revolution of 21 October: Its Causes, Its Objectives, Its
Achievements). Mogadishu: State Printing Agency.

1974   Diiwaanka Gabayadii, Sayid Mahamad Cabdulle Xasan, Mogadishu.

ISMAN, Mahammad Hassan.

1979   Adeegto. Mogadishu.

JAMAL, V.

1981   Nomads, farmers and townsmen: incomes and inequality in Somalia. Addis
Ababa ILO, September.

1988   "Somalia: understanding an unconventional economy," Development
and Change 19, pp.203-65.

JUNOD, H. A.

1927   The Life of a South African Tribe, 2 vols. London: Macmillan.

KAPTEIJNS, L.

1991   "Women and the Somali pastoral tradition : the corporate kinship and
capitalist transformation in northern Somali' African Studies Center,
Boston, Working Papers in African Studies No. 153.

KEENADIID, Y. C.

1976   Qaamuuska Af-Soomaaliga, Somali Academy. Mogadishu.

KIRCHHOFF, P.

1932   "Verwandtschaftbezeichnungen und Verwandtenheirat," Zeitschrift fur
Ethnologie 64, pp. 46-89.

KRIGE, E.

1950   The Social System of the Zulus. Pietermaritzburg: Shuter and Shooter.

KROEBER, A. L.

1909   "Classificatory Systems of Relationship," Journal of the Royal
Anthropological Institute, 39, pp.77-84.

KUPER, A.

1982   "Lineage theory: a critical retrospect," Annual Review of Anthropology
1982.

KUPRIJANOV, P.,

1973   "Somalian Village: Social and Economic Transformations." Proceedings
of Third International Congress of Africanists. Addis Ababa.

LAITIN, D and S. S. SAMATAR

1987   Somalia: Nation in search of a state. Boulder: Westview Press.

LAURENCE, M.
1954   *A Tree For Poverty*. Nairobi: Eagle Press.

LEACH, E. R.
1955   "Polyandry, Inheritance and the Definition of Marriage," *Man*, LV, pp. 182-184.
1957   "Aspects of Bridewealth and Marriage Stability among the Kachin and Lakher," *Man*, LVII, pp. 50-55.

LEWIS, I. M.
1955   [1969]   *Peoples of the Horn of Africa: Somali Afar and Saho*. London: International African Institute.
1955-6   "Sufism in Somaliland: A Study in Tribal Islam," *Bulletin of the School of Oriental and African Studies*, XVII 581-602; XVIII, 146—60.
1957   *The Somali lineage system and the total geneology: a general introduction to basic principles of Somali political institutions*. Hargeisa.
1958   *Modern Political Movements in Somaliland*, International African Institute, memorandum xxx, Oxford: Oxford University Press.
1959 (a)   "Clanship and Contract in Northern   Somaliland," *Africa*, xxix, pp. 274-293.
1959 (b)   "The Galla in Northern Somaliland," *Rassegna di Studi Etiopici*, XV, pp. 21-38.
1960   "The Somali Conquest of the Horn of Africa." *Journal of African History*, I, pp. 213-30.
1961 (a)[1982]   *A Pastoral Democracy*. London: Oxford University Press.
1961 (b)   "Force and Fission in Northern Somali Lineage Structure." *American Anthropologist*, 63, pp. 94-112.
1962 (a)   *Marriage and the Family in Northern Somaliland*. East African Studies No. 15, Kampala.
1962 (b)   "Historical Aspects of Genealogies in Northern Somali social struc-ture," *Journal of African History*, III, pp. 35-48.
1963   "Dualism in Somali notions of power" *Journal of the Royal Anthropological Institute*, 93, pp. 109-116.
1965 (a)   "Problems in the Comparative Study of Unilineal Descent" in M. Banton (ed.) *The Relevance of Models for Social Anthropology*. London: Tavistock.
1965 (b)   *The Modern History of Somaliland: From Nation to State*. London: Weidenfeld and Nicolson.
1966   "Conformity and Contrast in Somali Islam." In I. M. Lewis (ed.), *Islam in Tropical Africa*. London: Oxford University Press, pp. 253-67.
1969 (a)   "From Nomadism to Cultivation: The Expansion of Political Solidarity in Southern Somalia." *Man in Africa*. Edited by M. Douglas and P. Kaberry. London: Tavistock, pp. 59-77.
1969 (b)   "Spirit possession in Northern Somaliland" in J. Beattie and J. Middleton (eds.) *Spirit Mediumship and Society in Africa*. London: Routledge, pp.188-220.
1972   (a)   "The Politics of the 1969 Coup in the Somali Republic,"

Journal of Modern African Studies, pp. 383-408.

1972 (b)   "Somalia marched forward with confidence." *New Middle East*, December.

1975 (a)   "The Dynamics of Nomadism: Prospects for Sedentarization and Social Change." in *Pastoralism in Tropical Africa*. Edited by T. Monod. London: Oxford University Press for the International African Institute, pp. 426-42.

1975 (b)   *Abaar: The Somali Drought*. London: International African Institute.

1976   "The Nation, State and Politics in Somalia," In D.R. Smock and K. Bentsi-Enchill (eds) *The Search for National Integration in Africa*.New York: Free Press, pp. 285-306.

1979   "Kim Il-Sung in Somalia: the end of tribalism?," in P. Cohen and W. Shack (eds.), *The Politics in Authority*. Oxford: Clarendon Press.

1980   "The Western Somali Liberation Front and the legacy of Sheikh Hussein of Bale" in J. Tubiana (ed.) *Modern Ethiopia: from the accession of Menelik II to the present*. Rotterdam, pp. 409-415.

1982   [1961] *A Pastoral Democracy*. [Oxford: OUP] New York: Africana Press.

1986   (a) "Literacy and cultural identity in the Horn of Africa: the Somali case," in G. Baumann (ed), *The Written Word: Literacy in Transition*. Oxford: Clarendon Press.

1988   *A Modern History of Somalia: Nation and State in the Horn of Africa*. Boulder Colorado: Westview Press.

1992   "Continuing Problems in Somali Historiography," in K. M. Adam and C. L. Geshekter, eds. *Proceedings of the First International Congress of Somali Studies*. New York: Scholars Press, pp. 185-189.

LEWIS, I.M. (ed.)

1983   *Nationalism and self-determination in the Horn of Africa*. London: Ithaca.

1986(b)   *Blueprint for a socio-demographic survey and re-enumeration of the refugee camp population in the Somali Democratic Republic*. Geneva: UNHCR.

LOWIE, R. H.

1928   "A note on Relationship terminologies," *American Anthropologist*, vol. 30, pp. 263-7.

MCLENNAN, J. F.

1886   *Studies in Ancient History*. London: Macmillan.

MacMICHAEL, H. A.

1922   *A History of the Arab Tribes of the Sudan*. Cambridge.

MALINOWSKI, B.

1930   "Kinship," *Man*, pp. 19-29.

1929   *The Sexual Life of Savages*. London: Routledge & Kegan Paul.

MARCHAL, R.
1992   "La guerre à Mogadishu," *Politique Africaine* 46, pp. 120-126.
1993   "Formes de la violence et de son contrôle dans un espace urbain en guerre : les *mooryaan* de Mogadishu," *Cahiers d'Etudes Africaines* 2, pp. 295–320.

MARKAKIS, J.
1987   *National and Class Conflict in the Horn of Africa.* Cambridge: Cambridge University Press.

MASSEY, G.
1987   *Subsistence and Change : Lessons of Agropastoralism in Somalia.* London: Westview Press.

MILLER, N.N.
1981   "The Other Somalia Part I: illicit trade and the Hidden Economy." *American Universities Field Staff Report,* No.29.

MINOGUE, K.,
1967   *Nationalism.* London: Batsford.

MIRREH, A.G.
1978   *Die sozialökonomischen Verhältnisse der nomadischen Bevolkerung im Norden der Demokratichen Republik Somalia.* Berlin: Akademie Verlag.

MITCHELL, J.C.
1959   "Social Change and the Stability of African Marriage in Northern Rhodesia." International African Institute Seminar, Kampala.
1963   "Marriage Stability and social Structure in Bantu Africa" in *International Population Conference Proceedings, New York 1961,* Vol 2. London, pp. 255-262.

MOHAMED A. A.
1980   *White Nile Arabs.* London: LSE monographs in Social Anthropology 53.

MURDOCK, G. P.
1959   *Africa, its peoples and their Culture History,* New York.

MURRAY, G. W.
1935   *Sons of Ishmael: A Study of the Egyptian Bedouin,* London.

NADEL, S. F.
1947   *The Nuba.* London: Oxford University Press.

NEW ERA   (Mogadishu). March 1974, No. 13, pp. 9-18.
January 1975, No. 21, pp. 11-12.

NEEDHAM, R. (ed.)
1971   *Rethinking Kinship and Marriage*. ASA Monographs, London: Tavistock Press.

OCTOBER STAR Mogadishu: Government Printing Press.

PARKIN, D.
1980   "Kind bridewealth and Hard Cash : eventing a structure" in J.L. Comaroff (ed.), *The Meaning of Marriage Payments*, London, Academic Press, pp. 197-220.

PAYTON, G. D.
1980   The Somali Coup of 1969 - the Case for Soviet Complicity" *Journal of Modern African Studies*, Vol. 18 No. 3.

PESTALOZZA, L.,
1973   *Somalia, Cronaca della Rivoluzione*. Bari: Dedalo Libri.

PETERS, E.
1960.   "The Proliferation of Segments in the Lineage of the Bedouin in Cyrenaica." *Journal of the Royal Anthropological Institute*, vol. 90, pp. 29-53.
1967   "Some structural aspects of the feud among the camel herding Bedouin of Cyrenaica," *Africa*, vol. 37, pp. 261-82.

PRINS, G.
1980   *The Hidden Hippopotamus*. Cambridge: Cambridge University Press.

PRUNIER, G.
1992   "A candid view of the Somali National Movement; *Horn of Africa*, vols. xiii and xiv, nos. 3 & 4 and 1 & 2, pp 107-120.

RADCLIFFE-BROWN A. R. and D. FORDE
1950   *African Systems of Kinship and Marriage*. London: Oxford University Press.

REINING, P.
1972   "Haya Kinship Terminology," in P. Reining (ed.) *Kinship Studies in the Morgan Centennial Year*, pp. 88-112.

RICHARDS, A. I.
1960   *East African Chiefs*. London: Faber.
RIRASH, M. A.
1988   "Camel herding and its effects on Somali literature," *Northeast African Studies*, vol. 10, pp. 2-3.

SAMATAR, ABDI I.

1985   "The predatory state and the peasantry: reflexions on rural development policy in Somalia," in A. I. Samatar (ed.), *Africa Today: Somalia Crises of State and Society.*

1989   *The State and rural transformations in northern Somalia, 1884-1906.* Madison: University of Wisconsin Press.

SAMATAR ABDI. I. and J. BASCOM
1988   "The political economy of livestock marketing in Somalia," *African Economic History* vol. 17, pp. 81-97.

SAMATAR, AHMED I.
1988   *Socialist Somalia: rhetoric and reality.* London: Zed books.

SAMATAR, SAID S. (ed.)
1992   *In the Shadow of Conquest: Islam in Colonial Northeast Africa.* New Jersey: Red Sea Press.

1991   *Somalia: a Nation in Turmoil.* London:Minority Rights Group.

1982   *Oral Poetry and Somali Nationalism.* Cambridge: Cambridge University Press.

SAPIR, E.
1916   "Terms of relationship and the levirate," *American Anthropology*, vol. 18, pp. 327-337.

SAVE THE CHILDREN
1992   *Survey of Rural Somaliland.* London

SCHAPERA, I.,
1940   *Married Life in an African Tribe.* London: Faber and Faber.

1943   *Tribal Legislation Among the Tswana of Bechuanaland Protectorate.* London: Athlone Press.

1970   *Tribal Innovators: Tswana Chiefs and Social Change, 1795-1940.* London: Athlone Press.

SCHEFFLER, H. W.
1972   "Systems of kin classification: a structural typology," in P. Reining (ed.) *Kinship studies in the Morgan Centennial Year*, Washington D.C.: Anthropological Society of Washington, pp. 113-133.

1977   "On the rule of uniform reciprocals in systems of kin classification," *Anthropological Linguistics*, pp. 245-259.

SCHEFFLER, H. W. & LOUNSBURY, F. G.
1971   *A Study in structural semantics: the Siriono Kinship System.* Eaglewood Cliffs: Prentice-Hale.

SCHNEIDER, D. M.
1972   "What is kinship all about?," in P. Reining (ed.) *Kinship Studies in the*

Morgan Centennial Year, Washington D.C.: Anthropological Society of Washington, pp.32-63.

SERJEANT, K.B.
1957   "The Saiyids of Hadramawt." Inaugural lecture delivered 5 June 1956. School of Oriental and African Studies.

SERZISKO, F.
1983   "Uber Verwandtschaftxbezeichnung im Somali," *Sprache, Geschichte und Kultur in Afrika. Vortrage, gehalten auf dem III. Afrikanistentag, Koln, 14/15 Oktober 1982*, herausgegeben von Rainer Vossen und Ulrike Claudi. Hamburg: Helmut Buske Verlag, pp. 125-144.

SHAPIRO, W.
1982   "The Place of Cognitive Extensionism in the History of Anthropological Thought." *The Journal of the Polynesian Society* 91, pp. 257-97

SHEIK-ABDI, Abdi,
1981   "Ideology and leadership in Somalia" *Journal of Modern African Studies*, Vol. XIX.
1993   *Divine Madness : Mohammed Abdulle Hassan*. London: Zed Books.

SHIHAB ad-DIN,
1897-1909   *Futuh al-Habasha*, ed. and trs. R. Basset, Paris:

SIYAD, J.,
1973   *Khudbadihii Madaxweynaha—G SK-Ee Soomaaliya, Jaalle Siyad, 1969-1973*. Mogadishu: State Printing Agency.

el SOLH, C.F.
1991   "Somalis in London"s East End." *New Community*, No 17 (4), July.

SOMALIA, Ministry of Information and National Guidance.
1974 (a)   *My Country and My People: Selected Speeches of Jaalle Major General Mohammed Siyad Barre*. Mogadishu: State Printing Agency.
1974 (b)   *Our Revolutionary Education*. Mogadishu: State Printing Agency.
1974 (c)   *Somalia's Self-help for Self-reliance*. Mogadishu: State Printing Agency.
1975   *Directorate of Planning and Co-ordination. Revised Programme of Assistance Required to the Drought Stricken Areas of Somalia*. Mogadishu: State Printing Agency.

SOMALILAND NEWS   Hargeisa, British Somaliland.

SOMCONSULT
1985   *Report on inflow of remittances of Somali workers Abroad*. Mogadishu.

SPOONER, B.
1965   "Kinship and marriage in Eastern Persia," *Sociologie*, vol. 15, no. 1, pp. 22-31.

SRINIVAS, M. N.
1951   *Religion and Society among the Coorgs of South India*. Oxford: Clarendon Press.

STENNING, D. J.
1959   *Savannah Nomads*. London: Oxford University Press.

SWIFT, J.
1979   "The development of livestock trading in a nomad pastoral economy: The Somali Case," in *Pastoral Production and Society*. Cambridge, pp. 447-466.

TALLE, A.
in press   "Transforming Women into "Pure" Agnates: Aspects of Female Infibulation in Somalia."

TAX, S.
1955   "The Social Organisation of the Fox Indians" in F. Eggan, ed., *Social Anthropology of the North American Tribes*. Chicago: Chicago University Press.

THOMPSON, V., and ADLOFF, R.,
1968   *Djibouti and the Horn of Africa*. Stanford: Stanford University Press.

van VELSEN, J.
1959   "Notes on the History of the Lakeside Tonga of Nyasaland," *African Studies*, pp. 105-17.

VANSINA, J.
1965   *Oral Tradition*. Chicago.

WATSON, W.
1958   *Tribal Cohesion in a Money Economy*. Manchester: Manchester University Press.

WESTERMARCK, E.
1914   *Marriage Ceremonies in Morocco*. London: Macmillan.

WHITE, C. M. N.
1960   *An Outline of Luvale Social and Political Organisation*, Rhodes Livingstone Paper no. 30, Manchester.

WINTER, E. H.
1955   *Bwamba.* Cambridge: Heffer.

WOLCZYK, A.
1972   "Il "socialismo" Somalo: un industria per il potere." *Concretezza* (Rome) (January), pp. 23-6.

INDEX